A Short Cast Back

Kay Gardner

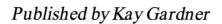

Published by Kay Gardner

First Published in 2000
By Kay Gardner

Reprinted August 2001

Written and illustrated by Kay Gardner

Produced by Windmill Graphics, Stroud, Gloucestershire.
Printed by the Alden Group, Oxford.

A Short Cast Back

Kay Gardner

Published by Kay Gardner

Acknowledgments

I wish to place on record my grateful thanks to all who have participated in this book, for their patience and hospitality. Thank you for trusting me with your innermost thoughts! I hope you will feel the result is worthwhile.

Illustrating this book would not have been possible without those who have provided photographs. Special thanks are due to Jim Meads who somehow managed to find just the pictures I was looking for from his archives. Some photographs have been provided by participants from their own collections, and I have made every possible effort to establish their origins and credit them where possible.

I am truly grateful to His Grace, the Duke of Beaufort, MFH for agreeing to write the Foreword, and for doing it so promptly.

My sincere thanks are also due to Martin Scott who has come to the rescue when I have been unable to find some of the less well-known hounds in my own records.

To Terry Crate for his good-humoured help with scanning the illustrations and page layouts I am also indebted.

Last but not least, thanks to all those who subscribed in advance, many of whom were not previously known to me. Not only has this helped in practical financial terms, but your faith in this project has been a huge encouragement in the moments of self-doubt suffered by all struggling writers.

Thank you, and Good Hunting, forever !

Kay Gardner
<u>September 2000</u>

Every effort has been made to establish the accuracy and authenticity of information provided by each person. To this end each Chapter has been approved by the individuals featured prior to publication.

Photographs for pages 8 and 9 : the author on horse, Terry Crate; the author on a snowy day with 'Tuppence', Ray Bird; His Grace the Duke of Beaufort MFH, Kay Gardner; His Grace the Duke of Beaufort MFH hunting, Jim Meads.

Contents

Author's Introduction

Over the last twenty years it has been my good fortune to meet a huge number of hunting folk countrywide. All those involved in our sport understand the 'one big happy family' fellowship which binds us all. I have as an enthusiast and occasional sporting hack been invited into the homes of many hitherto strangers, fed, watered, shown their hounds and even on occasion been lent their precious horses which have conveyed me with

admirable good humour. The last few years have probably been the toughest in terms of political threat and fanatical prejudice. That this has only brought out the true spirit of the countryman, his patient, quiet determination and a dignity few would maintain in the face of such pressure, speaks volumes. In this book I have tried to portray a variety of countries and characters. I have therefore missed out some notables in order to include some 'unsung heroes.' It is my small way of saying thank you, not only to those included, but to the way of life they represent. I dedicate it unreservedly to all those who have loved the Foxhound.

Foreword

by
His Grace, the Duke of Beaufort, MFH

```
Dadminton
   Glos


September 2000
```

I am delighted and flattered to have been asked to write a foreword to Kay Gardner's fascinating book on hunting.

I have been lucky enough to have known Kay since she was a child, when she formed a tremendous friendship with my late cousin, the 10th Duke. He quickly realised that they shared the same great passion - that of foxhunting. That passion has grown in Kay, encouraging her to produce this wonderful book. It is a book which depicts the sport and all who follow it to make it the most classless pastime, in which all comers are welcome.

There are some wonderful character studies from all parts of the country and well told anecdotes.

I could not have enjoyed it more.

9

Sidney Bailey. None have been at the top of the profession for longer.
(Jim Meads)

10

Sidney Bailey

There is no greater tonic than a day following Sidney Bailey and the VWH hounds. Just to watch him trotting to the meet with them is a joy. He has a quiet, easy way with them you could travel the length and breadth of the country to find. Indeed Sidney is a quiet man, almost to the point of shyness. Yet he is a man with many friends, sociable but not garrulous. He has a quality all too rare in the modern world - a genuine self-effacing modesty. Hounds hang on his every low whistle or encouraging word. Close to his horse, they look up, just waiting for an opportunity to please. I have been lucky enough to enjoy many happy days hunting with Sidney in the last fifteen seasons, and can honestly say that he has not changed a bit. From the moment he arrives, with that welcoming smile above the trademark cleft chin, there is a sense that this will be a day to remember. As a foot follower, it is not possible to be up with the action all the time. Even in familiar territory you can get it badly wrong. A Huntsman like Sidney is pure gold. He always makes a point of telling you where they are going to draw, what they did with that last fox, and innumerable other snippets which make the events of the day fall in to place.

I well remember a sweltering Opening Meet at South Farm. It had been a very dry autumn, the plough as parched and dusty as sand. Hounds found in the inappropriately named Snowstorm Gorse, hunting nicely inside. I toiled over the fields as they ran well left of me, and checked. I turned left up a hedgerow, and could see a fox running from where they had checked, along the next hedge, back towards the meet. He vanished at the junction with my hedge, and I thought he may have popped through away from me. To my horror the next thing I saw was the fox, coming straight to me. I literally 'bit the dust' flat on my face. I swear I have never been closer to a fox, as he jumped over my arm ! I watched him out of sight. Hounds had not opened, so I hollered, and soon heard the response of Sidney's melodious doubled horn. They could not speak at all to start with, then one bitch feathered and opened. The rest flew to her. Before blowing them away Sidney called over his shoulder, "Well done. That was good old Jealous '92." It was a moment so typical of hunting with Sidney. He often points out a hound like that, or one to look out for, when we are at the meet.

One of the best days I have ever had was when the VWH hounds went to the Quorn Monday country. On this busy and memorable day, I was fortunate to view their first fox away, and halt the traffic for fox and hounds on the main Nottingham road later on. Andrew Stirling and myself never used a car all day, and walked 24 miles, crossing only two ploughed fields, the country around Parsons Thorns and Muxlow Hill affording excellent views. Jack Littleworth would certainly have been proud of his nephew's performance that day.

Born to be a Huntsman

Sidney's mother was the daughter of Alf Littleworth, who hunted the Braes of Derwent for thirty years. His brother (Sidney's great Uncle Charlie) hunted the York and Ainsty for 'donkey's years'. Sidney's Uncles were the legendary Jack Littleworth, who hunted the Quorn, and Sidney Littleworth who hunted the Atherstone, and also enjoyed a spell hunting hounds in Ireland. As if this impeccable 'bottom line' weren't qualification enough, Sidney Bailey's own father, Tom was probably the greatest ever exponent of the trade 'Kennelman.' After 24 years as Kennelman to Sidney's grandfather (where he met Sidney's mother) he moved to Chipping Norton, where he was the renowned Kennelman of the famous Heythrop Pack for many years. A Kennelman then was

11

responsible for hounds' welfare and feeding, in rather the same way as a Kennel Huntsman would be today, "Not just a glorified knackerman", explains Sidney succinctly. Tom Bailey was responsible for 'putting to' all the visiting bitches. A huge number in this prestigious Kennel,"He was a great influence on me and a real character. Everyone respected him. He helped a lot of Huntsmen."

With such a pedigree, Sidney's future career was inevitable. As a child he would stand on the garden gate waiting eagerly for his grandfather, Alf Littleworth to return from hunting. He would then be placed on the front of his saddle, to return to the

This enchanting picture shows Sidney Bailey at three years old confidently walking out with the Braes of Derwent pack, hunted by his Grandfather Alf Littleworth. In his haste to be with hounds he has put odd shoes and socks on !

Kennels. He knew every hound by name when just three years old. The local newspaper carried a picture of young Sidney, with the following caption: *"Although only three, Sidney Bailey of Shotley Bridge County Durham has already started his first job. He's kennel boy to the Braes of Derwent Hunt at the Kennels at Shotley Bridge. Every morning, rain or fine, he turns out to help make their food, and exercise them. The hounds have taken a liking to Sidney, which is just as well, seeing the kennel-boy is just over a head taller than they are."* Showing me the cutting, and pictures of his childhood Sidney quips, "So you see I've been in it *most* of my life !" Though he passed his 11+ and got in to the local grammar school, he broke his arm the day before term started. The next six weeks were spent hunting every day, and he was so behind with his studies that he was relegated to the secondary modern school. More 'sick leave' did nothing to enhance his academic career, and with their son's future in Hunt Service already a racing certainty Mr and Mrs Bailey ignored the school's letters about his repeated absence. At 15, Sidney was expelled for non-attendance, "Well it was a waste of time. I always wanted to go in to Hunt Service." So, with never a thought of any other career in his head, young Sidney embarked on the single-minded course which has never caused him a moment's regret.

A First Class Start
There could have been few better places to start out than the Heythrop's Chipping Norton base at that time. As a country the Heythrop is second to none, and Captain Wallace was the greatest organiser of a hunting country. Percy Durno was Kennel Huntsman, his son Bruce, who latterly hunted the Fernie was second whipper-in. Sidney spent a year in the stables, then Bruce Durno moved on to the South Oxfordshire in 1955 , allowing him to move up the ladder, becoming second whipper in at the age of seventeen. This was a great time of hard work, second hand breeches and memorable sport, "You wouldn't get a greater hound man than Captain Wallace." After two years the spectre of National Service threatened to tear Sidney away from his beloved hunting. The Ledbury were advertising for a whipper-in, and he went for an interview, meeting Huntsman Nimrod Champion at the Kennels. Their new master, Colonel Warden, had just come out of the army. Sidney explained his predicament. Colonel Warden sent him to see a Doctor, who handed Sidney a letter to take with him when he went to Birmingham for his medical, "I had never seen him in my life before !" The letter explained that Sidney (surely one of the fittest of hunting men) suffered from very bad asthma attacks, which came on suddenly without warning ! Packed off home on the first available train, he was engaged as first whipper-in to the Ledbury.

12

Happy Years

So, whilst still a teenager, Sidney found himself whipping in to another legendary Huntsman, this time the professional Nimrod Champion, this family name one of the most prolific in Hunt Service, "The Ledbury was another wonderful country. Nimrod Champion was a great man. A good Huntsman, and a very good boss, one of the best. I really enjoyed working for him. They were three of the happiest years of my life." That this happiness was enhanced when he met future wife Carol is obvious. Still surely one of hunting's most devoted couples, Sidney and Carol were quite simply made for each other. Carol's Herefordshire farming family were all keen on hunting, and also very involved in racing and point to pointing. Her sister Monny worked in the Stables, and was not averse to putting in a day's work at the Kennels equal to any man. Carol's nephew is champion point-to-point jockey Julian Pritchard, and she takes a keen interest in his progress. "Carol is intelligent, has better eyesight than 99% of whippers-in, and has the best holloa in the country", Sidney enthuses, proving that this is true love indeed !

The Vale of the White Horse - Four Decades On

It was a happy day for hunting folk in this neck of the woods when Colonel Warden came down to the VWH, for he brought Sidney Bailey with him. Mr John White MFH was hunting hounds then, and Sidney was engaged as first whipper-in in 1960. Just before cubhunting, Mr White was driving with his elbow out of his landrover window when it was hit by a timber lorry, so Sidney started his first season here as whipper-in, by hunting hounds. Mr. White suffered from chronic asthma attacks, and Sidney would sometimes have to gallop up and catch his horse so that he could inject himself and carry on. The following Season, Mr White collapsed during the second morning's cubhunting. Sidney was handed the horn and hounds caught their fox. By the time they went home Mr White had died. Sidney was immediately put on as Huntsman, so although he was officially first whipper-in he actually hunted hounds from the time he arrived, aged just 22. At this time the VWH was still divided into the Cricklade and Bathurst packs. In 1964 it was decided that the two packs should amalgamate. The Cricklade masters wanted Sidney to stay, the Bathurst masters wanted to keep their Huntsman on, so to save any bad feeling both men left. Sidney went to hunt the Wylye

Sidney Bailey and the VWH Hounds move off from their meet in the Quorn country. (Kay Gardner)

Sidney Bailey with VWH Stallionhounds
(Terry Crate)

Valley. He married Carol the same year, and they had two enjoyable seasons there. Then in 1966 the VWH post became vacant again, and Sidney returned, "I shan't bother going anywhere else now", he tells me dryly, 34 years later, his serious expression belied by the smile in his eyes. He clearly enjoyed his years during Martin Scott's mastership, disapproving only of his smoking. Evidently the quality of the day could sometimes be judged from the amount of smoke emanating from a covert - the worse things got, the more the smoke. "Still", Sidney grins, "I soon fixed that. I used to do his valeting, and he would leave his fags in his pocket . . . well, you've got to brush those coats *really* hard. . . "

Hounds and the Huntsman

It is a well known fact that Sidney Bailey professes never to have favourite hounds, "A pack of hounds is a team. They all do different things at different times, on different days. I have been very lucky here to have such super hounds." When pressed however, it is interesting that without any prompting he nominates some of the same names Martin Scott came up with, "Bugle '76 was certainly one of the best bitches. She could take a line on roads or tarmac ahead of the rest."

Sidney Bailey at Honiton (Jim Meads)

Outstanding Stallionhound Guinness '92 (Portman Genius '87-Hannah '88) is also highly regarded. Not least for the day near Kemble when he hunted a fox alone, caught him single-handed, and immediately left him to hunt another which jumped out of the bushes, "He's been a good old dog." He has done a lot of other packs some good, getting progeny which are good looking and great workers. He possesses valuable longevity, and though now entering his ninth season is still fit and hard with excellent feet. The South Shropshire's Clever '97 (VWH Guinness '92-Claret '92) was the first of his progeny to take a Championship at Peterborough, securing the Bitch Championship in 1998. It would be no surprise to see the Duke of Beaufort's handsome Gunshot '98 follow suit before long. *VWH Guinness's grandsire General '80 also gets a mention. He escaped from Peterborough Showground, and was at large for six weeks, turning up fit and well in the Cottesmore country. Happily he was none the worse and survived to found an important foxhound dynasty. The pack has not shown at Peterborough for some years, but regularly take prizes at the popular West of England Hound Show at Honiton each Summer.

Close to Hounds

"To be a good Huntsman I think you have to be naturally 'doggy', the sort of person hounds go to readily. You have to be close to your hounds. Not everyone can be like that, however hard they try." Without looking up Carol mutters,

14

Sidney Bailey and the VWH Hounds in Cirencester Park (Kay Gardner)

"Temperament has a lot to do with it," from behind her newspaper, and her husband chooses not to hear.

A moving example of the bond between Huntsman and hounds is provided by a story about Sidney's grandfather. He lay in hospital just two fields from the Kennels at Shotley Bridge. One of the brood bitches went missing, leaving her whelps. Sensing that her beloved Huntsman was nearing the end of his life, she found him, defying the alien hospital smells, and numerous wards. She made her way unseen through the building, settling down under his bed. There she stayed until he died.

Like all truly great Huntsmen Sidney has genuine respect for his quarry too, "They are such clever animals. They can easily clap down and shoot away behind you. After so long in one country you do get to know the runs of foxes, or where you think they will go. Yet they still keep eluding me ! They are never in a hurry on a bad scenting day. I hate bad scenting days ! Foxes seem to know and just potter about. When scent is good they really straighten out and go," says the man who readily admits that the challenge is still just as great a thrill now as when he started.

Hunts and the Country
In such a long career there have been many memorable days. I ask Sidney to recall some of those that stand out most. Hounds once found at Williamstrip running to the Bratch, and on to Kilkenny, back right handed to Ladbarrow and caught their fox a field short of Burford Grammar School in the Heythrop country. There is a sense that Sidney always enjoys hunting in to their country. This friendly rivallry is mutual, the Heythrop's former Kennel Huntsman Tony Collins having whipped in to Sidney at the VWH, as did present incumbent Antony Adams, and his brother Trevor, now Huntsman and MFH of the Duke of Buccleuch's. One day Tony Collins was so eager to get to a road, when Sidney was hunting hounds in some thick stuff on his feet that he knocked Sidney over. Tony recalls, "He flew through the air and bounced. I thought I'd killed him !" Luckily Sidney escaped with stitches in his head, and quickly forgave his friend.

15

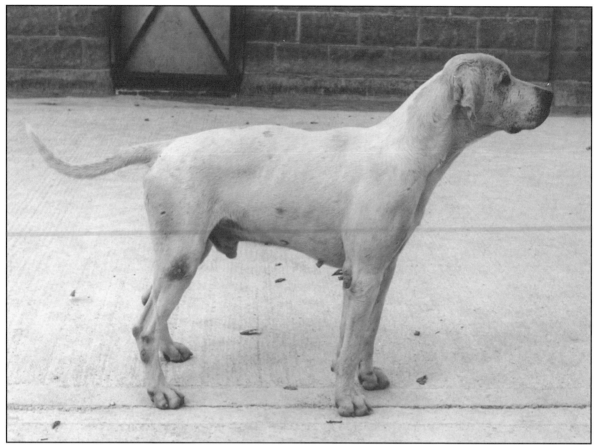

VWH Guinness '92, an outstanding Stallionhound still looking good nine seasons on.
Note the exceptionally good feet. (Terry Crate)

Another hunt he describes illustrates how much the country has changed in terms of roads and urban development, particularly around the Swindon end. From a meet at Lydiard Park whilst the M4 was being built hounds hunted across it, the Field jumping on and off it, catching up with the pack in the Car Park of Princess Margaret's Hospital in Swindon. Foxes in this part of the country now also tend to have urban bases and are far more inclined to run back in to Highworth or the outskirts of Swindon, "The country has changed tremendously, not only traffic, railways and urbanisation, but the farming. There is so much less grass, and where there is grass you find electric wire and sheep. Hounds have to contend with this and so much artificial spray and fertiliser now as well."

One of the most unusual occurrences took place from a meet at Sevenhampton, near Highworth. Hounds hunted well, and it was soon obvious that the adjacent Old Berkshire hounds were also enjoying a good hunt. Incredibly, the two packs hunted hard on opposite sides of a road, passing each other at full gallop, without even lifting their heads. The VWH caught their fox just a field from the Old Berks Kennels.

Time For A Pheasant

Carol recalls hollering a fox away from Eastcourt one day. He stopped, killed a pheasant, and ran on with it in his mouth. Carol hunts regularly, and daughter Karen follows often by car, "She can spot a fox two fields away on plough," says her father with pride.

If not riding, Carol often follows by car, sometimes with daughter Karen. When Tony Collins was whipping in she sometimes followed with Tony's late wife Junie, the four being great friends. One day the VWH hounds ran in to the Beaufort country on the Tetbury side. They came to a field surrounded by sheep wire, so Carol and Junie ran across to assist, and give Sidney some information. Sidney's

16

blood was up and he was not best pleased to be held up by wire. He swore at them, which they thought a great joke. The VWH disturbed the planned draw of the Beaufort for the following Monday, which the tenth Duke found rather less amusing at the time. He telephoned one of the masters and said that he found it wholly unacceptable that the VWH Huntsman had been seen shouting and swearing at two ladies in the Beaufort country ! When this was reported back to Sidney he remarked that it was a very bad job if he could not even swear at his own wife, and that of his whipper-in !

A Great Life

To think of Sidney Bailey without hunting is like trying to imagine a newspaper without print. He still has such enthusiasm for the sport, and his hounds, losing none of his flair with the passing years. He is simply a Huntsman through and through. When he broke a leg badly several seasons ago, many wrote him off. Every year since the rumour does the rounds that this will be Sidney's last Season. Each Season I ring to find out when they will start hunting, and ask Carol if there is any truth in the rumour, "What do you think? Silly old bugger. Of course he'll keep going !" It would be no surprise to see Sidney make his 40 seasons hunting the VWH. He still gets up bright and early, no matter how long a hunting day, or late the party. Carol accompanies him on summer bicycle exercise, and marvels at the enthusiasm he musters for each new dawn. At the Puppy Show with a new young entry, never a shy one among them, he seems truly immortal. Leaving his house after Carol's sumptuous repast last year I congratulated him on a particularly nice entry. His response was so typical, "They'll all be nice when they hunt foxes !" Retirement seems unthinkable, like holidays, "We go stag hunting. Beaches aren't really me. Squawking kids and fat women in bikinis ? No thanks !"

The Season begins with Sidney whistling through the early morning mist at Red Lodge, and ends on a warm Spring day in Cirencester Park to the same sound. Sidney Bailey is a contented man, "It's a great Life. I wouldn't change it." And so say all of us, for Sidney is the epitome of what makes the hunting world special.

Sidney Bailey with the VWH hounds at Ten Rides
(Kay Gardner)

* After this chapter was written, Duke of Beaufort's Gunshot '98 won the Stallionhound Class at Peterborough 2000.

Captain Charles Barclay and the Puckeridge Hounds in typical plough country
(Jim Meads)

18

Captain C G E Barclay MFH

Early in September 1998 I left home with owls hooting at 2.30am to attend a meet of the Puckeridge Hounds at Cave Gate Crossroads, Hare Street. I am sorry to say that hounds had moved off just before our arrival. I was later told they did so after Mr Peter Lyster, former master of the Meynell who regularly hunts with the Beaufort had said, "No need to worry, Kay could find a pack of hounds anywhere", which I found most reassuring. They had not reached their first draw, so all was not lost and they had in fact been very easy to find. Captain Charles Barclay was out in a vehicle, and in very cheerful order. The weather had been dry for some time, and the ground baked hard. This is very much a shooting country, but throughout the morning hounds found in every little clump or spinney. The landscape here is open and undulating, big fields but many small coverts in view. Midway through the morning it began to rain horizontally. We saw numerous foxes, all of which hounds hunted well. One abiding memory is of their fox crossing a large baked plough field in driving rain with every hound on the line and speaking hard. The Puckeridge hounds have long been renowned for their capabilities on plough, and this was a perfect illustration. A memorable morning was rounded off by an excellent pub lunch with the Barclay family, and Mr Lyster before the long drive home. I had first met Captain Barclay in 1981, as he judged the Duke of Beaufort's Puppy Show for over 30 years with Captain Ronnie Wallace. I had also spent a day's hunting in the hills near my home with him and Major Gerald Gundry.

One Hundred Not Out

"My family came to Brent Pelham in 1896, my Grandfather being the last in our branch of the family to be involved in the bank. He sensibly chucked it up to become an MFH. Prior to that we had our own pack of Harriers. We're all madmen really."

The Barclays have had an extraordinary involvement with hunting over the years including their own Harriers which hunted in Norfolk and Suffolk. These were based at Roydon, now part of London, and hunted some extraordinary places having been boxed from Tottenham Station. During the holidays, hounds were taken to Higham in Suffolk, where another branch of the family lives. Captain Barclay's grandfather was also a master of the North Norfolk Harriers. The best hunt he had on a hare had a nine mile point, 15 as hounds ran, and they had to be stopped at the end of it in Chesham Park due to shooting. Innumerable family members held masterships of the Trinity Foot Beagles over a sixty nine year period, and the mastership of the Puckeridge has now been in their hands for over a Century. Even more remarkably in modern times, all Captain Barclay's four children have gone into masterships. His youngest son James has been known to me for some years, a great enthusiast and innovative in his approach to educating people all ages about hunting. He is much in evidence this morning and is introduced by his father with a raven like laugh as 'the Enthusiast, who is rather good at PR.' James Barclay once told me that their family is an offshoot of the Berkeley family, "They fell out with us because one of my ancestors ran off with someone else's wife." A move to Scotland followed. The Provost of Aberdeen was boiled during a dispute over taxes, adding further strain to family relations, hence the change of spelling. I had hitherto regarded the Barclays as a most affable clan, so made a mental note not to upset them !

I asked Captain Barclay if he had found the prospect of hunting hounds a daunting one with such illustrious ancestors to follow, "Yes it was somewhat daunting, but father was still about when I took over in 1947, and did not die until 1962." That first year saw a unique mastership, Captain Charles Barclay, his father, and grandfather. His grandfather died that year. I wondered if a family mastership caused family disputes, and how the younger generation now feels about mastership, "We all get

19

along pretty well together now. It is unusual to have a whole family of Masters of Foxhounds I suppose. Perhaps no other family is as stupid as us ! I think my father might have disagreed with me now, as he was all for keeping the pure English hounds, which I have changed over the last few years." Pre-war hounds hunted four days a week. The pack merged briefly with the Thurlow, and then the two parted again, "We've some good keen hunters here."

My Way - Hunting and Humour

As a young man at Eton Captain Barclay whipped in to Captain Wallace with the Beagles. "He knows quite a bit about hunting", he grins impishly, adding, "But we'd best not tell him so !" The two Captains judged the Puppy Show at Badminton for a remarkable 35 years, "That had more than a hint of influence on my thoughts on hounds." When it came to hunting hounds, Captain Barclay tried to do

things in his own way, "I like to think I did it my way. I must admit though that one has to modernise a bit and change with the times. I have an open mind, no fads." He feels a good Huntsman requires patience more than anything, "Not that I've always got it !" What he has undoubtedly got however is a very thorough knowledge of the country, as might be expected of one who has grown up in it, "I know every farmer, and of course they know my lunacy well by now."

Captain Barclay hunted hounds from 1947-1985. For many years his right hand man was Kennel Huntsman Ned Paxton, "We first dug him up in 1936. When war broke out he went to work in a munitions factory at Broadway. He and I got on very well together. As a whipper-in, he was always in the right place, which makes things a lot easier when you're a silly old man ! " Captain Barclay was still at Cambridge when War broke out, where he was Master of the Trinity Foot Beagles, and whipped in. "Then I

Captain Charles Barclay (right) embarks on his first Season as a Master of Foxhounds with his father, Major Maurice Barclay (master since 1910) and Grandfather, Mr Edward Barclay (Master since 1896), who formed a three generation mastership of the Puckeridge in 1947, seen here on the morning of the Opening Meet outside Brent Pelham Hall (Jim Meads)

was sent for cavalry training at Weedon, where Major Bill Scott, Martin's father, was in charge. My Commanding Officer was Peach Borwick so I was able to get a little time off. That winter of 1939-40 was a bleak old time. A nucleus of a pack was just kept ticking over here with Ted Wilkinson as Kennel huntsman. Father was Chairman of the War Agricultural Committee. We built them back up again after the war." Captain Barclay whipped in again to the Trinity Foot Beagles briefly after the war, before taking up full time duties with the Puckeridge. Ned Paxton returned in 1947, "He knew what he was up against, as I had whipped in to him from 1936-1940 !"

The Essential Tour - the Gents' Loo

When I rang to arrange an interview for this book I was delighted to be invited to the Puppy Show, and Lunch at Brent Pelham Hall. The Hall is a joy for any foxhunter to visit. The walls are heavy with hunting pictures of every description, including many of the family to the present day. Sherman P Haight from Connecticut was one of the Puppy Show judges, and his wife Peggy drew my attention to the huge portraits on the staircase. Typically, Mrs Barclay took time to point out others to me, though preparing for lunch guests. In the Study where I talked to Captain Barclay there are books

from floor to ceiling and mouth watering paintings by Lionel Edwards and Peter Biegel celebrating his father's 50th year of mastership, and a charming one by Susie Witcombe, celebrating the family's Century of mastership. As we talked of hounds and hunting down the years Captain Barclay laughed that distinctive raven laugh many times, and is most insistent that I should be given a tour of the 'Gents' Loo.' James too is insistent that I undertake this unusual tour, "Before the others arrive" It is certainly a first, and seems quite a normal thing to do somehow in Brent Pelham Hall! Never one to balk at a new experience I followed the Captain and James meekly in to the 'Gents Loo', where all, they assured me would be revealed. Indeed it was, for here are the pictures of all the most fa-

Puckeridge Kennel Huntsman Wayne Reeder views a fox away on plough (Kay Gardner)

mous Puckeridge hounds. It is a wonderful collection which illustrates perfectly the radical changes in the conformation and 'fashion' of the foxhound from the 19th to the 20th century. How fashion ruined the good looking hounds of the early 1800s turning them into heavy over-knuckled caricatures. Then when common sense prevailed the foxhound's natural beauty returned, as we now see today, "All the hounds I've been most fond of are in here."

Bargain and an Earlier Deed

One hound in the loo 'Hall of Fame' is Bargain '24, "In father's day, in my youth we hunted a fox to the edge of a village. There were two alsatian dogs chained to a shed, and the fox crept in past them, up on to a shelf. He curled up, and old Bargain kept winding round, making it obvious a fox was about. She went in past the alsations, whereupon the fox jumped down and she nailed him." James entered and began another story about a fox which ran in to the back of Brent Pelham Hall and lay down in a pan of milk, where hounds caught him, "That really was a long time ago, the day my sister was born, in 1921", his father adds, "Grandfather complained that he had no milk for his tea !" James adds that the family graves often show signs of foxes visiting them, "Just remember who is being interviewed here, it's not you ! " , his father laughs.

Weathergauge - a Legacy

Weathergauge '22 was no bigger than a harrier, short, stocky and rather cobby, "Father was rather keen on those. We've tried to improve on that." One day Captain Barclay's father hunted 17½ couple of Weathergauge's sons, daughters, grandsons and granddaughters in 1931.

Notable Stallionhounds of the 1940s-1950s

President '48 (Workman '42-Peerless '45) won the unentered couples class at Peterborough with his brother Prompter, and also won the prize for best unentered hound. In 1951 he was in the winning two couple at Peterborough. Tan and white, in the field he was noted for his nose and deep voice, also possessing all-important drive and longevity. He was used by many as a Stallionhound including the Tynedale, Brocklesby, Old Berks, South Berks and Flint and Denbigh. Another closely related Stallionhound Playmate '50 was by Workman's brother Woodcock '42 out of Peerless's sister Peaceful '45. He was highly regarded by Major Maurice Barclay, who thought him the best looking post-war foxhound he had bred. He was also a brilliant worker with pace,

Puckeridge Playmate '50, Reserve Champion at Peterborough in 1951. (Jim Meads)

nose and voice. Reserve at Peterborough in 1951 where he was also one of that winning two couple. He was well used by other Kennels, including the Heythrop.

Puckeridge Ruler '50 (Brocklesby Rockwood '45-Willing '47) was not very big, but proved so good in his work that he was bred from as a first Season hound. His progeny were a great success in the home Kennel, and he was used at the Brocklesby, South Shropshire and Wynnstay. Puckeridge Racer '52 (Brocklesby Richmond '44-Canopy '47) was a strong deep tan doghound who hunted for a remarkable ten seasons, and whose feet remained in very good order. His particular forte was hunting on roads. He too was used at the Brocklesby, as well as the Sinnington and HH where his progeny proved especially low scenting on heather, even when burnt.

. . . and the 1980s

Puckeridge Grasper '75 was a most successful Stallionhound. A son of Heythrop Grossmith '71, Grasper's dam, Paragon '70 was a daughter of Brocklesby Cruiser '67. At Badminton, Grasper sired the well known bitch Duke of Beaufort's Wamba '78 (- Wagtail '73) whose daughter Whimsey '82, by Carbine '76, went on to be Champion Bitch at Peterborough unentered. Captain Barclay had in fact been given Duke of Beaufort's Woeful '60 (Woodcock '55-Tendril '56), from whom Wagtail was descended, as a brood bitch.

Puckeridge Gosling '80 (Wheatland Grappler '78-Gaylass '78) was used successfully in the early 1980s, "When he first went in at Peterborough he was shy, and didn't like it a lot, though he brightened up when the others came in. " He is regarded by Captain Barclay as one of the best looking hounds he has bred, and had a very good brother called Goshawk. Gosling's daughter Puckeridge Rainbow '84 (- Raceaway '79) was Reserve Champion in 1987. "Well you can certainly see how hounds have altered."

Puckeridge Devious 1987 Peterborough Bitch Champion 1989 (Jim Meads)

Peterborough Champions

The Puckeridge Peterborough Champions' photographs are all hung in the loo. Wizard '28 who won the Doghound Championship, alongside Bitch Champions Columbine '37 and Poetry '51 who won the Bitch Championship, all Champions as unentered hounds. More recently Pigeon '81 (Landlord '77-Pintail '75) won the Bitch Championship in

Captain Barclay's youngest son James Barclay MFH hunting the Granta Harriers
(Terry Crate)

1984 and Devious '87 (Portman Dayus '82-Cranberry '80) who followed up her Best Unentered Prize in 1987 by winning the Bitch Championship in 1989. With her litter brother Demon she had already completed a Championship double at the South of England Show, where the Kennel's hounds had all but swept the board to be leading pack at the Show.

Only Fools and Horses

The Barclay wit is never far from the surface. Who can forget the entrance of their Dellboy into the ring at Peterborough ? He was so named because, "Only Fools and Horses hunt with the Puckeridge "!

When Captain Barclay told his youngest son, then a master of the Fitzwilliam, that perhaps he ought to have some purpose in life other than foxhunting, James's response proved he is a chip off the Barclay block. He went out and formed a new pack of Harriers, the Granta ! I saw him hunt these hounds impressively for the first time out on the Fens during a four day Hunting Festival he had arranged.

From here we made a detour to the Captain's bedroom, to see yet more pictures, and where James appeared with his brother Ted, bearing his Grandfather's Hunting Diaries.

A Very English Occasion

Lunch as might be expected was a jolly affair with plenty of good British roast beef. Steady rain had fallen throughout the morning, but stopped in time for the Puppy Show itself, attended by honest hunting folk. The Captain sat beside his former Kennel Huntsman Ned Paxton, now in his nineties, and the pair obviously enjoyed themselves. Some Cottesmore sires have been used here, and a part-American Stallionhound was brought out. When asked by James, 'What do you think of him Ned ?' The flat reply, 'Not much' brought the house down. In the compact Kennels the feed room is well worth a visit. On the walls are boards detailing every Hunting Season back to the 1850s - days hunted, days lost and why, foxes caught and other snippets about the Season. The lawn back at the Hall makes a wonderful setting for tea with its typically English lavender, redbrick walls and roses.

23

Breeding Hounds for Plough - Maintaining and Improving

The breeding of hounds for this type of arable country is an art in itself, and Old English hounds do have a good reputation on plough. I asked how the good qualities were maintained, and what improvements were needed, "The Old English hounds had nose, but perhaps not the push needed. There's nothing to hunt on but plough here, so we looked for Stallionhounds with good reputations to maintain nose." Captain Barclay's father used to go and have some cubhunting at Badminton, and he would accompany him,"The late Duke, 'Master' was certainly an influence on my life. Though I never saw him hunt hounds regularly, just those early mornings, I saw his hounds. He was always very kind and keen to help the young. Seeing those Badminton Stallionhounds did make us change direction. All these things are tucked away in one's mind, they don't just happen on their own." Captain Barclay later visited Badminton with his own children, who enjoyed their stays enormously. One big step came in the arrival of the aforementioned Woeful '60 from Badminton as a brood bitch. She was a worthy winner of the Peterborough Championship as an unentered hound and had already founded a dynasty at Badminton, producing a succession of lovely, deep brood bitches. It is also a line which appears in the pedigrees of many influential Badminton Stallionhounds of the 60s and 70s namely Warden '68, Gaffer '68, Crowner '69, Cracker '72 and Monmouth '77. As well as the great quality this line possessed in looks, it is a pedigree full of low-scenting hounds - just what was needed in the plough country of the Puckeridge, There was just a touch of Welsh too in the top line via Brecon Petrel '32. "Of course, I judged their Puppy Show for all those years too." Continuity in masterships and consequently in hound breeding is a great bonus here,"I have been persuaded now to use a VWH Stallionhound. My advice from that part of the world comes from some fellow called Martin Scott ! " Captain Barclay's daughter, Mrs Diana Pyper MFH takes an active role in overseeing the hound breeding too, maintaining continuity for the future.

The Challenge of Plough

There is some lovely countryside here within twenty five miles of London. Surprisingly little has changed, though as elsewhere shooting continues to increase. "I regard the country as a good challenge. Hunting on plough can be very interesting." Foxes do not run as straight now because of the increase in traffic, yet the Puckeridge do not suffer from roads as much as other packs in the South East. One of Captain Barclay's best hunts was a nine mile point, 21 as hounds ran, in 1976. All but

Luke Neale MFH with the Puckeridge hounds in typical country
(Terry Crate)

Captain Charles Barclay MFH (centre) and his four children, all Masters of Foxhounds, outside Brent Pelham Hall. Left to right, James formerly Essex & Suffolk, Fitzwilliam and now MFH Cottesmore, Mrs Diana Pyper, MFH Puckeridge, Major Ted Barclay, MFH Puckeridge, and Mr Robert Barclay, MFH Puckeridge. (Jim Meads)

the last half mile, now close to the M11, would be possible today. Even that Motorway runs parallel to the main railway line, so has had little significance. It is far from 'one of the worst countries in England', as Nicholas Berry described it in 1888, "When my grandfather took the hounds there were fewer foxes, as can be seen in his diaries. They suffered from mange then. I have never seen a mangey fox here today." The country can ride very deep, and there is an abundance of deer and hares, which hounds take little notice of, "At least, we like to think not!"

Never a Bad Day

Though he confesses that he would think twice about taking on a mastership in modern times, Captain Barclay's love of the sport is still clear, "One could say it's not as good as it was, but it's not at all bad !" Summing up he muses, "There is no such thing as a bad day's hunting. I never had a blank day in 53 years. You might say I have had a mis-spent life but an interesting one." Not that mis-spent at all most would say.

Maurice Bell MFH with his Wensleydale Hounds in a snowy Dales landscape
(John Haigh)

26

Maurice Bell Esq MFH

I first encountered Maurice Bell on a murky October Sunday. His hounds had met at Semer Water in a lovely part of Wensleydale, a mixture of rugged Fell and stone-walled dales pasture. He was not hunting hounds himself that day due to a back injury, and gave me a lift. Hounds rattled a brace out of tussocky grass and had disappeared over the 2000 foot Fell top, where a thick mist suddenly descended. Pursuing his pack over uncertain terrain through the fog I was left in no doubt that here was one of hunting's truest enthusiasts. This no-nonsense farmer, as ruggedly made as any Dales rock speaks his mind, but would share his last crust with any true devotee of hunting. Impressed by his enthusiasm and the drive of his hounds I vowed to return and learn more about the Wensleydale pack he founded thirty years ago. Running a little behind schedule, I rang en route through the Dales. When I explained I was about ten miles away I was a little puzzled when Mrs Bell replied breezily , "We'll expect you in the next couple of hours then." An hour and twenty minutes later I was given more directions by a man with a trailer full of sheep. I found the right road out of Wensleydale, past the Creamery, and eventually the rough track which leads to the farm. Through a gate, down a steep hill, I lurched cautiously. My destination now clearly visible across the valley, I reached the stream. The ford consisted of boulders and holes probably only negotiable by a drunk in a chieftain tank. The more orthodox route was a bridge, of elderly sleepers, set at an angle, and only inches wider than my car. The drive had been a long one, determined to make the final ascent I walked my intended route as if competing at Badminton. It had to be the bridge, so I lined up the car, closed my eyes and drove. When I opened them, the thought briefly occurred to me that I would have to make the same trip back. I concentrated hard on weaving through sheep, opening the next gate, and the impending interview.

"Will You Walk A Puppy ?"

Maurice was brought up in the nearby valley of Snaisholme, in the Lunesdale country. He recalls helping his father with some fencing whilst still a schoolboy, "A fox came right by us, then hounds. Walt Parkin was hunting them then, and asked if we'd seen them, 'By, what a lovely place for hunting', he said, 'Are you keen on hunting ?' I didn't really know much about it then". Walt asked if he might send the Bells a pup to walk, "It soon went from one to six ! Then I became more interested." As Maurice grew up his interest became a passion. Walt Parkin proposed him for the Committee, and he took on organising Hawes, "I can honestly say that in those days the Lunesdale were the finest pack of hounds in England. They were unbelievably good, 100% genuine to drag, work and mark. It's a hard job to keep on top with a pack of hounds." Deeply involved, and now married, Maurice had set his heart on whipping-in. The job came up, he was encouraged to apply, but did not get it. Understandably, he was very disappointed. Then one or two people suggested that he should set up a pack in this home area, then unhunted, "It appealed to me, did that." It did not however appeal to many of the hunting folk he had hitherto regarded as friends, and he was hurt that his intentions were regarded suspiciously by some of them.

Uphill All the Way - To the Creamery

No-one wanted to give him any hounds, "My Uncle Jack had two trail hounds, then I was offered some from Scotland which had been rioting on deer. There aren't any deer here so I took them, because they were good hounds. Then we got some more." What he really wanted were some Fell hounds, but could not get any. Starting his first Season with eight hounds, they caught eight foxes. For his second season he had just 11 hounds. By strange co-incidence they caught 11 foxes. Maurice's assortment of hounds worked, but he desperately wanted more, as he had not managed to breed any pups. Hounds were now being kept in Hawes itself, which was not ideal. Then a major

27

Stone walls and sheep typify Wensleydale
(Kay Gardner)

breakthrough came in the shape of Kit Calvert who owned the famous Wensleydale Creamery. He lent Maurice a building and hounds were kennelled there very successfully. Then foreman of a tarmac construction company, Maurice was hunting hounds on Saturdays and Sundays, "Kit Calvert's a big Methodist man, and he approved of hunting on Sundays so that was good enough for me." They still hunt on Sundays, and attract a good following, many visitors travelling some distance. One regular follower comes every Sunday from Keswick, and particularly enjoys watching the pups he has walked.

The First Decade and Last Move for Farmer Bell

His roots firmly in farming, Maurice badly wanted to get back in to it. When West Duerley Farm came up he sold his place in Hawes, and moved out there, "It's a great place for hounds, ideally situated, and easy for them to find their way back to. You can walk out ten different ways," he enthuses, sounding like an Estate Agent's description of the Perfect Place For Kennels. By the end of their first decade he had some very good hounds. Then bad luck intervened; some were killed on a railway and a good bitch died whelping. He felt he had taken a big step backwards, and became increasingly frustrated by not being able to get more hounds. Maurice's farmers remained extremely loyal throughout some difficult times., "Many of them were my school friends and really wanted to support me. I had my own transport and did all I could for them. Hunting's all about give and take. You have to listen to people, talk to them and find out what they want." He has no time for those who shirk responsibility, "If there's any kind of trouble you must go straight away and apologise. If hounds run through sheep at a fothering or gathering you must go straight away. I am a stubborn man, but a fair one, and believe in speaking my mind. I'm a down to earth fella. I say what I have to say, and if it isn't liked, fair enough. I don't hold grudges. Tomorrow is another day, and life is too short to be at loggerheads with folk."

Recognition

Maurice built up a hard working Committee and had plenty of local support in this good viewing country, "Dennis Barrow from the Ullswater let me have some hounds, and now a lot of my hounds go back to those. Jimmy Mallett at the North Lonsdale helped me out with some hounds as well." From now on things really looked up. Hunt Chairman Mr Chilton was approaching his 80th Birthday and dearly wanted to see the pack recognised, which they now are, affiliated to the Central Committee of Fell Packs, which entitles their Master to attend one meeting a year.

Middleton Boost

The pack has gone from strength to strength, with drafts from Frank Houghton-Brown MFH at the Middleton providing a timely boost around 1988. "Some say we're Middleton Second String, but the hounds we had were too fast for their own country. We didn't get them because they were duffers. They turned our hounds around." Middleton Stylish '91 (Cottesmore Student '86-Middleton Ambush '86) proved outstanding, "John Nicholson said she was the best hound he had seen to work a fox." She had the Fell blood Maurice wanted and he bred from her. "By Hell her offspring have done us well. Her grandson Stormer is tremendous." Later another Middleton bitch, Alice '93 (Middleton Artist '86-Middleton Vernham '88), proved a star. She was also too fast for her own country, and a very sharp performer. She was so good Frank Houghton-Brown borrowed her back to breed from, putting her to a College Valley dog. She returned, with two of the resultant doghound pups, Bowler and

Briton. "I was afraid they might get too big, but they didn't and are 100% in their work. They've real mettle, not like pups, they worked well from day one. " Alice remains a real performer, only the previous Saturday having hit off the line and led the pack, "She's a really clever hound. All the Middleton hounds I've had have been genuine workers." Interestingly Middleton Artist '86 and Ambush '86 are litter brother and sister by Middleton Beaufort '81 out of Middleton Ardent' 83

Thoughts On Hunting

"My hounds have always been workers not passengers. I like to see them all go away from me in five minutes and cross the Fellside, and find a fox. I can't be doing with hounds following people about, it's no good to me. Hounds should find their own foxes, so I like to keep quiet and let them keep their heads down. I don't like hollering, unless you have to get them on away from a road. They know their job. I do like to watch them drag. Joe Weir once told me 'If you breed off hounds that will drag and mark, you'll have a good pack.' You must breed for work, not show. Looks is nowt to me. I like to see a nice looking pack but work's everything. I prefer light hounds as they're easier to see but I've used our black dog, Gazza, three times because he's brilliant." I was particularly struck by the size of the pack. They are small, not much bigger than harriers, and many have the distinctive Fellhound appearance. "They aren't big and heavy. They must be as fast up as down the Fellside. They are level headed to handle. I don't believe in ruling by the whip. If owt goes wrong then you must straighten them up, but they know when you're annoyed. They must have confidence in you, as well as you in

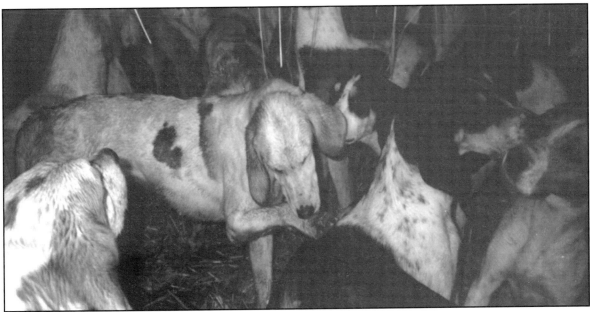

Wensleydale hounds make themselves comfortable at the end of the day (Kay Gardner)

them. We are fortunate to have a country that really lends itself to houndwork. We hunt foxes, not chase them ! My hounds hunt until the moment we go home. I am old-fashioned and not obsessed with the number of foxes hounds catch. We catch about 50 a year on average now but killing's not the be all and end all."

A Dedicated and Proud Team

Hounds thrive here and are genuinely cared about. Philip Bradshaw is an invaluable help, along with his brother Graham. Both are busy when I arrive, and join us for tea. They walk pups with their mother in Kirkbystephen, which always come back well educated and confident. "Philip does so well and keeps us going in kennels." Whipper-in Bill Braithwaite never misses a day, and has sometimes hunted hounds. "I wish I could turn the clock back thirty years ! I've got 40 hounds who all drag and mark," says Maurice proudly. Nothing makes him happier than someone admiring his hounds' work. A few years ago the pack paraded at the Great Yorkshire Show in a Fell hound pageant. "I was so proud they walked through thousands of people in the showground. They really enjoyed it, sterns up.

Maurice Bell boxes hounds up
(John Haigh)

I'm not a professional, but I walked back through that crowd with all 24 hounds, and one of someone else's. Philip's phone rang all night with people saying how they'd enjoyed it." Visitors are often surprised by the pack's ability in the field, "Anyone can come to see my hounds enjoying their job ", adds Maurice proudly.

The Pure Magic of Hounds

The first time Maurice hunted at Dufftown proved memorable. Hounds put off straight away and there was a lot of snow on the ground. They really got away and between 3pm and 6pm there was no sign of them. They had in fact crossed the Alston road. They all turned up in a farmyard, finding their way out of strange country in bad conditions.

A long hunt from Redmire saw hounds catch their fox beyond Middleham in the Lunesdale country one Christmas. They were three hounds short at the end, two pups and Willful. A search was mounted and the local keeper checked his snares. The pups appeared, but not Willful. Maurice waited an hour before returning home, where he found Wilful waiting for him ! This was a good 16 miles across mostly strange country in the dark.

Last Season, hounds met at Chapel le Dale, and marked one fox. They then hunted another onto a ledge above Ingleton Waterfall 150 feet up. Neither Maurice nor Bill spoke, letting them well alone. Their fox was just 6 feet below them, they were going round and round the ledge but could not get to him. Eventually most of the hounds came away, but they were worryingly two short, Magic and Trooper. Magic, with great presence of mind had found his way in to the Pet Shop at Ingleton, walking in as if he lived there, and demolishing most of their biscuits. The owner tied him to a display stand where he waited happily to be collected. Trooper was still missing, and Maurice informed the local police. He was seen on a road at midnight. Hounds were out again on Sunday, and Maurice hoped he would hear them. On Sunday night however he was reported as being near Settle. On Monday morning a roadsweeper saw him on the Settle bypass. On Thursday morning he walked back in to the farmyard, "He'd been to Long Preston, Malham, Kinsey and back. That was clever for a pup, he did a big circle until he got to places he had hunted in and recognised. He couldn't have known his way as he had gone out by vehicle from here."

Enviable Bloodlines

Maurice's pack now boasts some of the best Fell bloodlines available, "The Lunesdale had a hound called Glory who was outstanding. Both my litters of pups this year have lines to Glory." He pulls a

30

Mist comes down rapidy
(Kay Gardner)

pedigree from the shelf and rattles off some of those famous Fell hounds in it - Lunesdale Glory, Ullswater Truman, Eskdale and Ennerdale Tramper, Ullswater Tramper, Ullswater Misty, Blencathra Gallant, Pennine Token, Blencathra Talisman. . . "You have to follow bloodlines to breed hounds. It's no good just breeding from what wins at Rydal or Lowther unless you know the bloodlines. No matter who recommends a hound I like to see it, and look at how it has been bred over the last four generations. That's what will come out, good or bad."

The Real Meaning of 'Care'

There are records of Foxhounds in Wensleydale 300 years ago, as well as the Harriers. For a pack which has been established over just thirty years the Wensleydale is in good heart, "We don't have overheads of course, and farmers welcome us, especially for lamb worrying calls." Some things are more difficult though, like ignorance of those who move in. Maurice illustrates this with a recent example. The previous week hounds had been called on by a farmer with 800 sheep, who was having a fox problem. Maurice duly took hounds there at 5am, only to be reported to the police by the farmer's neighbour, who had just a handful of pet sheep, for sheep worrying ! He has also previously been reported as a badger baiter when seen out with hounds. For the last ten years lambing calls have been fewer than expected. This year he has been hard pushed to fit them all in between their own lambing. He firmly believes that lamping disturbs foxes greatly, especially when there are cubs about, and makes them more likely to take lambs. The farming crisis distresses him greatly, lambs now worth far less than they were four years ago, with no drop in feed costs.

"Those who are against Hunting say it is cruel to kill. When you are a farmer, you know all about it. All death is cruel but you have to accept it. I cannot kill one of my own lambs, or put my own hounds down, yet there are folk who would say you've no feeling if you hunt, or farm. I cannot rest if one of my hounds is left out at the end of a day. I'm not afraid of what they will do, because I trust them, but I want them home safe, in a warm bed, not out on a road somewhere. I really care about them," he says, eyes full of real feeling. Bringing himself back down to earth he plants his tea mug abruptly, to return to his lambs, "Hope you get up to see us again soon. Oh, and mind your radiator on the drive as you go out."

A View of Semer Water (Kay Gardner)

31

An atmospheric shot of Mr John Berkeley at the end of a good hunt
(Jim Meads)

32

R J G Berkeley Esq

It is not every day one pulls up outside a Castle, "Just come to the Outer Bailey and keep going" , were my host's matter-of-fact directions. Driving through these ancient portals seems faintly incongruous. Cannons guard a huge oak door set in the hard pink and lilac grey rock of this fortress which seems to have burst out of the surrounding meadows. There is a grand view here, the Kennels centre stage, as they have always been in Berkeley's long and illustrious history. As I step out of my car the eerie yet joyful sound of hounds singing drifts up to greet me. Inside the courtyard the stark sense of history is overwhelming, as if one has been transported into the set of an old Robin Hood movie. Inside, my host, known throughout Berkeley country simply as 'JB' soon brings me back to the present, "I'm afraid there has been a disaster", he beams looking remarkably unconcerned, bearing coffee and biscuits. My mind leaps to dreadful conclusions - flood, fire, crumbling ancestral masonry ? "My old labrador would not go to the Office for her elevenses and they're *dreadfully* upset", he explains, his face now etched with concern, mine I suspect, with relief that no worse catastrophe loomed. His contribution both to his Estate and the Berkeley hounds in particular is hard to calculate. The genuine affection in which he is held speaks volumes, and this is never more obvious than at the Puppy Show, which I have been lucky enough to attend on several occasions, held in the delightful 17th Century Kennels. Though relinquishing the mastership in 1984, he has maintained a keen interest in his hounds, which he continues to breed to a consistently high standard. Time passes quickly, or perhaps it merely stands still in such surroundings as we chat about the hunting world under the benevolent gaze of countless ruffled Berkeley ancestors. "You must put me in the stocks," jokes this most unlikely dungeon owner. It is not difficult to see why the words most often used to describe him are 'charming', 'modest', and 'genuine.' Over the years I have noticed too that this most unassuming man, like so many to the manner born, never forgets.

History and a Millennium of Hunting

The history of the Berkeley family and their hounds could itself fill several volumes. The family, who can trace their ancestry directly back to Edward the Confessor have been here since Saxon times. There are unique records showing that a pack of hounds has existed on the site since the 12th Century. Many old manuscripts and Day Books refer to hunting, first of stag and buck, and then fox in the 18th Century. A Millennium of hunting and a far more lasting monument than any fickle Dome. You will travel a long way to find a more level pack than this, predominantly light in colour and noted for toughness stamina and drive. There is also a unique colour which appears every so often called Berkeley Blue. This is a chocolate brown colour, akin to liver chestnut in horses which is hereditary but skips a generation before re-surfacing. The country which once stretched from Berkeley to Berkeley Square in London, requiring six kennels to sustain it, is now a long narrow strip beside the River Severn, just 30 miles by about six miles. When the first Earl Fitzhardinge, a great hound man, was dying in 1857, he asked for some of his favourite hounds, including the badger pied Cromwell 1855, whose head can still be seen at the Castle today. The Earl's last words to his huntsman, Harry Ayris were, "There are no better ones Harry", and would still be just as relevant today.

Early Memories

It was not until 1946 that John Berkeley began to hunt regularly. Pre-War he had lived at the family's Worcestershire seat, Spetchley. That first Season, Major Chetty Hilton Green hunted hounds, "I remember they found one fox at Sharpness, running right up to Gloucester. I was on a pony that wouldn't jump anything. I followed the hoofprints through Slimbridge and Frampton, only to meet them all coming back. I would have been about fifteen and felt such a chump !" This was hardly a propitious start, but there were many happier days, and it was not long before he began to take an

interest in the hounds. He would love to have hunted hounds, but the family had a long tradition of professional Huntsmen, "It would have been too awful to show bad sport to one's friends, and they would have been too polite to say so !" First wearing the famous family tawny coat in 1958, in 1960 he became a joint master with his father and Captain Brian Bell, considered very much 'on probation.' Up to 1960 this was still a four-day-a-week country. It was only after his father's death in 1969 that he became really involved with the hound breeding.

Breeding a Level Pack

To undertake the breeding of such a historic pack must have seemed a daunting prospect, "I was lucky to have so much help from Tim Langley. We would sit down together and work out a breeding policy. He knew far more about their working abilities, and would suggest bitches to breed from, and this was an enormous help." This system continues with his successor, Chris Maiden. Mr Berkeley likes to use his own doghounds as much as possible, " I like to think that you know their strong points and their failings far better. If a master really recommends an outside dog strongly, and I need to go out, I will go and see the dog, finding out more about him. We tend to try to keep in Kennel, and I like to think as a consequence we have a very level pack with plenty of drive and stamina." Mr Berkeley feels that the continuity provided by one family breeding a pack, and handing down information from one generation to the next is a great bonus these days when so many masterships come and go, "I am not an innovator. I know what I like to see, and that we have good working stock. I feel no need to go off at a tangent to America or the Fells. I leave that to other people ! I am full of admiration for those who do experiment like Ronnie Wallace, and Tim Unwin. I like to think these hounds are as level as you would find anywhere because one has not experimented, and used hounds we like." One reason why the Berkeley pack is so level is that it possesses just two female lines. That of War-wickshire Pitiful '52 being particularly dominant, "I breed closer than most people would approve of. If you are really certain of the qualities of a hound then there is no harm in that." The blood of Tiverton Actor '22 became lost in some kennels, but the Berkeley kept it going, and though diluted it still sur-vives today. Actor was full of old Berkeley blood, descending tail male from Berkeley Whipcord '12, a son of Four Burrow Whipcord '05. He was in turn by Lord Fitzhardinge's (Berkeley) Vanguard 1899. This line eventually traces directly back to Brocklesby Bumper 1743.

Mr John Berkeley with his hounds and Huntsman Chris Maiden
(Terry Crate)

The Berkeley Hounds with Huntsman Chris Maiden in the Castle Meadows.
(Jim Meads)

When outside sires are sought now they are usually only from the Duke of Beaufort's, Exmoor or Heythrop Kennels. Portman blood was used successfully in the past, Mr Berkeley's father having used Portman Sailor '52 (South Dorset Salesman '44 - Locket '46). More recently Portman Pilot '71 (Whipcord '67 - Pinafore '66) proved a great success. The Heythrop's well-tried Brigand '54 (Sergeant '46-Ludlow Bangle '46) and his son Craftsman '62 (Brigand '54-Crystal '59) nicked very well. One break with tradition came with the use of Limerick Seaman '76. This Old English doghound was recommended by Captain Wallace and had a lot of old Belvoir blood, "His progeny were not much to look at as he was rather a stuffy dog. This proved a very good nick though, and they were as tough as old boots, very good in their work and real foxcatchers. I now have a great lot of hounds going back to him and the stuffiness has bred out." With so many good workers it is hard to pick out the best, "Oh dear, there is such a panoply ! One *hates* to pick them out !" Tottenham '67 (Soldier '64-Tempest '64) was widely used, as was Freshman '84 (Exmoor Freestone '81-Delta '79), both especially highly regarded by their breeder. Further back Rallywood '56 (Cato '50-Random '52) stands out. He possessed the tail male to Brocklesby Bumper 1743 via Four Burrow Whipcord '05 and Tiverton Actor '22. In recent years David '81 (Waggoner '78-Doormat '78) has been the most influential, "I have probably got as nice a looking lot of Stallionhounds now as I've ever had." A lovely young doghound called Holster '98 (Godfrey '95-Hasty '93) is an exciting prospect. His top line goes back to the aforementioned Tiverton Actor '22, whilst his dam Hasty is by VWH Hackler '88, whose paternal grandsire was Berkeley Borwick '79. Few doghounds are kept now the country is only hunted two days a week. Those that are kept may be regarded as exceptional in their work, "With lovely bitches and very good doghounds it is really very difficult to go wrong" , says Mr Berkeley with typical modesty.

35

Work Not Show

The Berkeley hounds are traditionally not shown at the country's major hound shows. That they would win many good prizes if they were is indisputable. Their Stallionhound Denmark '95 (Duke of Beaufort's Daystar '91-Heroine '93) took part in a parade of non-showing packs last summer at Peterborough and looked very good indeed. Showing is something which Mr Berkeley holds strong views on, "My father never showed, and I never will. Absolutely not. We shall always breed purely for work." He adds with a disarming smile, "Anyway, I would be a terrible loser, and should hate to see an ignorant judge chucking out my lovely hounds !" It is very good news for the Berkeley that his younger son Henry joins the mastership on 1st May 2000, to ensure continuity, "I've knocked it in to his head not to Show too."

The Country and its Puppy Walkers

The best hunting in the current Berkeley country undoubtedly took place before the M5 was built. It was then possible for hounds to run up in to the hill country. As elsewhere, the country has changed in character, "When Tim Langley arrived there was far more undrained turf, which was better scenting. What we call the Marsh has changed tremendously because of the drainage scheme and as a result there is more plough." The famous rhines are mostly too steep to jump now having been dug right out to be arms of the Sea. "Some intrepid youngsters do jump the smaller ones. Personally I am rather relieved that they are unjumpable now. I well remember wondering if we would ever get out of some of them ! Traditionally, even pre-War, foxes have run up and down the Vale rather than across, so the M5 was not such a problem as it might have been. We still have the runs we had in the 1950s down towards Aust, but those hunts from Michaelwood to the hills just cannot happen any more. Then of course the M4 came too." The hill country has changed perhaps most of all, its wildness tamed and thick brambles tidied, with some Shoots springing up. The Vale still has relatively little shooting and is geared very much towards hunting.

The Berkeley country though diminished in size has lost nothing of its sporting spirit over the years. There is a particularly long tradition of puppy walkers who have undertaken this labour of love for generations. Some here have been walking puppies for over a Century, "In my father's day there were around ten farmers out towards Halmore, and on any morning you would hear hounds screaming around the woods. As soon as their walkers let them out they joined up and went hunting on their own."

Mr John Berkeley and the 10th Duke of Beaufort at a joint meet held to celebrate the Duke's 80th Birthday at Badminton House (Kay Gardner)

The Future

Mr Berkeley naturally worries about his lovely hounds and what the future might hold for them. The thought of destroying this wonderful pack would be as unthinkable as demolishing the Castle itself. The intransigence of ignorant urban MPs makes him very angry. Yet there is so much to be positive about. Contrary to popular belief not all farmers who welcome the Hunt are tenants. There are countless small landowners, "They love to see the hounds. With the exception of fishing, hunting is truly the most democratic of sports." He pays tribute too to the hard work in Kennels, " I have been very lucky with the Hunt Staff we have had here. Tim of course, I was extremely lucky that he stayed for so long. Hunt Service is a vocation - hard work, long hours, all weathers. You have to love it to do it. Still there are keen young men coming in to it which I think bodes well." The future of the Berkeley hounds looks assured as far as their owners are concerned. Mr Berkeley's younger son Henry hunts, and his elder son Charles is keen

36

Autumn morning with the Berkeley Hounds drawing the coverts beside the Castle
(Kay Gardner)

too, though he prefers to follow on foot. That Henry is joining the mastership on 1st May 2000 gives him great pleasure, "I am determined to teach him more about the hound breeding than my father taught me. I was pretty green when I took over and I feel it is most important for one Joint Master to be in charge of that side." He looks across the Castle Meadows, "These haven't changed much ! We had a whole day on this wonderful old turf a fortnight ago. The horses were so fresh at the end of it too. It was just like the old days." Somehow this seems to sum things up neatly, for although there has been careful planning, and great foresight about the future, good old-fashioned standards have been maintained. Just like the old days indeed.

Albert Buckle takes hounds to draw
(Jim Meads)

38

Albert Buckle

I had heard a great deal of Albert Buckle, legendary Huntsman and horn blower, not least from my old friend Albert Hickson. His real name is Alan, but he so idolised Albert Buckle, often saying, 'Albert wouldn't have done it that way . . .' that his friends called him Albert, the name he has now adopted. He had told me how he had been mad on hunting as a boy and as Albert was his local Huntsman had got in touch to seek his advice, "You'd better get down here." Soon he found himself helping out in the Kennels, and left in no doubt about how things should be done, "If you did something wrong out hunting you soon got a rollicking, but he always took time to explain on the way home just what you should have done, and told you to remember it ! He was marvellous with the young and always made time for them." Hickson too is marvellous (a word both Alberts use frequently) with the young and was paid the compliment by Albert Buckle that, "He does the job right." So how, I wondered, did Albert Buckle, who has influenced so many in Hunt Service, learn his own trade ? I travelled to his home in Bedfordshire to find out. It seems unbelievable that this dapper figure is now 85.

The Bookmaker, the Butcher and the Boy who Wanted to be a Huntsman

When Albert Buckle was at school, all he ever wanted was to wear a scarlet coat. His father had other ideas however, as proprietor of the local butcher's shop and, unusually Bicester's Bookmaker as well, "Father's butcher's shop was on the opposite side of the road from his betting office in Bicester and he apprenticed me to a friend of his in Oxford and I had three years there after school. They had some ponies they used to deliver the meat." This gave Albert his only interest at the butcher's shop, "One day father came in to the shop, I thought hello, what the hell does he want ? He said, 'Come on I'm taking you home. They say you'll never be any good at this job, as all you think about is horses.' At that time Mr Oliver Gilbey was joint master of the Bicester, and used to do a bit of business with father. Anyway he took me on and I started to take Mrs Gilbey's horse to the meet and bring their car back for them."

In Hunt Service with the Bicester

The following Season in 1934 Albert was sent to ride second horse to the second whipper-in at the Bicester Kennels. Riding second horse to the Huntsman followed, before he was put on as second whipper-in. "Clarence Johnson, Charlie's father could be a hard man. I used to go home and cry at night sometimes if he'd been at me all day, but I always hark back to his ways. He was a great man for discipline, and he did things the right way." The Bicester country was totally unspoilt then, "It was marvellous all grass. It was quite a sight to see a field of three hundred people jumping a hundred abreast. Colonel Blacker was the Secretary - marvellous man. You never even thought to look and see if there was any wire there, because you knew there wasn't. Major Field Marsham was very good to me, he was joint master of the Bicester when I first went there. He really was a smashing man and bred marvellous bitches. When I first came here they were all the Old English black and tan types. He hunted the bitches, and Clarence Johnson, hunted the doghounds. Sir Peter Farquhar bred marvellous doghounds. I remember going down to see the Portman hounds with Charlie Johnson when he was looking for Stallionhounds. They brought out five or six couple of bitches for us to see as well. They were all so alike, strong-backed and looked a treat. " After several years there Albert joined up to go to war and was in the Hussars," I was with horses first of all, which I thoroughly enjoyed. I was in the Army with the late Dick Deakin, whose son William later came to me as whipper-in."

The Hertfordshire - and Marriage

When Albert was demobbed he went to the Hertfordshire as whipper-in, "They were the wildest pack of hounds I've ever seen then. They'd hunt a blackbird up a bloomin' hedgerow. They were fast !" After two years Albert married having met his future wife at the Oakley Hunt Ball, "She was a physiotherapist, which came in very handy at times !"

Two Happy Years at the Duke of Buccleuch's

The newly weds moved up to the Duke of Buccleuch's in Scotland, "When I went up on interview we were stopped with frost here. We had a hell of a day. I whipped in to George Steele, who was leaving." Albert was clearly very much at home there, "We had a lovely two years. Tom Smith hunted hounds. He was a very good Huntsman, one of the old Smith family and died not so long ago. A lovely chap, old Tom." With fields of about forty and all grass there was much fun to be had. Colonel Scott MFH hunted the doghounds, Tom Smith the bitches. Another influence on Albert at that time was Jack Howells, "He was one of the best and hunted the North Northumberland for a long time. He was a great Huntsman and a wonderful friend who helped me as much as anybody. I was in the Army with him, though not the same regiment. He started off riding second horse at the Bicester too years ago." The Duke of Buccleuch's Kennels were in the village of St Boswell's opposite the Buccleuch Arms. "One day Colonel Scott's sister-in-law kept galloping in front of hounds, he said, 'If you do that once more I'll take hounds home.' She did, and he said, 'Come on Albert, we're going home. All this galloping about all over the place is no good.' He gave me a hell of a good reference when I left there. The old Duke was a lovely man, smashing."

The North Cotswold - Broadway Idyll

Albert's next step up brought him down to the North Cotswold in 1950. This was his first post as Kennel Huntsman, "I took over from Tom Watchorn who became a great friend of mine. He was a great help to me." Albert liked the country and they made many friends, "In those days if you didn't go somewhere once a fortnight they wanted to know where you'd got to, I really loved it. When the old bitches had whelps I used to let them lie out under the trees in Broadway High Street. You couldn't do that now, you wouldn't get down the drive on a Sunday !" Though taken on as Kennel Huntsman, Albert hunted hounds for two seasons when Major Fanshawe went, "We had a lot of fun and caught a lot of foxes." Then unbelievably it all came to an end, "One night it was snowing like hell and freezing cold. Lord Dulverton came to see me and asked me to go outside with him. He walked me up and down that yard in the snow and said, 'I'm afraid you will have to go.' It turned out they were trying to get Major Fanshawe to come back into the mastership."

To the Whaddon and a New Challenge

That was how Albert came to hunt the Whaddon Chase in 1954 with Dorian Williams, world famous show jumping commentator as master, "The Kennels in Ascott Park were absolutely lovely, and really easy to run." Albert set about the challenge of sorting out the hounds and breeding up a pack he could be proud of, "When I first came to Whaddon they were the worst looking pack of hounds I'd seen in my life. There wasn't one you'd want to breed from. Everybody kept on about this marvellous white hound which was always a field in front. The pack would run three fields, and with this damn' thing in front, instead of turning they'd go straight up to her. They had no chance of recovering the line. I got rid of her, and there was hell to pay with Major Drabble as he thought she was marvellous. I don't think any hound is that much better than the rest to be so far ahead all the time. If they're that far ahead, then you know damn' well they're doing something wrong. Either they're throwing their tongues, or not drawing, or they're just galloping about. The first six hounds can do more harm that way than the last six who are slower behind. They are often the ones you want on a bad scenting day."

Breeding Back to the Best Pays off - with Grimston '61

Albert set about looking back through all the Stud Books, "Sir Peter Farquhar had hunted them before the War and had a marvellous pack of hounds. There was just one bitch that went back to his breeding. I bred from her and that's how we got Grimston '61(Duke of Beaufort's Garter '55 - Wisdom '58)." Grimston's dam Wisdom'58 was by Portman Wizard '55, out of Gravel '56, a daughter of Portman Grossman '52 bringing in the two main Portman male lines.

"He was all blue mottle, a lovely looking dog." Grimston's fame spread and he was widely used, becoming the Whaddon's most famous Stallionhound, "I said to Captain Wallace that I had a dog here he ought to look at , as I thought a hell of a lot of him. I wanted Captain Wallace to try him. Well, he borrowed him, and gave him four bitches. They bred a lot of stud dogs from him. He was a marvellous dog to hunt. I'd seen him pull out away from the rest to kill a fox many times. I only wish I'd used him even more." One of Grimston's sons was Heythrop Peeler '67 who went on to sire Heythrop Peacock '73, whose own son Heythrop Brimstone '76 became another widely used, and respected sire. It is a line noted for strong, muscular backs. Heythrop Peeler's sister Perky '67 went to the Tiverton, where she founded her own highly thought of dynasty. Her name appears in some famous VWH pedigrees today.

Gallic Influence

Tom Smith's father, Frank, hunted the Dumfriesshire for over 20 years, "A proper old boy he was. There are two Dumfriesshire lines, one Bloodhound, one French. When I was at the North Cotswold we had two given us, one from each line. The Bloodhound line one wasn't very sharp, but the French line one was a hell of a good bitch. At the North Cotswold we had a hell of a hunt from Dumbleteon. She was in the first three all the way. Mrs Fanshawe was doing the breeding then and wasn't very keen on her, so gave her to me when I left. It was the best thing she could have done for me." The Dumfriesshire bitch soon proved invaluable," She half put these hounds right on her own she was so super. Sleek as a mole she was."

"He who Hesitates is Lost"

When asked what qualities a good Huntsman needs, Albert's reply is swift and positive, "Dedication, and more dedication. Using initiative is very important as well. One of my great expressions is, 'He who hesitates is lost'. It's no good dithering about. You have to make your mind up and go, it is so very important. Many masters ruin Huntsmen by interfering. With Mr Williams, whatever I did he would always back me. Not that I always did everything right by a long way, but if you *know* you have that sort of backing, you *know* you can always get out there and have a go. If you are always having to think, 'I wonder what the master will say if I do this, or that ?', it slows you down. You need a free hand to make your mind up and go. I was very lucky to be with Mr Williams. He really encouraged children to hunt too. The other thing that is important is to allow hounds to use their brains. If the whipper-in is always after them every time they make a move they'll never do anything for you."

Albert Buckle with Mr Dorian Williams MFH (Jim Meads)

41

No Smoke without Fire

"Lord Knutsford was a good man. We ran once into the Grafton country a long way. They'd gone really well, and checked. I saw a bonfire, and thought it had turned our fox away. When I held 'em round, I could see Lord Knutsford wondering what I was doing, as he wouldn't have seen the bonfire where he was. He apologised afterwards and said, ' I was just saying to the Field what the *hell's* he doing ? Then I realised'!"

Welsh Influence, Harrass of the Curre

Albert was clearly not afraid to try something different in his quest for good hounds, "One of the best hounds I ever hunted was a bitch called Harrass from the Curre. A fellow called Reg Dale hunted the Curre for many years, and when he retired he came up to live with his sister who had a big Nursery in Lincoln. When he asked if I wanted three of the best Curre hounds, I said yes, of course. The Curre were all so good in those days. Sir Edward Curre had bred them on the same lines for over a hundred years. You'd be a twerp not to have them. He gave me a rough one, Harrass, a smooth one and a broken coated one. Harrass, was a first Season hound. I bred, and bred, and bred from her. Eventually they came smooth coated again, and they were all good. When I first came here, all these coverts had been planted for hunting. Lord Knutsford cut and laid every one because we had a job to find that first Season. After that they were really thick. Drawing you'd suddenly hear, 'Raaaaaah', when this old bitch found. She ran up for eight seasons. When I went first to the North Cotswold we had a draft from them and they were all good too. Harrass was an ugly hound but she was marvellous in her work."

Albert Buckle takes a Hunt jump - there were none when he first came to the Whaddon Chase. (Jim Meads)

Puckeridge and Badminton Play Their Part

Other Stallionhounds also had a part to play in the pack's make up, "We used to use the Puckeridge Stallionhounds quite a bit and they used to nick in well. They hunted so well. Ned Paxton was Kennel Huntsman then. Their hounds used to be bigger when they used Brocklesby blood. Since they used the Welsh they got smaller." There is praise too for the Badminton blood, "In those days you could go to the Beaufort and pick any one of ten Stallionhounds. The old Duke was so good to us boys. You could always use any hound you wanted, or borrow one. He would give you good hounds too, and

they always hunted really well, they weren't just the tripe. We had Duke of Beaufort's Carbine '76 (Bugler '71-Crafty '72), and I hunted him several Seasons."

As Good as the Quorn

As word spread of Albert's slick style of hunting, and the Fieldmaster who liked to give the Field a real run for their money, the Fields began to increase, " A lot of characters hunted with us, from Lord Knutsford, to Victor Lowndes. Mr Williams was a good Fieldmaster. He always treated me as a friend, not an employee. Horses were his great love, and he let me get on with breeding the hounds". The country was unspoilt then by the sprawl of Milton Keynes and busy roads jammed with fast moving traffic, "When I first came there was no such thing as hunt jumps. On a Tuesday you would never cross a ploughed field, it was all grass. We had a marvellous time. Then when people started growing winter corn we had to have hunt jumps put in. It had been a marvellous country before the war, and they often got fields of three hundred. It was the best country near to London, and before my time there were Stables in every house near Leighton Station."

Milton Keynes Changes Everything

The development of Milton Keynes was a dreadful blow to the countryside here, "We'd had tremendous fun. It was easily as good as the Quorn country. Then all coverts and hedgerows were pulled up, when the town was built and it just keeps growing." The strain on the country was intolerable, and just two years after Albert retired, the Whaddon Chase amalgamated with the Bicester and Warden Hill, his beloved Kennels turned into a private house, "It's a job for them to get one day a week this end now. Mentmore Golf Course is now on what was Lord Rosebery's estate. All the big woods left near Milton Keynes are too close to the town to draw now. Even in these villages the traffic night and morning is terrible. You'd get every hound under the sun killed around Bletchley and Buckingham now in no time at all." Albert hunted the Whaddon Chase hounds for 26 Seasons, and then stayed on three more with David Barker, "Just to teach him the ropes !"

Legendary Horn Blower - and a Command Performance

Albert's prowess on the hunting horn is legendary. At the Horse and Hound Ball he won a cup, three silver hunting horns, and a car mascot, "We had some good times at the Horse and Hound Ball. A gang of us would go up together." This fame led to him being invited to give a rather special horn blowing performance, "It was years ago now. When the Duke of Beaufort was Master of the Horse he used to entertain 40 of the Royal Family at Buckingham Palace every year. Anyway, he rang and asked if I would go and blow the hunting horn while they were having dinner. The first man I met when I got there was his butler, who I knew from their puppy shows. He gave me a couple of good whiskies while I got changed. After I'd blown all the calls, they all came to thank me. I had another drink afterwards, and left. It was past midnight and there was no traffic about. I went down Baker Street, and as I went over the first set of traffic lights it turned red, and the next did the same. When the third one did the same too a policeman came up, and the conversation went something like this: 'Did you know you went through three traffic lights ? It's gone midnight. Who are you, and what are you doing ?' 'I'm a Huntsman', 'A what ?' ' A Huntsman, and I've been to Buckingham Palace to blow the hunting horn for the Queen. ' What?! Bugger off, before I pinch you.' I don't think he believed me somehow. Luckily he seemed in a hurry to get home !"

A Unique Occasion - Carrying the Horn again at 80

On his 80th Birthday Albert hunted the Bicester with Whaddon Chase hounds. It was a unique occasion," Ian McKie let me do it. I can't think of any other master who would." Even Albert wondered how the pack would react to a strange Huntsman, " I worried a bit that they might not go with me, but as soon as we started to draw they went. We had a lot of luck and they caught a brace. " Albert had hunted regularly until then on a horse given to him when he retired and several others. He decided to end on a high note, "I haven't ridden since. I chucked it after that. If you are old and have a fall you can't roll and get out of the way. You'd just lob there and the old horse would be on top of you." A Birthday Party followed in Winslow Village Hall, attended by many including his old friend Jim Bennett former Huntsman to the Vale of Aylesbury, Mr and Mrs Peter Stoddart, Mr Derek Ricketts, Bicester Secretary Jamie Judd, John Rawdings, Mr Bill Shand Kidd, Mr Ian Mackie MFH, Patrick Martin the Bicester's current Kennel-Huntsman, and Brian Pheasey who he succeeded.

Albert Buckle Whaddon Chase Huntsman 1954-1980 cutting his 80th Birthday cake at a party at Winslow. Watching are Mr Peter Stoddart MFH (Heythrop), Jim Bennett, retired Huntsman Vale of Aylesbury, David Randall, Badsworth Huntsman, and Patrick Martin, Huntsman to the Bicester Hunt with Whaddon Chase. (Jim Meads)

"Mr and Mrs Stoddart have always been very good to me. Mr Stoddart joined Mr Williams in the mastership after fifteen years and we got on very well. They went to live in a lovely house in the Heythrop country. They always have the Opening Meet at their house and have a very good covert where hounds always find. I go over and stay with them every Summer, and they have a wonderful party for me, inviting many Huntsmen and old friends from that part of the world, which I really look forward to."

Tracker Lives up to her Name

"Tom Watchorn who had been so good to me used to have our draft hounds when he was at the Essex. We had an old bitch called Tracker '62, who I'd bred several litters from, and I asked Tom if he would like her, as she was a good old bitch. I took her and met him at Hatfield." Three days later a man going to a meet of the Hertfordshire rang to ask if Albert had lost a hound, as he'd seen one cross the road. " I said I hadn't lost any, and was he sure it wasn't a puppy at walk." The man said it was definitely an older hound, "When he said it was yellow and white, I rang Tom and sure enough he said he'd lost Tracker." Instead of returning to the Kennels she made her way back to the Warrens down the road, who had walked her, "She'd crossed the M1, A1 and I don't know how many other roads, and her old pads were a bit sore." It was a remarkable journey of around 70 miles over strange country, "She'd gone there by Land Rover, and was back here in just three days! It turned

44

out Tom had taken her hunting and she'd tickled off. " Tracker habitually made a detour to see the Warrens when Albert had walked hounds out, and as nothing would deter her he had let her get on with it, "In the end I'd just pop back later and pick her up. Anyway, I couldn't send her away again now." There was no doubt that Tracker had made her own mind up about where she wanted to live, "June Warren kept her for us as a brood bitch. She used to lie on the sofa and stink ! She's buried in their garden now." He recalls another 'homing' incident from his early days at the Bicester, "We sent a bitch down to the Aldershot Draghounds. I went into Kennels one morning, and there she was waiting at the door, all the way from Aldershot. They're like pigeons !"

From the Chase to a View

Albert shows me his pictures and we talk of hounds and rough coated terriers. Since his wife died eight years ago, Albert has lived alone," I had to fend for myself, mind you it's surprising what you can do if you've got to. I'd never cooked before !" His daughter farms just outside Aylesbury, and his son lives in Milton Keynes. He now plays golf several times a week, "I'm not the best golfer in the world but I enjoy it. When you've been active all your life you've got to have something to do, else you'd be six foot under before long. You must have an interest in life especially when your job has been your main interest. A lot of people I'd dealt with in town who hunted played. Everyone at the Club knows what I did, and pull my leg about hunting." The golf club is just ten minutes away, "I'm the oldest playing member in the Senior Section. I am very lucky to be doing what I'm doing at 85. I've got a lot of friends in the country, and know a lot of people about." He shows me the view from his garden across to High Haven one of his favourite coverts, and the first draw from the opening meet, "Christmas Gorse, that was another good one just a field from the Bicester country. Then you could get cracking a bit for the Quainton Hills. I've had a good life and met some marvellous people you know. "

45

Captain Simon Clarke, Judge at Peterborough.
(Jim Meads)

46

Captain Simon Clarke

The passing of another Hunting Season is always a poignant time, a time for reflection on that which has gone before. Hunting's canvas is an ever shifting landscape, as people move from place to place and hand over the horn to make way for new blood. I attended Captain Clarke's last meet as master of the New Forest Foxhounds on a glorious Spring day near Godshill. I had first met him many years ago, with his stepfather Major Gerald Gundry, who had been influential in nurturing my own early interest in hunting. I soon realised that here is a man who makes a lasting impression, not in a brash, garrulous way, but through a genuine interest in people, and a truly dedicated love of his hounds.

Beginnings

Simon Clarke's father was killed in World War II. He recalls following Stanley Barker and the Pytchley hounds by bicycle from their home with his cousin Jimmy Shaw (later MFH West Norfolk Foxhounds) around 1942. One day Jimmy's leg was broken by a kick from a horse, and the Field, to young Simon's horror simply passed by. When his widowed mother re-married Major Gerald Gundry Simon Clarke's foxhunting future took clearer shape. He has vivid early memories of hunting here, first at Garden Plantation, Westonbirt, "I got frightfully excited when I saw the fox, to everyone's embarrassment !"

Subtle Influences

Up to now there had been little in the way of male influence in young Simon's life. Major Gundry had tremendous character, irrepressible humour and a great understanding of farming and the countryside. He was exceptionally good with the young, who were invariably drawn to him as a result. His influence on Simon Clarke is clear to all who knew 'the Major', who had himself been hugely influenced by his grandfather Parson Milne. The Major had a tremendous interest in, and memory for people, their families, dogs, children, ponies and problems. It was an almost pastoral care. Captain Clarke also has this insatiable interest and memory, frequently astonishing those whose countries he has visited by remembering details and people's names, "My stepfather had such infectious enthusiasm which knew no bounds. We had such fun hunting then, especially in the Park. The late Duke was also wonderful with the young of course, although I was rather in awe of him. He was always keen to give us some good hunting during the school holidays." The fact that he was witnessing some rather special hunting had yet to dawn on him - it was just what he had grown up with.

Major Gerald Gundry DSO,MFH
(Kay Gardner)

47

Eton College Beagles and Upward

Against such a background it was small wonder that he became Master of the Eton Beagles for the 1953-54 season. It was only now he began to realise that the late Duke made handling hounds look rather easier than it was in reality ! There is nothing like the tireless enthusiasm and unfailing charm, of those cheerful little hounds to strike a chord with the budding hound man. Little by little, the inevitable course of his life was being mapped out. During the holidays he was able to take the Beagles home and kennel them in Estcourt Park, a short distance from Major Gundry's home, "We had a lot of fun. I remember one wonderful hunt in the Dauntsey Vale. We found near Miles' Gorse and caught our hare at Great Wood. You would never do it now with the Motorway and Railway. It was a four and a half mile point, and I lost my horn in the River ! People were so kind and we had good meets in the VWH country around Brinkworth, and in the Berkeley country too." In the Season before he went to Sandhurst he also enjoyed some hunting with Captain Wallace at the Heythrop, "He had been there three or four seasons, and was at his peak." At Sandhurst he continued his association with Beagles, hunting the Sandhurst pack. This included a trip to Northumberland with them, which he enjoyed very much.

Army, Leicestershire and Ireland

Serving with the Blues after a spell abroad he was sent to Melton Mowbray, "I was lucky enough to have something like 76 days' hunting, some on my own horses and many on the black horses. George Barker was still at the Quorn, Jim Webster had just started at the Belvoir, and Bob Hoare was in the first year of his Cottesmore mastership." Thanks to this wide experience he became an accomplished horseman playing polo, point-to-pointing and winning the Army prize in the Melton Hunt Club Ride. He confesses that at this time he was more interested in the riding aspect of hunting, than the houndwork. Fate then took a hand. In one week's leave Simon Clarke and fellow Blues Officer Hugh Pitman had six days' hunting in Leicestershire, before a foot and mouth outbreak struck. Mrs Migs Greenall said she could send one of them to Ireland. The two men tossed a coin, and Simon Clarke won, "I saw a lot of hounds over there and had wonderful sport. I hunted with Lord Daresbury's Limerick hounds four days a week, and others on the remaining days." For thirteen days he hunted every day, "I had second horses every day. Lord Daresbury alone had twenty hunters. I am eternally grateful to Migs Greenall." His appetite for sport now thoroughly whetted, Simon Clarke's future as a Master of Foxhounds was sealed. He continued to hunt whilst in the army, and kept horses with Badminton's famous and sorely missed tenant farmer the late Jack Windell.

South Dorset 62-69

Like many young men before and since he began hunting foxhounds in the delectable South Dorset country. He quickly earned a reputation as a down-to-earth farmers' man, and a great ambassador for foxhunting. His dedication lasted all year round, and much time was spent doing the essential groundwork which gives such a crucial insight into a country. He would be made welcome at many a farmhouse table, and was always more than willing to lend a hand. This is a man who responds to those who appreciate good hound work. He first encountered some woolly Welsh lines here, "To my stepfather's horror, I rather took to them !" He had inherited a good working pack here, carefully bred, "Captain Mike Wellesley Wesley was a great friend of Captain Jack Evans from the Brecon. The famous Sire South Dorset Salesman '44 was bred here during his mastership. I learned a lot from those hounds and took some with me when I moved on to the Cottesmore."

Cottesmore 69-76

In 1969, plough had yet to make its presence really felt in the Cottesmore country and Captain Clarke showed himself able to provide good sport both in the fashionable Shires grass, and in the less 'high pressure' Lincolnshire side. He may have been impressed that his teenage stepsister Jane was always up with him whenever she came up for a day. Jane told me however, that on his big strong hunters, she had little choice ! Using New Forest Medyg '69, bred by his great friend the late Sir Newton Rycroft , who had taken the New Forest, they began to exchange whelps. The hounds he brought from the South Dorset provided the basis for his hound-breeding policy. The 'woolly' influence he began continues successfully at the Cottesmore today.

Duke of Buccleuch's 76-79

After seven Seasons of the hard riding Fields of the Cottesmore, Captain Clarke's next move took him to the wilder country of Scotland. Though foxes endured a harsher attitude North of the Border and were by no means abundant, much fun was to be had in this more open landscape. He found himself hunting yet another type of country, where the style of hunting hounds was necessarily different. He also gained first hand experience of the Old English hound, and its lower scenting qualities. "I could not influence the way hounds hunted in those hills. They had to draw wider." Here he had the opportunity to watch the College Valley pack in action, "I was impressed by the way they drew wide, and got together very quickly when they found." He was subsequently lent a bitch by Martin Letts MFH. The Liddesdale also impressed him when they visited the Duke of Buccleuch's country for a joint meet, "They brought eight couple and I took eight couple of ours - a big pack for them. It was at the end of the Season and a very hot day. Late in the afternoon they checked on burnt ground and my hounds got fed up, going off to drink from the burn far quicker than theirs did ! True, they had cooked flesh, and mine ate raw, but I was very impressed with their tenacity." The lure of the South proved too great however and after just three seasons Captain Clarke moved to the South and West Wilts.

South and West Wilts 79-90

The Wiltshire country of this pack enjoys a variety of open downland, woods and more open country. In many ways it is similar to that of the South Dorset, and these two countries would be the most similar Captain Clarke hunted. The variety of country he hunted speaks volumes for his diversity as a Huntsman and hound breeder. It is significant too that the packs he has been connected with are well-established, requiring careful breeding to maintain high standards. Here he inherited the wonderful bloodlines established by Mr Ikey Bell, so instrumental in the introduction of Welsh lines, through the Brecon. Again he was able to successfully blend in the bloodlines of his own hounds. Mr Tim Unwin former Master of the Cotswold told me, "He was a great assessor of a hound's capabilities, nose, voice and constitution." He certainly had a wide reputation for being able to place draft hounds carefully, in countries he thought would suit their individual qualities, and his judgement in this was highly respected. His Kennel Huntsman John Tulloch found him easy to whip in to, as he instinctively knew which hounds were on with him. His memory for hounds verges on the photographic, and once he had seen the young entry, he knew them.

Captain Simon Clarke MFH taking the Cottesmore hounds to draw, January 1971 (Jim Meads)

New Forest 92-96

After an uneasy two year sabbatical hunting the New Forest country provided a new challenge, "It is a different art. The country is 40% wooded, 60% open. Where foxes used to be found out in the open, lying in bogs and so on, the ten million visitors have pushed them back in to the covert." With the majority of foxes found in the woods, he realised the value of really good cry, "I think this was the first time I really took notice of voice, and concentrated on breeding for it." The pack's deep booming cry was certainly an impressive feature. He clearly enjoyed the pure venery here, "Yes, they were a very happy four years." There is a certain magic aura about the ancient Forest, where hounds hunt under the watchful gaze of the ponies, and doubtless innumerable spirits of Monarchs and their hounds who hunted it from Norman times.

*Captain Clarke and the New Forest Hounds at his last meet. Mr Alastair Jackson
and Sir Newton Rycroft on foot (Kay Gardner)*

Sir Newton Rycroft's legacy could not have been in more capable hands, than of this man who so clearly cherishes hounds. On numerous visits to other countries they never failed to give a good account of themselves. They visited the Beaufort country when Jane Gundry married Philip Tuckwell, for a joint meet with the Wynnstay at Clayfields. Despite Robin Gundry's horse depositing him unceremoniously on top of hounds at the meet, a thoroughly enjoyable morning ensued. A busy day ended practically at dusk, most of the Monday country having been covered. In his last Season hounds were taken to the Curre country in frost, and to the Berkeley's hills on a hot Spring day. Many would have handed hounds over to their Kennel Huntsman at the box without another thought. Captain Clarke, mindful of hounds' need to please took time to make much of them at the end of a hot and difficult day.

Part of the Family

When his daughter Clarissa married Captain Tim Forster's Assistant Trainer Henry Daly, whose own late father was a master of the Ledbury, Captain Clarke was understandably delighted. Clarissa told me, "He was so excited, and wouldn't tell us what he had planned for our going away after the wedding." All became clear when the New Forest hounds arrived, clearly enjoying the occasion as much as anybody. "We were to 'go away' behind hounds of course, how else ? It was brilliant. You see hounds were always part of the family, he just adored them."

Thoughts on Hound Breeding - and Quality

On hound breeding his views are characteristically concise and clear. His views are sought after and freely given by this most approachable of senior foxhunters, "We used mostly Exmoor and Badminton blood at the South and West Wilts." That is not to say however that he subscribes to wholly orthodox lines. Like many he is a fan of the New Forest Medyg '69 line, "I have always had some. He served us very well. The only problem with it is that unless you have a Kennel with size, like Badminton, it is apt to get very small bitches. Once you lose size it is very difficult to get it back." He also mentions the other relatively 'modern' woolly line of Vale of Clettwr Fairy '73, introduced at the Bicester by Captain Ian Farquhar, "It is very effective. The Bicester bitches are tremendous. It is a very good scenting line with good cry and great perseveranco." He describes his practical knowledge of the Fell lines as 'Rather limited', but has had success using a College Valley bitch. One experiment from his New Forest days was the introduction of a part French dog called Bonaparte '94 (Dumfriesshire Bordeaux '92-Countess '89), now with David Palmer at the Worcestershire and showing encouraging signs. He is outstandingly low scenting, and has some pleasing offspring who have inherited his great voice, "It isn't that new, the Duke of Beaufort imported a French hound which had won the Paris Hound Show in the mid-nineteenth Century. I felt it was a wonderful way of sealing cry which is so important in a country like the New Forest. Those French hounds can be somewhat plain and ponderous, so you do need to be careful. The key is to keep quality up all the time. To lose size is a bore, but to lose quality is *dreadful.*"

Trust, Observation and Tact

On hunting hounds too his thoughts are equally sensible, "Trusting your hounds is the key to success at all times. The moment you think you know more than they do is the moment you come unstuck !" Once told that his hounds were on a hare, he replied only, "Aren't they doing it *beautifully* ?" Such confidence in his hounds was proven when after a good hunt, the 'hare' was marked to ground ! Unsurprisingly, for a man who clearly knows his own mind, decisiveness ranks high in his estimations, "You've got to get on with whatever you have decided to do, whether it is making a cast, taking hounds to a holloa, or choosing which fox to go with." Observation is an important quality for a Huntsman to possess. This hints at Major Gundry's influence , for I had often heard him remark that no reconnaissance is ever wasted. Captain Clarke's explanation confirms this, "There were at least three different ways of getting from Clayfields to Badminton. My stepfather made a point of varying his routes there and back every time. He would say, 'You might notice a new drain, or see a fox, or meet someone who gives you useful information.' That is so true. As a Huntsman, or master, you should be observant all year round. You must know *absolutely* what is going on around your country. More than ever nowadays tact is important too."

An Eye for a Hound

As a judge, Captain Clarke lacks nothing in integrity. When he makes his decision you feel that he has done it fairly and for all the right reasons. He is never afraid to explain his methods to anyone who asks, however publicly. He laughed when I put this to him, replying, "Well, I always think the longer you give everybody else to look, the more criticisms they will come up with !" His modesty belies an eye for a hound developed at an early age. At Badminton the young hounds were looked at every week by 'Master', Major Gundry and any guests they happened to have. To be present at one of these appraisals was pure gold to anyone who loves looking at hounds, and Simon Clarke had ample opportunity, "Yes, I was very lucky. Gerald Gundry walked the doghounds out, and His Grace walked the bitches out. Then on Sundays at three o'clock we would go to the Kennels and the young hounds back from walk would be produced." When he came to judge hounds himself, he says that he received help from many people, "That's the great thing about hunting people, isn't it ? Two in particular were a great help. The late Major Bob Field Marsham was a wonderful judge who helped me, and Captain Ronnie Wallace who was never dictatorial to me. I think judging with lots of different people is a good way to learn. I was lucky enough to judge my first Peterborough with Sir Rupert Buchanan Jardine."

Some Notable Hounds

I asked about hounds - those that have done exceptional or unusual things. "The late Duke of Beaufort said it was very difficult to compare hounds pre- and post- War. In my case I think I tend to be less critical of my early hounds. I had a dog called Falstaff '65 who was no looker but had tremen-

Judging the Cotswold Puppy Show in 1999 with Mr Martin Scott. (Kay Gardner)

dous nose and voice. I thought the world of him, but it is hard to know just how exceptional he was - maybe the rest just weren't very good !" He came to an untimely end. Borrowed by the Heythrop, he was a bit off colour one morning so they left him behind. He escaped and found hounds seven miles away. They ran like fury all day, Falstaff determined to be up there. Plainly all was not well however and he died that night, however his blood came strong at the New Forest. Captain Clarke had a dog called Beckford '72 at the Cottesmore, by a Tynedale dog, out of Duke of Beaufort's Beeswing '66, who had been walked by the Akermans, and given to him. Beckford's shoulders weren't the best, but he was a very honest dog. Sir Newton Rycroft used Beckford at the New Forest, "He sired New Forest Buccaneer '78 (- New Forest Maxine '73) who was plain but exceptional in his work. When I was at the South and West Wilts I borrowed Buccaneer, who had rather a good week - four bitches and three days' hunting! Major Gundry came out one of the days on the Somerset side. Buccaneer was always the first to find the fox and had a very distinctive voice, he was in the top three or four couple every day. " As Captain Clarke points out, New Forest Buccaneer '78 still features strongly in many pedigrees. Another he deems worthy of mention is New Forest Floater '92 (Cottesmore Falmouth '88 - Primrose '85)," He was bred by my predecessor Stephen Sherwood and was a very high class dog who only died this Summer. New Forest Champion '93 (S & W Wilts Dorian '91 - Chaffinch '90) was a better sire though. He was used at the Cotswold and got some good ones." Another, South and West Wilts Democrat '86 (Bacchus '88 - Deluge '80), who went to Essex was a 'Hell of a good dog', as I had already been told by John O'Shea. Captain Clarke sums up neatly, "I have been blessed with wonderful hounds, and had jolly few bad ones." It might be added that they have been blessed with a master who understood them as individuals, and placed those that did not suit their own country where they could fulfil their potential.

Hyde Park Rules - Passion and Commitment

Not one to sit idly by after retirement from mastership Captain Clarke was soon at the forefront of campaigning for hunting's future. Actively involved in the then British Field Sports' Society, he was eager for action, "I kept banging on that we had to *do* something. In the end of course they said, 'Well get on and do it then !' That's when we thought up the Hyde Park Rally." I well remember receiving an enthusiastic telephone call from Captain Clarke during that time. I had worked in a voluntary capacity with his daughter Clarissa, our Regional PR Officer. He was bubbling and eagerly gathering support, bouncing ideas off fellow enthusiasts, keen as ever to pool knowledge and develop a sense of involvement. What he did not envisage was the extraordinary success of the Hyde Park Rally,

The Hyde Park Rally, 10th July 1997 (Terry Crate)

which was to become the watchword for subsequent gatherings, the phrase 'Hyde Park rules' now well established in our vocabulary, "Major Mike Parker who ran the Tattoo and the Queen Mother's Birthday Parade this year came in and was brilliant. The balloons were his idea. We were thinking we might get 30,000." From early morning on 10th July 1997 there was a feeling of anticipation, and apprehension. "Then more and more people kept coming in. We had 100,000 badges printed, and when they ran out we were all very excited. It meant a lot and was such an exciting day. It was wonderful and when it was all over there it was on the front page of the London Evening Standard, 120,000 people." As he busied himself dealing with press and personalities behind the stage, one journalist described him somewhat incongruously as a 'butterfly', "Rather *large* butterfly," he retorted dryly. Of the future he remains very optimistic, "There is a lot of hard work, to be done, most of it boring like lobbying MPs. Not all of it can be glamorous. The foot soldiering is so very important. Passion and commitment will win through."

Percy Huntsman Don Claxton
(Jim Meads)

54

The late Don Claxton

Alnwick is a place I had heard much about but not visited until the Spring of 2000 when I took my furthest trip North to interview Don Claxton, former Huntsman of the Percy. Once off the Great North Road, with time in hand I took a leisurely drive along the coast, where I walked my terrier through white grass against a backdrop of a dark and angry North Sea. There is nothing to stop the merciless wind here and it batters all in its path damply. The coastal country is open, with big arable fields. As I made my way back to Alnwick the country softened in to leafy lanes. The Castle town of Alnwick itself, entered through impressive stone gateways feels more welcoming than forbidding. Its wide street affords ample parking and has an easy, comfortable atmosphere. The Kennels are tucked away through another soft grey gateway down a drive which ultimately leads to the River. No sooner had I parked than Mrs Claxton appeared at the door of the cottage, just across the Kennel yard from their old home now occupied by son Martin. Don appeared from the garden, instantly recognisable from the many years I had seen him at our Puppy Show, deftly discarding boots and overalls, seeming to shake my hand and usher me in all at the same time. In an accent deep and distinctively North Eastern, he talks quietly and rapidly, perhaps a little nervous of what he has let himself in for.

Of Keepers, and Bowler Hats

Don Claxton was born just outside Northallerton, in Hurworth country. His father was a gamekeeper, and it was his grandfather who had a smallholding, and took horses for breaking who taught him to ride. As a boy he hunted with the Hurworth, whose Huntsman at that time was Ned Littleworth, brother of Alf, "It was lovely country, all that Thurrock side, and around Barnard Castle." His father was not keen for him to go in to Hunt Service, "He wanted me to be a joiner, because the woodwork master at school said I was good at carpentry. Anyway, when I got to 21 I decided I would do what I liked !" After Don's grandfather died he did National Service, and then spent a Season looking after two horses for Mrs Schofield, "My father had never worn a bowler hat in his life. The first time he saw me in one he said, 'You look just like a rat peeping out of a sink hole'!"

A Northern Grounding

He then went to the Zetland as second horseman for one season, whipping in to Captain (later Lord) MacAndrew for another season. Whilst here he met his wife Rosemary, whose father Hubert Dunn was Stud Groom for many years. He then whipped in to George Knight at the Badsworth, before moving on to the North Northumberland to whip in to Jack Howells, "That country was similar to this one, but I would say a better scenting country than we have. Jack Howells was a great influence on me." In 1958 Don went as first whipper-in to the Middleton, under Denis Sturgeon, "The Middleton was a good country. They had amalgamated by then with the Middleton East. Up on the Wolds the plough was chalky and if they found a fox he had to go, as there was not much covert. We had a lot of fun there, especially in the autumn." This brought back memories of a day I spent hunting on the Wolds in October 1996, co-incidentally when the College Valley-North Northumberland visited the Middleton.

Huntsman to the Atherstone

In 1960 Don was appointed Huntsman to the Atherstone, "It was a great country to ride then, not all split up in parcels by the terrible roads they have now. It was a big country to cross, with a lot of ditches." Don enjoyed five years here, "Colonel Morrison, one of our joint masters was friendly with the Duke of Northumberland, who used to come and stay for the Puppy Show and he told me the Percy job would come up the following Season, 1965. I told him I was quite happy where I was."

Colonel Morrison went on to explain that things would never be the same again, "The first stage of the M1 had just been finished. He told me, 'That won't be the end of it, you know.' The Duke was coming to see him that Sunday night. He called to see me, and we had a drink. He said, 'Are you coming to Alnwick, Claxton ?' I really wasn't sure, I'd never even been to Alnwick. I had Rosemary and our boys, Martin and Tim to think about." It was arranged that they should go up the following weekend for lunch, and a look round the Kennels and house. The Duke promised to ring the following night at six o'clock. "Bang on six the phone rang, it was him, 'Are you coming to Alnwick Claxton ? We'll see you on May 1st.' I thanked him and that was that. Rosemary said, 'By, you're a soft 'un, you haven't even discussed the terms !' I knew we'd be all right. He was so genuine, a real gentleman." Another good sign was that the previous incumbent, Fred Kinch had stayed for over twenty years as Kennel Huntsman.

Hunting Hounds at Alnwick for 31 Seasons

Don hunted the bitches, and the Duke the doghounds. There were two professional whippers-in. "I whipped in to the Duke then and if he was away on business I hunted his hounds too. The best move I ever made was listening to Colonel Morrison." When Don arrived the Percy country was 75% grass, "Now it would be 75% plough with the coastal side all arable. The West side used to be the Monday and Thursday country, but is the more popular side now as there's more grass, so we swapped around. It's just the way the farming's gone with those big arable fields in the East. It certainly rides a lot lighter than the Atherstone, though it's heavier South of Alnwick than North. You need a horse that is a good timber jumper, as there are hunt jumps rather than hedges and walls. Hunting can be fast here. There's a bit of forestry out by Rothbury, but nothing colossal." The open, chalky coastal land, with its salt breeze is not the best scenting country, "You've got to have hounds that'll really hunt, that's why we've still got the Old English hounds."

Don Claxton and the Percy Hounds. Alnwick Castle makes an impressive backdrop
(Jim Meads)

Maintaining Old English Lines, and some Memorable Hounds

When Don arrived he was told that he would be breeding hounds, and that he was to stick to Old English lines as much as possible, "We've just gone on that way. I was used to the Old English hounds at the Atherstone." Don used some of their dogs to start with, as he knew them so well, and wanted to get away from the Kennel's own lines a bit, as they were becoming a bit close, "They nicked in quite well actually, then I used a dog called Heythrop Alderman '73 (Meynell Archer '70-Dogma '71). By, he nicked in champion. They were corkers." They next borrowed a white dog from the Duke of Beaufort's, Clasher '74 (Crowner '69-Canopy '70). "The Duke of Beaufort used to ring up every second Sunday to find out how he was getting on. I said, 'He's brilliant, Your Grace. He's no Peterborough hound but he's a cracker to hunt.' He was a brilliant hound." The Duke of Beaufort stayed at Alnwick every year and judged the Puppy Show, "He would always come to see me, and have a drink." Don did not go to Peterborough, but was surprised when reading about it to see that Clasher had been in the winning two couple ! "Next time I saw the Duke of Beaufort I said how sorry I was to have condemned Clasher. He said, 'That's all right, he was the worst of the four !' and we laughed about it. Clasher got us some very good pups. Then we crossed the Aldermans and the Clashers, which made a very good cross." Don came down annually for the Beaufort Puppy Show, "Last year, 1999, was the first time I had missed. I always stayed with Phil Hale, my old Stud Groom at the Atherstone, but he had a hip replaced last year." Another hound remembered fondly by Don was Ringer '56 (Richard '51-South Atherstone Warfare '49). "No oil painting mind ! But a brilliant dog. One day we drew a bit of rough stuff on the side of a road, with a gate in the corner. Ringer struck up and a fox came flying out under the gate. Ringer jumped clean over the gate and landed on him Brrrrruhhhh ! " He shakes his head vigorously from side to side to demonstrate Ringer's swift despatch of the fox, "Then the other hounds struck up on another fox, so he dropped his and jumped straight back over the gate to join in !"

The most unusual circumstances surrounded a young hound called Leveller '62 (Braes of Derwent Lexicon '58-Charming '59), "I've never had one like him. The very first morning the young hounds usually look at you a bit, or wander in. He went straight in like a fourth season dog." On this particular morning they never stopped hunting. They ran around covert well to mark their fox in a small place. When the fox had been accounted for, Leveller fought an old dog for the mask, "It was a very warm morning, and we hacked seven miles back to the Kennels. Every now and then he'd put it down and have a good pant, 'hahahahah', and pick it up again." Leveller took that mask right home, only putting it down when he went to feed. Don was so impressed with him that he wanted to breed from him, "The Duke had never bred from a first Season hound. I told him I'd never had one like this before. He was such a corker I wanted to breed from him, in case anything happened to him. The Duke agreed to let me do this, so I gave him a bitch." The following Season, the new star was no more than average. By his third season he was very disappointing. "He was useless, he just didn't pull his weight at all. I've never known anything like that. It's usually the other way round. He's the only one I've ever known like that." Luckily, all his progeny were good, "They were never as brilliant as he had been in that first Season, but they didn't tail off as he had."

Born, Not Made

Don regards the ability to hunt hounds as something you are born with, "If it's not there, you can't put it in. You either have it, or you don't. You pick up bits from this one and that one as you go along and develop your own style, of course. Good Huntsmen are born though, not made ." He feels that he has been especially fortunate with masters over the years. Captain MacAndrew, Lord Halifax, Colonel Morrison, the late Duke, they were the old guard, you know ? I never even had to apply for this job, I was asked to come here." He has few pet hates, except perhaps showing and hound parades. "I showed at the Great Yorkshire once. We were the only Old English pack there, and first out ! We used to have a hound parade at the local show, and the county show. I have shown hounds at one or two local shows but didn't really like that. I'd rather leave it to the likes of Bill Lander and Brian Gupwell, they'd show hounds like anything, they were so good at it. His tenure as Huntsman here was both long and happy. "The people here are super. I could go in every field. I was never warned off a single field, not once. There's quite a bit of shooting, but we all got on well together. Over the years it has been something of a family concern too, for prior to Martin, Don's younger son Tim whipped in for four Seasons too. Fearful however that good jobs were few and far between he decided to make a fresh start and now works for an oil company, "He still likes his hunting mind, and

Don Claxton and son Martin
(Jim Meads)

has the best hands of the three of us." Don clearly has a quiet pride that Martin has taken over his role as Huntsman here, "We got along very well when he whipped in to me." Don was in no hurry to relinquish the horn however. One day, Lady Victoria Cuthbert MFH (daughter of the Duke) told Don that she had been looking at the books, and discovered he was due for retirement, "I said, 'But I'm not ready to retire yet, madam !' She said, 'Good, we don't want you to !' Anyway, we had a pact, I said, 'I'll tell you when I'm ready, and if you think I should go before then, you tell me !' " When Don felt it was time to step down, at the age of 68, he went to see Lady Victoria in the Spring, "I told her it was time for a younger man, and that I wanted to make the following Season my last. She had tears in her eyes." Her first thought was to offer Martin the job, "I told her that was nothing to do with me, it's the masters' job to hire and fire! ! He took it on anyhow. I told him, 'Once I walk out of those kennel doors that's it.' I would never interfere, but he knows where I live if he needs anything." Don smiles, adding with feeling, "He's doing all right."

In Safe Hands

I could not leave without seeing these historic kennels, and famous Old English hounds. Don's response to my wish was typically professional, "I'll just go and ask Martin if that's all right." He took me to the Kennels, and handed me over to his son, "I'll leave you to it then. Thank you very much. " A swift touch of the cap, a handshake and his slight form had disappeared.

Martin's enthusiasm for hounds is clear from the outset, and he takes great trouble to talk to me about them. Though uniformly 'Old English' in colour the first thing that struck me was the enormous variety of facial shapes and expressions as they peered at their inquisitive visitor through the Kennel bars. Martin has continued the Old English breeding policy, using outside sires such as Brocklesby Speaker '91(Limerick Pugalist '86-Sprinkle '88), Belvoir Pageboy '86 (Warrior '81-Paleface '83) and more recently Duhallow Claymore '94, by Muskerry Claymore '92. Two York and Ainsty South Stallionhounds, York and Ainsty South Tradesman '93 (Saddler '90-Treasure '91) and York and Ainsty South Ruler '93 (South Devon Rumour '87-Reckless '88) have proved successful here in the last few years. The pack's own Stallionhound Sportsman '97 by Brocklesby Speaker '91 out of Pastel '92 , whose own sire was Belvoir Pageboy '86, has been much in demand. The York and Ainsty

58

South, Atherstone, Fernie, Fife, and Thurlow have all used him, with more bitches lined up this Season.

Old English hounds are not always renowned for the softest of temperament, which makes this story Martin told me even more interesting. One evening, he spotted a movement on a ledge above one of the lodges. It turned out to be a stray cat, which must have been either very brave, or rather foolish. Fearing that in the confines of their own quarters the temptation could prove too much, Martin hoped it would make a quick exit. His astonishment can well be imagined when he found it curled up among the doghounds, sleeping happily the following morning. They have accepted its presence, and it lives contentedly with them to this day.

As I left Martin spotted my terrier watching from my car window, "You can walk her down by the River if you like, but don't catch all the rabbits as my greyhounds need the exercise !" So after our long drive North we strolled along the peaceful banks of the Aln to the famous Lion Bridge. It is not difficult to see why the Claxtons have settled here for so long.

Martin Claxton and friend
(Kay Gardner)

Just a few weeks after my visit, Don Claxton died suddenly. I felt privileged to have had such an insight in to the career he was so modest about, and I am indebted to his widow Rosemary, sons Martin and Tim for allowing me to include this chapter.

Harry Colbeck and the Portman Hounds in the Vale.

60

Harry Colbeck

Born beside the Badsworth Hunt Kennels two years before the outbreak of World War I, this son of a Pontefract butcher is no stranger to hardship. As a result of war duties his father contracted Tuberculosis and was forced to live in a hut beyond the village, a pony and trap providing communication with the outside world. By the time he was four his father was dead. The Colbecks however were bred tough, Harry's sister having traced their pedigrees back to Cavaliers who rode proudly from Hull. Beer wagons propelled by steam had just been introduced when he was at school and a real treat was a ride on a solid wheeled charabanc to 'Donny' Races.

Yorkshire Cavalier

Harry's first job was for the Chief of Police, looking after his horses in 1928. The Chief's post then afforded a fairly luxurious lifestyle allowing for a groom, chauffeur, gardener, and hunting with the Badsworth. After leaving the Chief of Police Harry worked for Major and Mrs F E Wright. Mrs Wright was a joint master of the Rockwood Harriers, Major Wright also hunting with the Badsworth. "Badsworth mud took some shifting. Horses came down cart tracks and were well plastered up. We'd rub them with straw. There was no hot water then mind." Stainless steel bits and stirrups all had to be cleaned , dried and burnished. Labour intensive seems an understated description. Taking the traditional route in to Hunt Service, Harry then rode second horse at the York and Ainsty North for three seasons in 1932. There were no riding schools then apart from the army, "I never went to riding school. If you got bucked off you got your backside kicked and got back on." Hours were long, "We were on the wheel", Harry explains, on duty for a week at a time in Stables, "You couldn't leave the place." In Kennels he was allowed every third night off, "Anyhow, you didn't have your bus fare home !" he chuckles. A normal Saturday began at 6am and ended at 10pm. Second horsemen got new leggings, a mac and smart checked waistcoats every year. It is hard to imagine how the volume of work could be accomplished. One man would be employed solely to clip horses - a day long job with clippers operated by a turning handle in those pre-electricity days. Riding second horse to Charlie Goodall, then Lord Mountgarret, he graduated to second whipper-in in 1936. The York and Ainsty was a good country, and hounds hacked everywhere, often 16 miles to a meet, Boroughbridge being its biggest town, "You worked muscle on a hound. In my opinion most hounds are too fat nowadays." Harry is also a firm believer in the old method of second horsemen who worked their way up in to Kennels, "That way you always have someone to whip-in when needed." Lord Mountgarret was all of 6'6" and could cross the country without jumping a twig. The Rivers Ouse and Humber ran through the country and Harry recalls what happened if their fox crossed, "There were these old boats on chains. They put the horses on, side by side. I couldn't swim, and often thought if one of the horses jumped we'd capsize ! It was the only way across, so we had to go. Across the River wasn't our country, so when hounds checked we had to repeat the performance to get back !" Each of these hair-raising journeys took around quarter of an hour, "It felt a very long time" says Harry with feeling. In all his time as a whipper-in Harry never had a second horse, a situation not uncommon then.

Whipper-in to VWH Bathurst

In 1937 Harry made his first move away from his native Yorkshire to the VWH Bathurst, their magical Kennels situated in Cirencester Park. Then it was possible to hack to Tuesday meets through Cirencester, along Blackjack Street to the Abbey Grounds, across the main road to Hare Bushes and Bibury. Hounds were out three days a week. To get to the Friday country they would hack the other way to Ewen and beyond, as far as Somerford Common. Bye days were spent in the woods. The VWH Cricklade were also out four days a week, illustrating how much this country has shrunk over the years. The roads then were unrecognisable from today's fast highways, villages often consisting

of little more than farm cottages," You could walk hounds out such a lot too. We didn't need grass yards." Many happy hours were spent in fields where the school and bypass now stand. Harry met his wife Heather whilst here, her family walking puppies.

Lord Knutsford hunted the Bathurst, and is remembered warmly, though he had a somewhat erratic attitude towards bill paying. He also allowed knackermen to take much of the flesh so often only the worst of it was left, "Every few months, the gas man would be waiting with his spanners on a Saturday. That was us with no hot food for the rest of the weekend. We always knew what had happened, because Lord Knutsford wouldn't call that weekend until the Monday to tell us, all smiles, that we were going to be reconnected. He always said he didn't know if it was best to look at your bills before you went out, and make a bad day worse, or spoil a good day by coming back to them !" Ted Goddard was Kennel Huntsman, "He was a grand chap."

At the VWH Bathurst, Kennel-Huntsman Ted Goddard,
Lord Knutsford MFH, Harry Colbeck and Stud Groom

World War II
In 1939 Harry moved to the Warwickshire to whip-in to noted lightweight horseman George Gillson. Snow put paid to hunting for months, "You could only just see the coverts. Hounds caught a lot of foxes on exercise near the Kennels at Kineton, as they were often in the drifts." The outbreak of war meant that Gillson was called up, Will Maiden came to look after hounds, and Harry too went in to service. In 1941 however he was invalided out due to a shoulder weakness, and went to the Portman in Dorset.

Wonderful Hounds and a Legendary Mastership
Harry's association with the Portman lasted a long and happy fifteen years. For the first five seasons, during the war Harry hunted hounds. Lord Kildare took them for one season. and then Sir Peter Farquhar moved to Turnworth in 1947. In 1949 Major Bill Scott another noted hound breeder rejoined the mastership, remaining until 1952. This heralded an extraordinarily successful period for the Portman, which was to benefit hound breeding for generations to come. These two fanatical hound men produced a plethora of fine looking hounds proving themselves both in this hard riding country and on the flags and Harry remembers them all vividly, "Playfair '51 (South Dorset Salesman '44-West Waterford Playful '48) had a toe down when he was a pup. He still beat all the other hounds at shows

Harry Colbeck receives a prize at the South of England Show
(Frank H Meads)

because he was a class apart. It didn't stop him hunting either. He was a very good dog in his work." We admire a whole shoe box of photographs, "Friar '47 was a smart dog. Outstanding in his work." Friar's best known son Portman Freshman '49 now appears in many illustrious pedigrees, "Lorimer '47 (Meynell Painter '43-Locket '43), he was used a lot, but I thought his brother Lovelock '47 had the edge in his work, a very independent sort." Portman Grossman '52 (Duke of Beaufort's Grimston '49 - Lollipop '49) was a striking mottled dog with a distinctive deep voice, particularly well known at a mark. He had been walked by Lady Farquhar and due to an injury sustained as a pup had wasted muscles behind which gave him a slightly odd gait. Harry recalls how Sir Peter would tease his wife every time Grossman was heard baying, "He won't come out again if there's nothing in there !" Portman Latimer '51 (North Cotswold Landlord '44 - Frolic '47) won the Peterborough Stallionhound prize and Championship, shown by Harry in 1953. There were numerous showing prizes at this time, with Planet '54 taking the bitch Championship at Peterborough in Harry's last Season at the Portman in 1955.

The Best of Fun

Sport at this time was superlative. Traffic was minimal and only one farm in the Portman country had wire, "You didn't have to play follow-my-leader like you do now. You could go where you liked. Few people would know how to ride a country like that nowadays." This is no idle criticism, but a statement of fact, so greatly has the countryside changed. Harry rues the 'wall of steel' traffic creates and hates to see vehicles driven across country. His descriptions of hunting are mouth watering, long points so frequent as to be regarded normal, "Hounds really never checked, they were driving on all the time. In the Vale you could really fly, catch a brace and go straight on with another. Foxes would often jump out of the 'doubles' ahead of you. There was no shooting to speak of and we were welcome everywhere. You couldn't get the points now what with motor cars and artificial sprays. There was a man on every farm to do the stopping as well." Hounds were out five days a week. I ask Harry if he ever got the chance to hunt hounds, "Not after the War. No-one was ever ill !" Though he does recall one occasion when Major Scott took a heavy fall, and came to tell him he could hunt hounds the next day - on the horse which had given him the fall. He evidently possessed a dry sense of humour. He saw Harry laughing at his predica-

Harry and the Portman hounds. Major WWB Scott MFH is behind him
(Frank H Meads)

ment with a difficult horse one day, "If you had to ride a horse like this I'd help you, not laugh at you", he exclaimed with heavy irony as Harry passed, flat to the boards on a blood weed bought out of a seller in Ireland. Harry's favourite horse was a little black cob, immortalised by Peter Biegel, which would jump anything, but did not care for open water.

One day the hounds were really flying and Harry got the cob going fast enough to clear the Stour, "There were only four of us left. Like a fool, I looked back. There was Sir Peter crawling out, Major Scott and Lady Farquhar all stuck in the water, so I had to go back. You could put him at anything, we once took seven gates in a row. He was very handy but just lacked a bit of scope if the take off was poor." The black cob only gave him one bad fall, when he got a foot stuck in a cut double and went tail over end, "Sir Peter was seeing someone about his back and I said I couldn't see straight. He arranged for me to see this chap. Turned out I had a broken neck", Harry says in a surprisingly matter of fact tone, "Sir Peter was a real gentleman, a tough nut but fair. He was a real hound man, who would never draw down wind, or go in half way along a covert like you see some doing now. He rarely took more than 17½ couple out." Lady Farquhar's merry sense of humour and violet blue eyes endeared her to all who met her. One day someone told her Harry was lying on the ground by a hole. Sure enough, he was laid out flat, "He's listening for a terrier" said Lady Farquhar, with confident assurance. In fact he was unconscious, his horse having put its foot in the hole! Harry admits he missed the North, but he was a contented man, "If you are engaged as First whipper-in and Kennel Huntsman you accept it for what it is, and get on with the job of turning hounds. There's no room for jealousy, if you want a Huntsman's job you should move on." He cites the example of Bert Pateman, "There was no better man with hounds, and he was a first rate Kennel Huntsman."

Educating the Cotswold Pony Club with Mr Bob Phillips MFH

Back to Gloucestershire

When Harry finally did move in 1956 it was to the Cotswold, again as Kennel Huntsman, this time to Sir Hugh Arbuthnot, another master he admired greatly, "You knew where you were then, it must be very hard for some today who have five or six masters to please." He also enjoyed whipping in to Mr Bob Phillips who arrived in 1964.

The Cotswold Hills, with their deep wooded valleys and high brashy fields could hardly have been more different from the Portman, "What we would have called a poor scent in the Portman would be good up there." This too was a good pack and many fine hunts are recalled, "I remember one when we found a fox in Notgrove and hunted him to Trafalgar in the North Cotswold. Hounds came to an ivy covered wall, and one, Countess, put him out and they caught him there."

One day visiting the Kennels at Badminton, Harry heard an unmistakable voice, "That's Portman Grossman!", he exclaimed to Bert Pateman. Sure enough Grossman '52 was there on stud duties. Harry got on the 'phone to Sir Hugh, "Grossman's at Badminton. Ring Sir Peter and see if we might use him too." The Cotswold duly sent a bitch and she produced a son, Cotswold Grossman '60, with the most beautiful prominent mottling, captured in a painting now on Harry's wall.

Sadly, after eleven seasons, things did not end happily at the Cotswold for Harry and he found himself with-

Cotswold Grossman '60 - "I always reckon I bred him !"

Harry and the Portman Hounds on exercise

out a position through no fault of his own, after a lifetime of hard work in 1967. This left him unsettled for some time, and he drifted into taking a local pub, followed by several part time jobs before settling down in to happy retirement, and enjoying some hunting again. He is a familiar figure now at many a local meet and Puppy Show.

Then and Now

Harry feels Hounds don't often run up together now, and tend to be more strung out than in the past, "It's no good to criticise, as I do understand you just can't do the road work now like you could pre-war. You had more chance to get hounds really steady then too hacking home through hares and all manner of stock." He feels hounds do not appear to be bred for cry, though he was recently impressed by the Warwickshire, who still possess 'double notes'. He feels that some young men are impatient to get to a Huntsman's job too soon, "You can't

The beauty of the Cotswolds is typified by this shot. Harry, in the foreground is on the most expensive horse he ever rode. Bought by Mrs Jackie Brutton MFH it cost £120. (Frank H Meads)

Harry shows hounds at a Portman Puppy Show

beat a thorough apprenticeship." He is too tactful to name the best Huntsman he has seen in action, and feels it is essential for a Huntsman to be a diplomat, "He must get on with everyone and not show quick temper. You need everyone's support, car followers and all." Knowledge of your hounds as 'people' is first and foremost, as is knowledge of the country, "Enthusiasm for the job is everything. You are lost without it. I never slept the night before hunting for thinking about where we might find the next day." Not all change is bad. Hunt Servants can now go to far more Puppy Shows than in the past and see many more hounds. He greatly approves of the Cotswold recently having second horses brought to hounds, as in the old days, "Taking hounds *back* to second horses is such a waste of time. What's the matter with these young men ? We never had to stop for tea in the middle of the day !" He chuckles with a twinkle in his eye, which is evident throughout, no tone of criticism apparent, merely statement of fact about a world in which even hunting has changed. Any bitterness about the past has healed, leaving Harry to enjoy the rest of his days, "There's nothing worse than Hunt politics. It's the true enemy of hunting." He loves to go out and see hounds, sometimes spending a short time with three packs in one day. He enjoys good food 'proper meat' as you would expect of a butcher's son, and home grown vegetables. Sadly Harry's wife Heather died twelve years ago, but he looks after himself well, cooking daily and having friends or family over for roast beef and Yorkshire pudding at weekends, "Not bad for someone in their 89th year?", he smiles, pouring another cup of tea. A pretty good advert for honest British food and fresh air too.

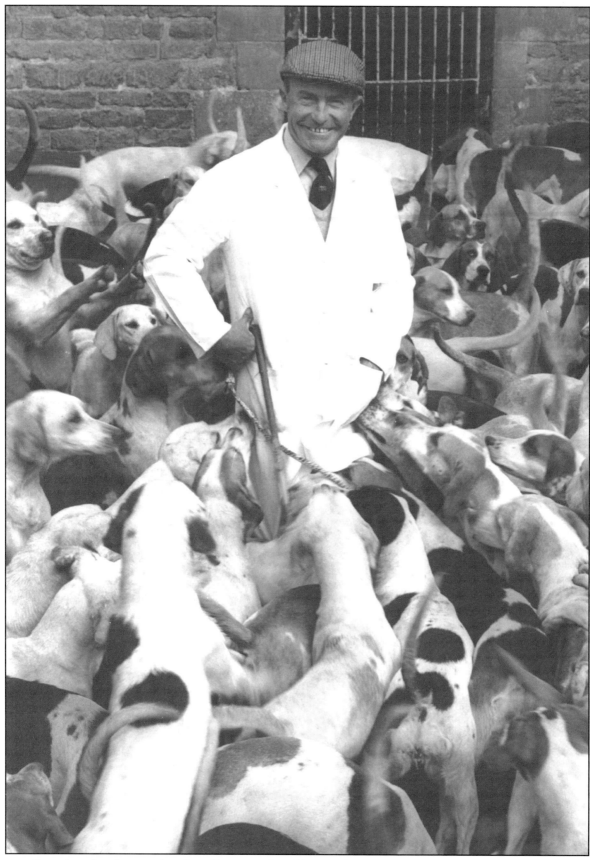

Can a happier picture exist of any Huntsman than this one of Tony Collins and the Heythrop Hounds ?
(Jim Meads)

Tony Collins

Tony Collins seems truly to be the Peter Pan of Hunt Servants. Over the years I had never seen him without that happiest of smiles, and he always has some funny story to tell. He has always struck me as a very happy-go-lucky man who is not easily ruffled. His is not a conventional story, as he made a very late start in the world of Hunt Service. That he was still able to rise to the top of his profession speaks volumes about him, and his love of the foxhound. I visited him and his delightful wife Junie on a wet Spring morning, soon brightened by Tony's irrepressible humour.

Early Days at the North Cotswold

Tony's father bought him a very good pony when he was about eleven, "I started hunting, and would lie awake at night thinking of nothing but galloping after Major Scott and the North Cotswold Hounds." A little over two years later, Tony was galloping towards a winning post.

Apprentice Jockey Rides His First Winner

At the age of just 13½ Tony became an apprentice jockey at Newmarket. A year later he rode the winner of an Apprentice Flat Race for Mr Harry Peacock in 1942, "I was just a kid who'd never seen more than 7/6 d. I was put on a train, driven to Leeds to stop in a hotel, and driven to Stockton Racecourse. That night I was back in Newmarket. I'd never been further than Evesham before !" After the race Joe Taylor and the owner Mr McKinley came to see him, "The race was worth no more than £120. He gave me £25. Collins kept his hands firmly in his pockets when all the lads started playing cards on the train home !"

Over the Jumps and in to the Cotswold Country

When he became too heavy, his father bought his indentures for £100 and Tony went to Mr Hector Smith who had just bought a yard at Snowshill. He sent out a lot of winners over the jumps from that yard in the 40s and 50s. Tony rode the first for him, over hurdles. After a spell at Aldbourne with Major Powell he did National Service in the Army with Don Claxton and Bill Lander who both returned to Hunt Service. Tony went back to racing, working for Mr Gerry Wilson at Andoversford in 1949. This yard was next to the Cotswold Hunt Kennels. Captain Wallace had come to hunt hounds, and Tony began to follow, walking many miles, often with terrierman Charles Parker. He began to help two Irish lads who worked for Mrs Brutton MFH, and decided to leave the Wilson yard. Tony had yet to break the news to Mr Wilson. Mrs Brutton did this, unbeknown to him on August 12th. "Next morning, riding out Gerry said, 'So you're leaving ?' I said, 'Well, I shall get some hunting.' 'Fair enough. We're having a swap. She's having you, I'm having a brace of grouse. That's all you're worth' ! " Tony was very happy working for Mrs Brutton, becoming great friends with Kennel Huntsman George Knight, and his Kennelman Bob Clements, "They had decided I should go in to Hunt Service."

Jockeys' Valet

Also at this time however Mr Fred Taylor, well-known jockeys' valet, with his son Phil, died suddenly. So in 1952 Tony went North to be a Jockeys Valet, "Most of the meetings I went to were in the North, but when there weren't any there I would go to Sandown and the southern courses. I looked after George Slack, Dick Curran, Tim Moloney, Martin Moloney, Dick Francis, as well as National winners Arthur Thompson, Jimmy Power and Bryan Marshall great jockeys and really great gentlemen." Tony was on duty the day Devon Loch collapsed under Dick Francis when he looked set to win the National for the Queen Mother, "He chucked his saddle on the table, and sat with his head in his hands." The weighing room had a great buzz about it. "In those days everyone was allowed in, owners would bring the Missus' handbag in, umbrellas. There was always a quid on the end of it. One

day everyone's coming in, having coffee. A gent comes in, Wetherill suit, bowler hat, the lot. Asks me to look after his bag. He came back for his mac and galoshes when it started raining. After racing I was clearing up ready to go. He comes back, 'Where you off to boy?' ,' Shifnal Sir.' 'Mind dropping me off, it's near my home ?' " The man was Jack Lawrence, former Huntsman of the Heythrop who had been on gate duty at the course.

Back to Gloucestershire, and a Boy Named Adams

In 1959 Tony was working in the Weighing Room , and was told a lady was asking for him. He went outside to find Mrs Brutton, who asked him if he would consider going back. "After I gave up, Bryan Marshall, I mean *the* best, came up to me at Cheltenham and said if ever I was out of a job to let him

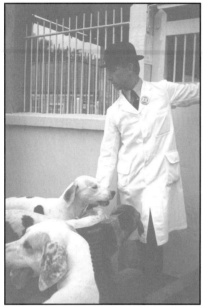

Antony Adams (Kay Gardner)

know. That's how they were." Tony still did the odd weekend valeting after this. One May 1st he arranged to go to Wincanton, where he would be the only valet on duty. "I took a young lad with me to help, about thirteen years old. He was quite pleased, as he saw a fella called Fred Winter ride two winners, and he gave him a quid." The lad's name was Antony Adams.

When Tony was going to leave Mrs Brutton's yard, he contacted Bryan Marshall. He spoke to Colonel Warden MFH VWH Cricklade, who asked Sir Hugh Arbuthnot MFH Cotswold about Tony. Thus Tony was engaged as whipper-in to Sidney Bailey at the VWH Cricklade.

Starting Out With Sidney Bailey

"When I did start with Sidney Bailey I didn't realise at the time that I had started with a very fine professional. Sidney, Carol, Junie and Collins, we all became great friends. His father was famous as Kennelman at the Heythrop. There was a very good Kennelman at the Cricklade then too called Sid Franklin. A proper Kennelman, not just a knife sharpener." The six Seasons Tony spent here were very happy, "It was good country, organised by good masters." Tony remembers Major Gar Barker whose wife was master at the time as a wonderful gentleman,"Very smart, very proper. He bought me a new horse. We came to some rails in a brook near Swindon. Everyone popped over it, bar Collins on his new horse. I suppose I was saying things I shouldn't have ! I caught up when they caught their fox in a field at Purton. Major Barker rode up and put his arm round my shoulders, 'Tony, my boy, we think the world of you, but if you carry on like that, you'll have to go.' Well, he rode a wonderful horse called Charlie, who was perfection itself. About an hour later Charlie was misbehaving and Major Barker was not at all happy with him." Tony rode quietly by and muttered, 'See what I mean Sir ?' disappearing before he could explode ! Other good masters followed Mr John White, "Major Jock Mann was another fine gentleman who would be so proud of his children's involvement now." When amalgamation came, Derek Goddard hunted hounds for two seasons. It was now that Tony got his first chance to carry the horn, and made an interesting discovery, "Derek was laid up, and hounds stuck to me like glue." On that first day Tony rode a horse he shared with the Huntsman. The second day however with Alex Mason whipping in on one of the Huntsman's horses was rather different, "I never had a hound with me hacking to the meet, until I swapped horses with Alex !" It was a busy day, and when hounds marked for the second time Mr Gregory Phillips uttered those famous last words, 'It's only a small place, we'll have him and finish early'. At 4pm the horses went home and from then on things did not go to plan. The fox bolted, "We stopped at the pub in Purton at 10.20pm with hounds. They never even caught their fox and I was in trouble with Sid Franklin." Sidney returned for another two happy Seasons, when Tony felt it was time to move on.

Otterhunting Interlude

During his valeting days Tony had the opportunity to get a lot of otterhunting in during the summer months. He hunted with the Hawkstone when hunted by Captain Wallace, and mainly with the Wye Valley with Sir Hugh Arbuthnot and Harry Colbeck, "The first time I held hounds was for Harry at

Honiton." When a young man called Captain Antony Hart arrived, Tony would drive him and his friends, "One boiling hot day Mr Hart was hunting them. I loaded up hounds and all these girls and boys. We drew for miles and miles, not a touch all day. I'm going along in front with hounds. There were 11½ couple, some woolly, some a bit shouldery, some old and not quite sound. They came to a stick pile and up jumped a lovely gurt fox. I promise you the Beaufort, the Heythrop, the Quorn bitches never went faster in their lives! They went miles, and I was driving the lorry. We eventually got them back and Captain Hart told me to stop at the first pub. You thought nothing then of going to a pub with hounds and letting them out in the car park. We had a lot of fun." Sometimes young Ant Adams accompanied Tony on his otterhunting outings.

Going West

Living in Gloucestershire Tony had come to know the West Country very well, "I love it, always have, always will." He applied to Mr Bob Phillips MFH, who wanted a Kennel Huntsman at the West Somerset, "I didn't know Mr Phillips at the time. I arrived on May 1st and by August we felt we'd been there all our lives. Nothing to do with me, but we had followed a good set up, and hounds were welcome anywhere. No disrespect to anyone else, but those two Seasons could have been twenty two." Tony loved the country down there, "It was real hunting country. It wouldn't suit the ladies and gentlemen because there was not much jumping." At that time farmers tended their stock on ponies, not quad-bikes, "All the gates practically opened for you, like a posh hotel !" Though staghunting remained the first choice for many to ride to here, the support was still good, "It was a wonderful time. Harry Holt was my kennelman/whipper-in. His father had whipped in for the West Somerset and he was a great help. Sometimes Mr Phillips could not manage a day, and Tony would deputise with Harry's help, "We were like puppy dogs with 50 tails, hacking home in the moonlight over the Brendon Hills without a care in the world." Mr Phillips proved a model master, "He had been at the Garth and South Berks and the Cotswold, then bought the Anchor Hotel at Porlock." Tony and Junie wanted for nothing. Mr Phillips had the place done up and left instructions that Tony was to ring Mrs Fosse at the Anchor to ensure a ready supply of refreshment in their house at Carhampton for friends and farmers. There were some nice hounds here, and in 1969 Tony went to Ardingly. They were second in the entered couples class, and took Reserve Champion with a dog called West Somerset Garth and South Berks Capital '67 (Heythrop Carver '63 - Cotswold Woodlark '63). After two years Bob Phillips told Tony he was leaving, "I was bloody miserable. He told me not to worry as he was speaking with Captain Wallace at the Cotswold Supporters' Dinner, and he would see what he could do. The following day, Saturday I was sitting at the meet, 'Well, what did the great man say ?' I asked him. 'A week Sunday you can go for interview' , he said. 'What for?', I asked. Well, when he said the Heythrop job I just bust out laughing. We all knew Bill Lander was leaving but the thought of applying for that job never entered my head."

Kennel Huntsman to the Heythrop

Tony duly went for interview, "We drove to the Kennels. Junie was to look at that wonderful house. Do you know Captain Wallace knocked on Bill Lander's door and *asked* if he could take me in to the Kennels. Driving back he said, 'Tony, if you do come, you know it will have to be 'Collins' don't you because that's the way it is.' He also asked whether Tony had any ideas about who could be engaged as whipper-in. Without hesitation he recommended Antony Adams, whose father, grandfather, and uncles had all hunted there. Within ten minutes of arriving home the telephone rang. It was Antony, "How did you get on mate? We all know where you've been." Captain Wallace promised to let Tony know in a week. True to his word he telephoned on Tuesday morning, and came to see him. After a brief look at the Kennels, he offered Tony the job, "At the West Somerset Puppy Show he told everyone what a good chap I was, adding, 'I suspect that'll be the last time I say that.' Twelve years ago, on my last day he spoke to the crowd there and said, 'Collins has kept the standard up.' I reminded him it *was* the first time since that day in Somerset !"

Mr Bailey Senior Brings His Influence to Bear

"One of the first things I asked at the interview was what Tom Bailey was doing. He'd been there since 1946. I was told he would stay for two Seasons." It may be thought that the prospect of working for Captain Wallace would be daunting, "For me, Tom Bailey was harder ! He was such a marvellous man. He was a great man for early mornings, in Kennels at 5.30am every day. Well, to Ant's disgust, I am an early morning man as well. Sometimes if Tom was just in front of me he'd run to get

there first, or if just behind he'd run to catch up. Now remember he was the Kennelman and I was the Kennel Huntsman. After about three months we were swilling down, and he said, 'Well, lad', not Mr Collins, or Boss, Guv'nor, or Sir. 'I thought you were a new broom sweeping clean, but I think you'll be all right.' Ever after that I was 'Boss' if anyone was about. He was a wonderful, wonderful man. A lot of Hunt Servants in my position wouldn't have bothered to ask him things. He was an extraordinary man." He was at the Heythrop Kennels for the best part of thirty years. When Hunt Servants retire, there is always a whip round, and presentation of some kind. It is not usual in the case of a Kennelman. Tony organised a whip round among the Hunt Servants for Tom Bailey and went to see Lisa Sandys Lumsdaine to commission a painting. She refused to take any money, so Tom was given a painting of Heythrop Lurcher '67 (Craftsman '62-Lottie '63) and the money. The painting was given to Tony by Sidney Bailey after his father's death, "I cannot say enough about the help Tom Bailey gave me." Another kennelman, Paul Firmore left to join the Church, "I think I must have been a good influence, what with Mr Lambert becoming a Reverend too !" Kennelman Ralph Stubbings was an important addition to the team, and stayed for eleven Seasons.

Tony, Ant , and a Few Surprises

In the early days Ant lived with Tony and Junie, "One day I called down from the bathroom, 'Hey, Ant what do you think the great Jack Lawrence would say if he knew a jockey's valet was sat on his throne ?'" Tony and Ant became a great double act, and firm friends to this day. Captain Wallace was full of surprises, "He was the easiest man in the world to work for. Out hunting I was often told 'It's nothing to grin at!' One day I was late. Then Ant arrived, "You two ride about like a couple of broody hens !' Well, if you can't grin at that you're a miserable sort of devil" , says Tony, grinning broadly.   On a more serious level, Tony learned a great deal. Still there were surprises, "Our first Season we were hunting around Christmas time." Tony was puzzled, as the Captain had hardly mentioned the hounds all Season, "He came to the meet, got on his horse and went. This particular day he came to the box and said, 'Just a minute Collins', pulling a piece of paper from his pocket. On the paper were the names of $3\frac{1}{2}$ couple of hounds. He said, 'I haven't seen these out lately.' " He may not have asked, but had obviously noted the hounds' absence. He very much left the Kennels to Tony, and when taking Chairmanship of the MFHA warned that he would find himself alone a lot - in summer at any rate, "I don't suppose he came on hound exercise more than half a dozen times a year in the seven Seasons I was with him." Here, Tony believes, apart from his flair as a Huntsman, lay the key to the success of his mastership, "He knew it was no good coming to the Kennels and chucking biscuits about. That was my job. He got out there and ran the country. You can say what you like about good Huntsmen, good packs of hounds, and good country. Only one thing makes it work and that is the way the whole thing is organised. That was why the Heythrop had the edge. He made the country his for every hunting day."

As time went on Tony was told he would be able to hunt hounds a bit usually on Fridays, "I can tell you if Collins was hunting hounds on Friday, Ant wasn't whipping in to me, it was a day out for the pair of us. It was ! Tom Bailey, Ant Adams and Collins. We were a real team."

Who's Coming With Me ?

"I'm a silly sort of bugger. People go on about long points, and how many foxes they caught. Other things give me pleasure." Tony's first day hunting hounds here was unexpected. Captain Wallace was hunting hounds in Hensgrove. It was raining and very windy. Tony was in his place outside, "I kept just creeping in to make sure he hadn't crept off." The Secretary Colonel Chamberlain galloped up. Tony followed him to find Captain Wallace had run a blackthorn into his eye, "The Field were gathered. The hounds were sitting all around him. Nobody else would remember this but I do. He told me to carry on with hounds, and which bits he hadn't drawn. I got off my horse and just said, 'Who's coming with me then?' All those hounds followed me straight away. That's not to get one over on him at all, I don't mean that. It was between me and those hounds." Tony's horn had not been out of its case in four years, and he was dismayed when he blew it, "I've never considered myself Harry James on the hunting horn. I looked at it, and saw there was a crack. Then it broke clean in half !" Ant Adams' father was despatched to the cars to see if anyone had a horn, "He came back with a kid's plastic trumpet. I tell you, this was the *Heythrop* !" Colonel Chamberlain found Captain Wallace and gave Tony his horn, inscribed with the name of his first Peterborough Champion, Harper '53. Hounds found and after 40 minutes they heard the distinctive holloa that could only belong to the

master, who was still following by car. Once when Captain Wallace had a fall Tony hunted hounds for the last fortnight of the Season. He met Major Gerald Gundry who said, "I hear you had a good time? You must have done because when I asked Captain Wallace how you'd got on he said 'Rather well'!"

What Jim Meads Missed

One part of the Season Tony really enjoyed was the month in Spring when hounds were taken to Exmoor, "One day on Dartmoor we'd not done much, it was boiling hot and as we came to Princetown a lady bought ice-creams for myself and the Captain. I wish Jim Meads had been there to catch the pair of us trotting through Princetown eating ice-cream !"

Jim Meads didn't miss this shot ! Mr Goschen's Huntsman, Ted Rafton tries to encourage Tony with a biscuit at Peterborough (Jim Meads)

What A Huntsman Needs Most - A Good Wife

" A Huntsman needs a good helpful wife. I've been so lucky with Junie." Tony and his lovely wife Junie met at the Frogmill Inn at Andoversford, where he later proposed to her, "Before she met me she hardly knew what a horse was. She was wonderful on the telephone and could defuse things so well. I never needed an answerphone ! When I went to the Heythrop I heard Captain Wallace had told people, 'He's got a very good wife.'" Tony adds, "I could not have done what I did without her help, it's as simple as that."

Some Memorable Hounds

"We had a very good bitch called Pebble '67 (Whaddon Chase Grimston '61-Pansy '62). The Captain never bred from her and when I asked why he said he wanted her hunting with him every day. I was very fond of Rockwood '80 (Latimer '74-Rockdove '77), who I showed a lot. We never won a Peterborough Doghound Championship in the seven seasons I was there with Captain Wallace. I thought Pixton '75 (Grossman '71-Pillow '69) would win for him in his last Season, and I was disappointed when he was reserve, though he won the following year, 1977. He was a very fine foxhound as well as a real looker." I had always been an admirer of Heythrop Berry '78 (Fulmar '75-Breakfast '76) who won the Bitch Championship at Peterborough in 1980, "Ah yes. bless her. Her dam Breakfast '76 (Peacock '73-Old Berks Brandy '72) was one of the first to be frightened to death of electric wire, and Berry became the same. They'd only have to see kale and go right round. People often said, 'That thing's useless' but I knew why she did it. Look and see how many Champions go back to Breakfast '76 and Berry '78." Breakfast had been Reserve Champion at Peterborough herself. "One of the finest doghounds I ever hunted was Author '80 (Draycott '77-Acer '77). He was always second to Rockwood '80, but I thought he was better. A real looker he did win the Championship at Harrogate." Author took a very bad kick from a new horse one day, which sent six hounds flying. Author was short at the end of the day, and Tony found him in kale, his front caved in. Carried to a stable and covered with straw, time and patience saw him recover.

Heythrop Berry '78, Peterborough Bitch Champion in 1980 . This photograph was taken at the Kennels, as having won, she refused to pose at Peterborough ! (Jim Meads)

A Lucky Man

"I considered myself lucky to get the job at Chipping Norton. I had a lot of good friends so didn't worry when the moans about the Huntsman started after four seasons, which always happens." When Captain Wallace left for Exmoor Mr Stephen Lambert joined the mastership, and shared hunting hounds with Tony, which worked well. Few things annoy Tony, except people who criticise

Tony Collins at his last meet as Huntsman with Paul Larby, Ralph Mankee, Colin Hicks and Matthew Puffer, all Huntsmen who whipped in to him. (Jim Meads)

hounds that have been shown successfully without justification. "People will say, 'the showing's taken over.' It's a load of rubbish. If someone's with a pack a long time and gets them looking right it means they are doing their job. To my mind there's no such thing as breeding for show."

Tony feels that he has been a lucky man, and appreciates all the masters he has worked for over the years. His is an extraordinary story, as he was already 32 when he began whipping in with the otter-hounds. He regards his starting with Sidney as another very lucky move. He enjoyed his time at Chipping Norton greatly, "I had such a great gang of lads there."

Above all, what shines through my morning with Tony Collins is the dedication between him and Junie, and his love of hounds. Small wonder the man some Hunt Servants refer to as 'Uncle Tone' is in demand for Kennel sitting during the summer months, when he cares for no fewer than seven different packs whilst their Huntsmen are on holiday. Before I left Tony showed me his favourite picture. Not an illustrious Champion, or himself hunting the famous Heythrop Hounds. It is of the Heythrop hounds snoozing happily in a heap before the puppy show, "I liked to pop them in together beforehand to get them relaxed." It is a picture of canine contentment.

Sadly, Tony's wife Junie died shortly after this interview. The regard in which she was held was reflected in a packed Church at Broadway, full to the brim with a huge number of Hunt Servants and Masters present.

George Cook and the Bilsdale hounds in 1983. The Farm where they were kennelled at Chop Gate can be seen in the background. (Roy Parker)

76

George Cook

When I told my old friend Winnie Morton about this book she said, "Now you must come and see George and Nancy. I'll sort it. You must come and stay." I knew Winnie's organisational abilities of old, and certainly had no hesitation in accepting the invitation. Winnie's company is worth a guinea a minute, any guest is assured a warm welcome, and will certainly never go hungry. I have stayed here before, and fell under the spell of the wild beauty of the North York Moors, and their hardy, enthusiastic packs of hounds several years ago. Before staying here I knew nothing of those wonderfully keen hunting folk, where hounds are often kennelled on a farm, and every day's sport is worked hard for. I confess I knew nothing of the Bilsdale, as I suspect few in the South would. Winnie has lived here for years, her first home at Hawnby, "One day I was driving home, and there was this mini driven by a very tall man, and the woman in the passenger seat was blowing a hunting horn out of the window. In the back were a couple of foxhounds. That was the first time I met George and Nancy, who were looking for some hounds." Winnie's encounters with the Bilsdale hounds soon became more personal. One dark winter night she went outside for some wood, and was almost knocked over by a hound coming in through the door. The hound made straight for the Aga. She had been walked at Winnie's home, and impervious to the fact that its ownership had changed, she still regarded it as her home. Winnie was happy to feed her and return her to George the next day which became quite a regular routine. Winnie once arranged a day for me with the Bilsdale, where current Master and Huntsman Alan Caine and his wife Sheila provided me with a perfect steed. To say the country is breathtaking is a gross understatement. The views afforded are spectacular, and on that clear day the patchwork of Yorkshire countryside spread far beyond, with no discernible horizon. The modern world seemed far away, and we could have been transported back a century or more. It is said the Bilsdale is England's oldest pack founded by the Duke of Buckingham in 1668. Its history has been colourful, and full of characters. Like Bobby Dowson, a fanatical former Huntsman, who died in 1902 at the age of 86. The local parson, an exception to most in those days refused to have his headstone in the churchyard as it was adorned with fox masks and crossed whips. It was duly put at the Sun Inn, the hostelry, known locally as Spout House, and can still be seen there today, The Sun Inn is still in the Ainsley family who hunted the pack for many Seasons. The pack continues to flourish, cared for on the Caines Farm, and fed on leftovers from a local bakery. Saturday Fields number around thirty and there are numerous social events. Winnie is still enthusing about the Hunt Breakfast, something of a marathon - champagne, Full English, porridge, toast, followed by tea and cake at the meet and strawberries and cream for tea, "By, they do themselves well," says Winnie, who knows a thing or two about food.

So what of George Cook, and Nancy ? How do they fit in to the Bilsdale's rich history. George and his family have been a part of the Bilsdale for many a year. Winnie invited him for lunch. He arrived in pouring rain, bare headed, tall and upright. A no-nonsense honest working man, what you see is what you get. His tales of hunting Bilsdale told in a Yorkshire burr as deep as it is soft are easy on the ear, and paint a crystal clear picture in the mind's eye.

A Story Which Began Five Generations Ago

In 1924 George's father whipped in for the Bilsdale to Huntsman Tommy Bentley. He later gave up riding, but would take his son out on foot whenever hounds were nearby, and they would walk many miles. George's earliest memory is of hounds hunting on Carlton Bank, "We stood behind a wall, and while we listened a fox got up from the heather. We watched him, and told William Edward. They hunted him to the bottom of the hill where they caught him." Another time he saw a fox bolt, hounds right behind him, "He was off like a bullet. It's not always how the antis say it is. They never caught him !" That night they had a drink at the pub in Carlton before catching the bus to Stokesley at

77

6.30pm, and walking home from there. "It was just before Christmas, and all the shops in Stokesley were lit up which was quite a sight for me. I'll always remember it." A sight indeed, as at that time there was no electricity at all in the hills where George lived, a situation that continued until 1958. Hunting is in George's blood, for his Great Great Grandfather George Bell, and Great Grandfather, George Bell Junior were both Huntsmen to the Bilsdale, then a trencher fed pack. In his father's childhood hounds were still trencher fed, and hunted by Joe Garbutt. His father would go out on a hunting morning , walking through the valley with a horn. When he blew, hounds appeared joyfully over the hills from their walks in all directions. Those who cared for them on the farms said they always sensed a hunting morning, and would become restless long before the first notes of the horn were heard. He would then walk hounds three miles back to the Kennels. At the end of the day hounds were returned to their walks. George's father also went out with the neighbouring Farndale.

Will You Be Our Huntsman ?

In 1962 Mr Willie Coates and Mrs Hutton Wilson came in to the Bilsdale Committee. The pack had always been traditionally Fell bred which works well in the country, but the breeding policy had been changed, and many felt it no longer suited the country. This had caused a bit of a 'to do' and George was approached to see if he would be interested in hunting hounds. He applied and with the majority of the committee behind him he took them on in 1963, kennelling them at his farm. That he was successful is proven by the fact that this arrangement lasted 23 years. He decided only to send pups out to walk, rather than the older hounds as well, as fewer people had the time or facilities to care for them now, and traffic was increasing in summer. He and his wife Nancy, who he met when she came to Stokesley as a Land Girl, cared for hounds. Nancy did the majority of kennel work, between raising a family, whilst George ran their tenant farm. This they did for the princely sum of £300, out of which they had to feed the pack as well. George would go to Great Ayton and Ingleby Greenhow slaughterhouses, to get tripes and offal which weren't wanted, "I got that for nowt and boiled it. We still had to buy flaked maize, which cost money. Then there was the petrol. There wasn't much left for me out of the £300 !"

The Bilsdale Field in typical country, autumn 1996.
(Kay Gardner)

The Season did not begin until September or October, but George exercised hounds on the Moor all Summer, "My first priority was to get them 200% steady with sheep. In this country they can get away from you on a fox, and you may not see them for some time. You had to be happy that even if they got left out they would never touch a sheep."

Building Up

Fields at that time were sparse, consisting of a few locals. George often found himself with just the whipper-in for company, "We had a lad called Billy Wilson who came over from Cleveland. We rode to most meets, but he had a wagon, so sometimes we went in that. He had it fitted out to take the hounds, and stayed about 15 Seasons." They had a good system, based on the following understanding, "If I was on the bottom of a hill, he would be on top to get away with hounds, if they went that way and I had to catch him. If however they went away at the bottom it was up to him to catch me. It worked ! We went on to have some good hunts, and we had a good pack put together."

Music - the Brilliance and the Tragedy

Some of the Fell hounds had been given away by a previous master to the Wensleydale Harriers, and George managed to get them back. One, Matchless could never be cured of hunting hares. Music however was one of his best hounds, "One of the best I ever had was Music. She was really true to fox. She could hunt a fox when no other hound could. At a check they all looked to Music and the moment she spoke they flew to her." One day, drawing a wood in Scugdale, Music collapsed. George put her on his horse and rode to a nearby road to call for the vet. Sadly Music died before he got there, "It was a tragedy. A very sad loss to Nancy and I and everyone in the Field. Our daughter Margaret remembers it vividly. It was all due to careless use of strychnine by a gamekeeper." When they arrived home and unboxed the hounds, another three were affected, "Mr Sinclair, who was the Hunt vet injected them so that they would sleep for 12 hours. He said if they came round they would be all right, and thank God, they were. Music was such a brilliant hound a black cloud stayed over the Kennels for a long time." The Wensleydale Harriers were being hunted then by Frank Buck, well known there and in the Lunesdale country. Then they went to Scotland for some hounds, to the Jedforest, "There'd been connections since the 1930s when William Edward had the Bilsdale and used to trade hounds with Mr Harker MFH at the Jedforest. His son said 'I'll get in touch with Mr Harker and see what I can do.' We only had half a dozen good hounds when I started." After hunting all day with the Jedforest George duly returned with five hounds, all good Fell types. Only one of these failed to fit in, "They did us a lot of good." As word spread of the pack's improvement, and the sport they were providing hunting with the Bilsdale became popular. Fields were numbering 70 or 80 on Saturdays, which would be a tremendous number in these parts even now.

Of Grouse Moors and Keepers

Bilsdale country in common with most of the North York Moors has a relatively sparse fox population. Hounds must really stick to their fox, as they may not find another. They need the confidence to range away from their Huntsman, and drive on without him. George was now well pleased with their abilities, but in the 1970s, when the trade in fox pelts was at its peak there were many blank days. He found himself apologising to the Field, but most of them were happy just to be riding through this glorious country. It is not a galloping, jumping country, except for the Thirsk end. There were many jumps at Mount St. John, home of Brook Holliday, whose father was Master of the York North. This was an oasis, full of foxes, and no digging was ever permitted, "Keepers always used to keep foxes and pheasants. We always found plenty at Kepwick Hall and on Lady Feversham's estate where there was plenty of shooting. I only had one place we couldn't go until February." Lowesby Hall was the venue for the Boxing Day Meet, and four generations of the Cameron family hunted. He was frustrated that in the 70s many of the Keepers became one-track minded. One even took a fox from a snare quite deliberately as hounds were about to draw his wood. He feels shooting and hunting are pulling together more now, "Some of them then would have killed the last fox on the moor if they could, yet we would move pheasant nests when we were mowing. It was all one way."

The annual joint meet with the Farndale was much enjoyed, and there was great friendly rivallry between George and Farndale Chairman Alf Brown as to whose hounds were in the lead at various points.

George and the Bilsdale hounds at Silton Forest 1972

The Art of Hunting the Moors

Hunting the North York Moors is an art, requiring patience and no small amount of skill. This is rewarded with some wonderful houndwork in some of England's finest scenery, "You've to be a true hunting man in this type of country. It isn't a matter of ability to hunt hounds, because these Fell types hunt themselves. They have to, as you can't always be there to help them. They must get used to putting themselves right. If you are lucky enough to have two or three really true hounds, and get to know their voices, you will know that they are right." He recalls a hound called Sampler, who was very good, but became apt to babble. The others mistrusted him for it. One day George just caught a flash of something silvery running along a fence. Only Sampler spoke at first. The rest then joined in and 3 1/2 hours later they checked on a hill end where the wind was blowing hard. A girl riding home was stopped by a man quarter of a mile on who said, 'Just pop back and tell George his fox went into the wood here.' She did, "I held them on over the Moor to the wood, which was about quarter of a mile long and full of old jet working holes, so I thought he would get in. He didn't though and came back to the top farther on. I sent my daughter on. Hounds ran well and she said Gaffer, a dark foxhound was in the lead. The fox sat tight and then went over the forestry fence. They viewed him then and caught him two miles later. I often wonder why he didn't go into the jet workings where he would have been safe. When we caught him, he was a very unusual colour, his back was silver, so that's what I had seen. We could have trusted Sampler after all."

A Foot Follower's Knowledge

George hunted a lot as a young man, and I asked if anyone in particular influenced him. His answer was an interesting one, particularly for those who follow on foot, and often manage to see a lot of houndwork, "I think the knowledge I gained on foot was vital, it really helped me to hunt hounds." As a boy he hunted on a pony, "The whipper-in on the top would say 'Just pop down and get those hounds on.' I would hop off, dead keen, and slide down on my bottom, put the hounds on, and then be faced with a steep climb back up to where he was waiting with my pony !"

Where Duty and Pleasure and Sport are as One

In those 23 years George had a lot of fun, but their hunting really had to be worked for. On a hunting day they would need to leave home by 9.30am or 10am, having first attended to the farm stock. Despite this he was a stickler for punctuality. He would try not to be too late home, simply because of the amount of work, "Our Chairman then, Wilf Thompson hunted on foot. At half past three or four o'clock, if hounds weren't hunting I would be starting to think of what needed doing at home. Then he'd say, 'Just try one more place.' That was fatal of course, you'd always find, scent had improved and by 5pm I'd be left on my own as everyone else had sloped off home. Luckily, after five years or so, we had a good box to get back in, but there were often 14 gates to open on the way." Nancy would have all the feed ready and waiting, and once hounds and horses had been dealt with, they would begin on the farm work. If hounds were missing, George preferred to go looking for them that night, rather than break in to the following day as well. It made for some very long and arduous days, "Many a time I've been sat up on the East side at midnight. Those hounds really did hunt, and if they found a fox late in the day, they kept going." On one rough snowy night they almost did not get home. Police had closed the Clay Bank road as so many trucks had become stuck. George pleaded that he had to get hounds and horses back to his farm where stock needed tending. They let him try, and luckily he made it. Weather can be harsh up here. Once George set out for a meet on Snilesworth Moor, in thick fog. Billy Wilson met him at the gate one and a half miles from the farm. They set off across country, inevitably getting lost, each blaming the other. Eventually they followed a stream. George wanted to go right, Billy said, 'It must be left, look at the way the water's running.' George conceded and Billy was proved correct, taking great delight in telling all his farmer friends in Cleveland that George thought water ran uphill ! "It was a long time before I heard the last of it I can tell you."

George Cook

Support Along the Way

Local farmers were all very supportive, and George remembers just one farm where they were not welcome, "Being a local lad I think they knew they could trust me, that my hounds would be sheep proof and the like. Very few of them hunted, or even followed, but they loved to see hounds come through their yards. It was lovely really, to feel they were behind you like that."

Hounds were welcome too in the little market town of Thirsk," We used to meet at South Kilvington just outside, and then ride through. Everyone came out to see us." Thirsk housed the veterinary practice so well known through the books of 'James Herriot.' Siegfried Farnon was in fact the late Donald Sinclair, around whose home I had ridden during my first Bilsdale day. He was a very keen hunting man, at one time having his own beagles. He was a master of the Wensleydale Harriers, and gave George a couple he had acquired from John Bulman Master of the Windermere Harriers. One of these, Talisman was brilliant, and could turn short with a fox if he doubled back along a wall when the rest would go on over it. Mr Sinclair was very popular and is warmly remembered locally, "If we went through his yard he would always come out and want me to stop for a drink. I'd say, 'But I'm here to hunt foxes, not drink whisky !' A very popular man he was, everybody liked Mr Sinclair."

George Smithson hunted with the Bilsdale all the time George was hunting. He had a little bay mare, which was also his farm horse. She must have had great stamina to work on the farm and hunt, for he rarely missed a day. Bad weather never deterred him, and he would appear even on days when hounds couldn't go, "He would ride to all the meets on her, perhaps an hour's ride. You couldn't keep up with her on the banks. He used to like to stand on top of the hills." The country had a fair amount

81

The Bilsdale hounds with current master Alan Caine, near the home of Mr Donald Sinclair. The ear on the left belongs to the author's horse. The finest view in Yorkshire, perhaps ? (Kay Gardner)

of forestry and the foxes used this to lie up in, rather than out on the open Moor, It was not always easy to tell what was happening in the forestry, especially when windy and George knew that if Smithson was still visible on the top hounds had not gone, "We once hunted a fox from Skugdale into Arncliffe above Ingleby and lost him. Coming back they picked up a drag. They dragged down and down, and I let them just keep dragging on. Someone heard a holloa." George asked, "Up yonder?", "Aye", came the reply,"That'll be George Smithson. Pop up and see", said the Huntsman. The Hunt Chairman, Frank Wood went. When he came back he said to George, "I can't understand a word he said, but I think he's seen the fox." As they hunted nearer Smithson, George called out, and asked if he'd seen him, "Aye, quite an hour since", came the reply. He had waited all that time. Hounds hunted on more strongly, "You knew he was always right. Sure enough they put up their fox, hunting right away to Over Seaton." When Smithson died a picture of him on his horse was etched on his headstone.

Another regular was Mr Dent from Ribston Hall, who hunted with all the York packs, "A grand fella was Mr Dent."

"A farmer from Coxwold, Mr Myers hunted with us regular, he was a relative of the lad that whipped in. He brought a friend from Great Ouseburn one day to a meet at Spout House." Evidently the visitor took one look at George and said to Mr Myers, "Not much chance of us getting left today with him on that horse." Typically, the day started slowly with a long draw, then hounds put up a hare. Chances of impressing the visitor seemed remote. Then a fox jumped up, "By God, what a hunt we had !" Just George, Billy Wilson, Mr Myers and the visitor were up with hounds. He soon fell by the wayside in this demanding terrain, "When we finished hunting and came over the road by Chop Yat he was two mile away going back to his box." George clearly enjoyed this poetic justice, and laughs heartily , "Nah, we never heard tell of him again, we didn't ! He never come back."

Change and Inevitability

Even up here, George has seen the countryside change, and not for the better. Increased public access has given many more people the freedom to walk the Moors, but in places the sheer numbers, and disturbance they unwittingly cause has made a big difference, "You don't see the wildlife you used to. No you don't. Easter weekend we could hardly hunt for walkers sometimes."

Popularity certainly has a price and as word of good sport spread, and the Bilsdale Fields swelled, more and more who came hunting from outside the country knew less about hound work, "More and more were just hunting to ride, and Bilsdale country was never that way really. Not to my way of thinking." Increasingly foxes were headed by little parties going off on their own, "There was nothing worse than finding a fox, only for him to run straight in to five riders coming the other way." There was more pressure to show sport, and no-one wanted to wait if a fox got to ground after a difficult hunt, for hounds to be rewarded. "Everyone was always in a hurry for things to happen. It wasn't good for the hounds. And it wasn't much good for me neither !" For a man so dedicated to the needs of his hounds above all else, and with the patience to let them get on with it in such difficult country, it took the fun out of it. A reluctant victim of his own success, he decided to give up in 1986, after 23 enjoyable years.

Under a Cloud - In the Happiest Sense

George has in his possession an old Bilsdale Hunt button, flat, not curved like modern buttons. It portrays the letters B.H., a running fox, and above him a cloud. I drove on northwards across the wide open Moors. There was snow on the tops and daffodils under the walls, the sky above a searing bright blue. In this huge sky, skudded big woolly clouds, throwing fast-moving shadows over the heather. Whoever designed that button many years ago knew a thing or two about Bilsdale country.

John Cooke and the Eridge hounds

John Cooke

It would be all of ten years ago I first met 'Cookie', probably at a Puppy Show, or local race meeting. He is one of those people who is always about. On a warm Spring afternoon of blue skies and daffodils I travelled to his home beside the Windrush where he and wife Shirley walk puppies for the Heythrop and Bicester, to learn more about his career in Hunt Service.

'Butcher's Boy' to whipper-in

Before the war John Cooke's father was a Stud Groom in Thimbleby, Lincolnshire. With his father away during the war, and then waiting to be demobbed John left school at 14, to start a job his mother found as clerk in an auctioneer's office. The local parson, Reverend Lawrence, a hunting man, enquired how he was getting on, "I told him I didn't really like it and he told me Mr Butcher wanted a boy." Mr Leslie Butcher later took the Grove and had also had his own pack of beagles. When war broke out the South Wold had divided into the East, kennelled and hunted by Mr Frank Dawson and West, or Farmers', taken by Mr Butcher. This had kept the pack going, "He was a nice little man who described himself as a 'pest officer'. I became kennel boy terrier boy and general facto-tum. Someone only had to shout 'Shit!' and I'd be there with my shovel !" He vividly remembers being bundled in to a horse box to abet in a scam to get people to the Hunt Ball, "They thought it would look better with a boy in front too. Petrol was rationed after the war, and people wanted to go to the Ball at Revesby Abbey, about nine miles away. You weren't supposed to use petrol for things like that. We bundled about seven couples in to the back, in all their finery and set off." Inevitably the police stopped them, "Old Bert Parrish told them we were going to pick up a dead horse. They stopped us on the way back too but luckily didn't look inside." After four years, he did National Service with the King's Troop. As soon as this was over he went straight back to hunting, going as second whipper in to the Linlithgow and Stirlingshire. Miss Annette Usher was MFH and Huntsman, "I may have been young and impressionable but she seemed to do a very good job, and really could blow a horn." Alf Gee was Kennel Huntsman. After two Seasons he moved south to whip in to Charlie Mitchell at the Burton for a further two seasons, "He was a top class plough country Huntsman who taught me a lot." His next move was as single handed whipper-in at the Newmarket and Thurlow in 1955.

The Icing on the Cake

Two Seasons at the Wilton followed before he moved to the sought after post of whipper-in to George Gillson at the Meynell in 1959, which made so many Hunt Servants' careers, "To spend two years with him, well it was marvellous." Hound exercise began without fail on the first Monday in May on bicycles, then ponies by mid June, "We were only little chaps so always took the Farquhar girls' ponies." Joint master at this time was Colonel Mike Farquhar (Sir Peter's brother) and the girls are Angela Meade, and Daphne Pardoe. "Leaving at 7am hounds never returned before 3pm. They were jumping out of their skins with fitness. Gillson never liked a whip near them, he used to say, 'Hold 'em with your eyes' !" A knack he obviously had. "He could fix you with a look all right. By July we'd box hounds up and go miles up in to the stone wall country around Ashbourne. It was nothing to stop at farms and have perhaps a dozen cups of tea through the day. Once we boxed back at Sir Ian and Lady Walker-Okeovers'. They came out with tea and madeira cake. We'd been out all day and my belly button was touching my backbone. I saw this cake, and like a fool looked up. George just stared at me. I felt I had to say no ! Another time I saw this big Vulcan aircraft, and said ,'Did you see that aeroplane ?' 'No Jack. Any hounds or foxes up there ?' I was too frightened to laugh !" George Gillson was a great man to work for though, and could laugh at himself. A real affection runs through all John's stories about him, "He used to judge the Puppy Show at the Barlow for Miss Elsie Wilson. It

John Cooke (Jim Meads)

was quite a do with a bullock killed for lunch, and hunting starting the next day. Poor George, off he went all dressed up. He'd gone a week early ! Dear old George, how we laughed about it." John remained to whip in to Mr Dermot Kelly MFH for one Season, "I had probably become too influenced by George Gillson really. When I was growing up he was *the* man, and a brilliant horseman. When I whipped in to Tom Kirkby at the Newmarket and Thurlow he had spent a season with George and urged me to do the same if I could. I felt so lucky to achieve this. He did everything just right. He was a sharp little man with a lovely voice and horn. All day long it would be 'Quick, quick. Good, good'." One of his greatest pieces of advice concerned not nagging hounds: 'You know what you're like Jack if your Missus gets on at you. In the end you don't take any notice.' He would always go and get his hounds too, not blow for them. Never trailed them about."

Gillson's own apprenticeship had been a tough one, to his uncle, Frank Freeman, to whom he whipped in for eleven seasons, "He must have been hard. Apparently one day the second whipper-in, who couldn't swim, fell into the Braunceston Brook. Poor little beggar somehow got out with watercress all over him, soaked to the skin. When he caught up Freeman just said, 'Where's your whip, boy ?', 'In the brook Sir', he shivered, 'Well you're no use to me without it. Go home' ! Even George who was his nephew was never once invited in to his house." Gillson handed on one of Freeman's kennel coats to John, and a pair of the 'clomping' army boots which he habitually wore.

One hunt of this period stands out in John's mind, "It was March. Cold with that drying wind. Hounds hunted steadily and we never went out of a trot, popping a place here, opening a gate there. They quite literally walked up to that fox. It was a hell of a hound hunt, and had a 4½ mile point. Miss Elsie Wilson was out, and Ted Hill her Huntsman."

Huntsman to the Wilton and Newton's Lore

This fascinating apprenticeship complete John was eager to hunt hounds and secured his first Huntsman's post back at the Wilton for Lord Folkestone, "People buckled around him, he was popular and did us well. He was terribly crippled but really brave. He never missed a day, and no day was ever too long." Foxes weren't over-plentiful but two days a week were enjoyed. The chalky downland was poor-scenting and John set about improving the pack, "I mustered hounds from all over. Sir Peter Farquhar had just finished and let us have some, we had some from the Meynell and Fitzwilliam. Sir Newton Rycroft was very kind to us as well. Jim Bennett gave me 1½ couple from the Vale of Aylesbury which were very good." So good in fact that Sir Newton asked for one to breed from. John admired Sir Newton's abilities as both a Huntsman and hound breeder. One day a week he would whip in to him which proved as informative as it was entertaining. Sometimes Sir Newton would just roll off his horse and run with hounds. Harry Lenthall was Kennel Huntsman. John enthuses, "You look at the New Forest, full of foil; sheep, deer, pigs, ponies, and those hounds of his would hunt true through the lot. They were catching about 60 brace a season, which takes some doing. He was ahead of his time, really, him and Mrs Bridget Scott with their hound breeding. I felt this good bitch he wanted may have been a little light of tongue, and his pack had such good cry. He took the trouble to write to me and tell me how she was getting on. Years later, not long before he died I saw him at the Dummer Puppy Show and he remembered that bitch." Sir Newton had great trust in his hounds, and John believes this is a major factor in any Huntsman's success, "All great Huntsmen have it, George and Charlie were the same. George Gillson used to say, 'Don't lie to your hounds and they will never lie to you. Trust 'em, never kid 'em.' "

I ask him about memorable hounds, "Everything hounds do amazes me. I don't take much amazing !" That infectious chuckle follows again, "I was given an old dog called Badger '56 (Portman Freeman '51- Portman Ballad '53) to help me out a bit. He was Portman bred, of Major WWB Scott's bloodlines and had been given to Colonel Mike Farquhar by his brother, Sir Peter. It was late March and we'd had a bit of a hunt round the woods but they couldn't make much of it, so I went on to draw elsewhere. This old dog was short. I went on drawing. There was no sign of him and about an hour later I went back to give a blow. When we got out of the forest to some gorse, there was Badger. He came out of a gorse bush, dragging a big old fox. He was about a seventh season dog then, and must have persevered to catch that fox alone, and wasn't going to leave him."

Eridge - Foxhunting Paradise

After four seasons at the Wilton, building up a pack, learning from this and from those days with Sir Newton 'Cookie' was ready to move on. When Brian Gupwell was asked to go to Badminton, he applied for the Eridge post and got it. All Brian's sentiments about the country and its people are underlined by him, and he clearly enjoyed every minute there. Except perhaps for the morning of the Centenary Puppy Show. Such an important occasion of course merits even more hard work and prepara-

John Cooke and hounds in Eridge Park

tion than usual. The tenth Duke of Beaufort and Captain Ronnie Wallace had been invited to judge. The Kennels were situated in an idyllic spot surrounded by woodland. All was ready for the afternoon and as John gave his hounds one last walk out in the sunshine they looked a picture, washed and groomed. Then they picked up a line. John saw a fox cross a ride and stood helplessly by as the entire pack, puppies and all tore round in full cry through the thick rhododendron covert. When they finally checked he got them up together. One can only imagine the panic he must have felt wondering if he would get them all back in time. The hot tired dirty hounds who trooped back to the kennels looked rather different from the pack which set out. There was nothing for it but to set to and bath them again. It was already 11.30 am. John's biggest worry now was that the puppies would be too

John Cooke receives a cup from Mrs Richard Barlow at Ardingly in 1975 where Actor '74 won the Championship. (Jim Meads)

tired to show themselves properly. In fact they were so pleased with themselves they really showed off and all was well. Apparently the Duke made some cryptic comment about hounds having been in good voice when he arrived for lunch !

John believes that the way things had been left by Brian when he arrived had a major bearing on his own success. Nothing was out of place, 22 pairs of couples were all soaped and ready to use, "There were six litters of pups, the young ones were already off couples. He had even marked up a hound list with comments about each hound's abilities and given them star ratings. That's what you call A1." Major Field-Marsham had bred a lovely pack of hounds, having already taken a Peterborough Championship and things were done in style, "I never really aspired to showing glory" , Cookie chuckles, "But we got to the last three in the Peterborough Championship with a bitch called Fizzle '73 (Ghurka '65-Fidget '67) . There was me, and the two green coats." Fizzle had won the brood bitch class at Ardingly however and the pack had much continued success there. They won the Championship in 1972 with a red mottled dog called Growler '68 (Tipperary Growler '64-Freda '66). The Queen Mother presented the Championship, and stayed with Lady Abergavenny. About a year later Cookie got a phone call to say Her Majesty wished to attend their meet in the scout field opposite the Kennels. Few other people recognised her, as she studied the hounds in her headscarf and brogues, "There's Growler" she exclaimed to John's astonishment as she walked through the pack to pat their Champion. They also won the Championship in 1975 with Actor '74 (Cottesmore Actor '71- Eridge Wistful '66.) Cottesmore Actor '71 was a very good dog given to the Eridge by Captain Clarke, such a good judge of hounds' capabilities. Cottesmore Actor '71 had proved too sharp for his own country, and Captain Clarke felt the thick Eridge woods would steady him, which they did.

There could scarcely have been a more perfect setting for Kennels than this peaceful 'glade' amid the woods. The morning birdsong was out of this world and the three herds of deer - red, fallow and roe - would simply part for hounds to walk through them, "It was marvellous country to hunt, with very little riot." Good hunts were numerous, "I remember one they went really hard about eleven miles as they ran which takes a bit of doing in forestry. We passed the Hook Green pub to Lambhurst over the stream and back to mark at Wylie outside Wadhurst."

The Role of a Good Whipper-in, and Doghounds

John believes that having a good whipper-in can make all the difference to how many foxes a pack catch, "He should be wherever you aren't." In this respect he was very fortunate at the Eridge. Amateur whipper-in and farmer Bill Swift knew the country like the back of his hand and could cross any part of it without jumping. He had whipped in to Will Freeman and Bob Champion. Bob Street, later Tiverton Kennel Huntsman also earns praise, "He was a masterpiece as a whipper-in. He'd been at the Puckeridge and Thurlow before and spent a lot of time otterhunting. He was very sharp which you have to be in a wooded country. If hounds divided he could have them back together before I even knew !" John is very proud of his whippers-in's own achievements. He goes several times each Season to see Martin Thornton, "He helped me catch a lot of foxes. I admire him a lot and he is a hell of a horseman." As is Thornton's son, National Hunt jockey Robert. Another who whipped in to

John was John Goode, now with the Brocklesby, "It's interesting that those two both ended up with Old English hounds. I think you have to be a certain type of person to hunt them well." John's own thoughts on what makes a good pack are also interesting, "I could never see the point of hunting just bitches or just dogs. A pack of all bitches tends to flash on a bit. I liked to have some doghounds out always as I believe they are a good 'brake' for a pack."

Eridge country remained well foxed, with its four big estates, and the support of real foxhunters, "We had a lot of fun. From the meet at Wylie we always popped the chestnut railings. Three of us set at them first with hounds. All three of us tipped up as if synchronised and I found myself rolling around like an apple with Lady Rose Neville (Lady Abergavenny's daughter) in front of the whole field. She was only about twenty and shrieked, 'Quick John get up or they'll all be talking about us' !"

Sadly all good things must come to an end and after thirteen tremendously happy Seasons here John's marriage broke up and he moved on. Fate dealt him a good hand however, as he was able to go home to the South Wold.

Full Circle

So at the beginning of the 1980-81 Season John Cooke found himself Huntsman to the pack where he had started as Kennel boy, the South Wold. His personal life took another very happy turn, for here he met his wife Shirley, "Bless her. Her family have walked hounds since at least 1930. " South Wold country was crossed by big drainage ditches, similar to those in the Berkeley country, "I remember one hunt, all across the Marsh for about nine miles. Galloping on towards the dunes of the Golden Sands I passed a big sign saying 'Welcome to Mabelthorpe' !" Recovering from the laughter this induces he adds, "We caught our fox." Brian Dobson MFH was a good man, and sadly died of

cancer. When the mastership changed ten years later, Cookie did not fancy being a Kennel Huntsman, so decided to retire.

Retirement and the Heythrop

Lord Rotherwick was looking for someone at Cornbury Park, and was happy for Shirley to carry on puppy walking, which suited everyone very nicely. The couple stayed there for ten years before moving to their current home, next to the lovely River Windrush. Shirley still walks plenty of puppies for the Heythrop and Bicester which gives them

'Cookie' at the Heythrop Puppy Show in 1975, flanked by Peter Wright who hunted the Cottesmore and Tom Normington who hunted the Grafton (Jim Meads)

both a lot of pleasure. Their home is full of photographs of their puppies. Shirley is joint secretary of the thriving Heythrop Hunt Club and they both take an active interest in fundraising. They enjoy four or five days by car each week throughout the Season, and attend many puppy shows. Faction '95 (Angler '88-Fashion '92), walked by Shirley was Reserve Champion at Ardingly in 1997 and the home pack always provides plenty of interest at the major shows.

"I never wanted to do anything else. I'm very lucky really", grins this most genial of men as he watches my terrier weaving in and out of his daffodils, the Spring sunshine dancing off the river below.

Brian Gupwell
(Jim Meads)

90

Brian Gupwell

Many recognise captured in the slim figure of Brian Gupwell, immaculately turned out in his green coat, distinctively seated on a hunter of a certain type, the epitome of the word 'Huntsman'. Such timeless embodiment is something akin to the very best of sporting art. Most of my own formative days in the hunting field were spent following the Duke of Beaufort's hounds during his twenty two Season tenure there. In a curious twist of Fate, just days after I interview Brian in his cottage at Badminton, this picture is brought sharply into focus again. For the first time in a decade, Brian's green coat comes out of its mothballs, as he is asked to whip in on a busy mid-Season Saturday. Brian still very much enjoys his hunting, though past his three score years and ten, and hip replacement notwithstanding the years have been kind. Hopping in customary fashion from his first horse on to his second without dismounting, he grins, "I'm only on trial you know. Don't think I'll get the job." Brian does not suffer fools gladly, but appreciated anyone with a genuine love of hounds and hunting. I well remember as a teenager, when Brian realised I made the effort to learn hounds' names, how he would point out individuals, or tell you little things they had done. Following on foot, or bicycle, he would always tell you the next draw, and what had happened to each hunted fox. In the haroosh of the chase it is often difficult to be appreciative of help given. Brian would always remember later on, though and thank you for a holloa, or information given. On my sixteenth Birthday I made the sensible decision to go hunting rather than to school. Few late March Birthdays fall on good hunting days, after all! I walked to the meet across country, just a few miles from my home in our hill country. By pure co-incidence, just 16 couple of hounds were out - a very unusual number. The rain came down in stair rods all day, and I slithered around the banks of Boxwell like the proverbial drowned rat. Hounds hunted nicely in the Box Wood and caught their fox after about half an hour of lovely music. As he brought them out, Brian called up to me to do the gate for him down by the stream. I ran down, and as he trotted off he muttered, "Happy Birthday." There on the gatepost was the brush of that fox, which still hangs in my hall today.

Beginnings

Brian's father Walter Gupwell hunted the Middleton and latterly the Fernie. His grandfather was Stud Groom at the Old Surrey and Burstow. Although Brian learnt to ride at the Middleton when a boy, things did not always go his way. He recalls one pony, Bo Peep, who would stop at the odd fence, where the second whipper-in would come to his rescue, jumping off his horse, and riding Bo Peep over. Brian's father was sent in to the Yorkshire Hussars by joint master Lord Grimthorpe, who sent all able bodied staff and half the hunt horses to the regiment. Joe Wright, then first whipper-in was not passed fit, and it was this good horseman who got Brian going. This was followed by a spell in racing stables where 'You had to ride to stay on the blooming things.' Although he never officially whipped in to his father he would do so unofficially whenever he was at home.

Middleton (East)

Brian's memories of his two seasons whipping-in to the widower, Alf Hoare are particularly vivid. The Kennels were in 'the coldest place in East Yorkshire.' Winters there invariably produced snow, and never more than in the notably atrocious winter of 1947, "The night the snow fell, hounds could have walked out of the yards, as it was level with the top of the railings." This bad weather went on right in to April, and Brian recalls riding over gates. The horses were only used for the staff to ride to a nearby farm for their customary midday meal, and for Brian's nocturnal courting expeditions! Alf was great fun to work for, always encouraging, "He would say things like, 'Go on Brian, I'll give you a pound if we catch this fox.' " The use of strychnine was still widespread, and to see a hound take this lethal poison was a sight to chill the blood, "We carried soda to put down their throats, but you'd

never have time." Another horror still prevalent in those days was the gruesome gin trap, "I watched a fox run a furrow, and could hear this clanking noise. There he was running with this gin trap clanking on his leg. It was a terrible sight", he recalls with a revulsion few 'antis' would begin to comprehend.

At the end of that all too long winter Brian spent a holiday with his father, then hunting the Galway Blazers. He had gone there directly after the War, and told his son that the going there was so good that they could leave Kennels at 8am and return at 8pm, all on one horse! It was now early June, and the snow still lay on the northern side of those hedges in East Yorkshire.

The Belvoir and Beyond

Brian's next appointment was a prestigious one, as second whipper-in at the Belvoir, but Huntsman George Tongue, an undoubtedly brave man who had won the MM in the First World War was, putting it mildly, very difficult to work for. It was not unusual for no word to be uttered by him all day. Brian stuck this out for one season, and second whipper-in Dick Perkins was promoted to be first whipper-in when he left. A measure of the situation may be taken from the words of Colonel Colman (of the mustard family) who was a master at that time , "Congratulations Perkins. You are the only whipper-in to stay for two seasons in the last thirteen years" ! Brian liked the Belvoir, and had it not been so unpleasant working in such an atmosphere he would like to have stayed, "The work was hard enough in those days without that." Indeed it was, for all the brickwork had to be scrubbed down by hand with soda, and with no antibiotics, hounds with septic feet had to be held in buckets of salt water. The only available medication was something called 'M & B Tablets'. "There was no such thing as walking out, it was running out. You had to run and run to keep hounds up together." Disillusioned, he joined the Navy, but this did not provide the open air life he had envisaged, and the lure of hunting proved too great. He returned home to be second horseman to the late Major Cowen at the Fernie for a year, before seeking another post in Kennels.

Brocklesby

Happily, this time Fate was kinder, and appointed first whipper-in in at the Brocklesby in 1956, he had a far better time, "The Huntsman there, Ron Harvey was a great chap who had been a prisoner of War, captured at Crete." The Old English hounds were, and remained, to Brian's liking, "People descry them, going through fads with the welsh and so on, but they have proven themselves. They will draw the thickest of covert." This open plough country, where fields of over one hundred acres were the norm, had an abundance of hares. At that time the area near the River Humber was especially good scenting, with its marshes, now sadly built over all around Immingham and the docks. This open plough was vastly different to the well fenced grass country his father hunted at the Fernie. During the period 57-58, a lot of foxes were dying in the Brocklesby country. Birds were also dying unaccountably, and hunting was stopped during February. Lord Yarborough instructed his keepers and hunt staff to dig as many foxes out as they could, and inoculate them, as a liver complaint was suspected to be the cause of the problem. The cost of the exercise was not inconsiderable, each inoculation costing 7/6d. Brian did not feel that the liver complaint was the cause, as no such problems had occurred in grass countries, such as the Fernie, and he became convinced that dressed corn was a more likely culprit. Subsequent tests carried out at Newmarket on dead foxes and birds, proved his theory correct. Dressed corn was being eaten by the birds, which were then eaten by the foxes. When the substances responsible were banned all was well once more.

Huntsman of the Eridge

Brian's next interview was in another plough country, the East Essex, in 1961. He travelled on under the Thames for an interview at the Eridge, and as soon as he arrived his heart was set on this country. Heavily wooded, with thin hazel coppices and small grass fields, it proved full of foxes, "You meet nice people all over the hunting world, but you will go a long way to meet such super people as were in the Eridge country." He succeeded Major Field-Marsham MFH as Huntsman, and he proved the greatest help and influence. "It was not easy catching foxes , as we could not do much stopping. If ever we caught a leash on top he would send down a bottle of champagne." He was a very thoughtful man, and always gave credit where it was due. In 1964 Brian showed a bitch called Eridge Freedom '60 (Portman Playfair '51 - Freda '55) at Peterborough Royal Foxhound Show. She won accolades and the Bitch Championship. Brian's mother congratulated Major Field-Marsham, saying, "This

Brian Gupwell with the Duke of Beaufort's hounds at Worcester Lodge 1980
(Kay Gardner)

must have made your day ?" His response, "It has made my Life" leaves little more to be said. Except that in an act of typical unselfishness he gave the cup to Brian to keep in his house, rather than taking it to his own.

Style

Brian's relatively quiet style of hunting hounds had to change in the Eridge country. At Christmas he was approached by Joint Master Miss Brooke with the words, "We do like you Gupwell, but we wish you'd make more noise. If you could make us aware of where you are we would all be happier." Brian explains, "Before that, I was like these modern huntsmen. I learned then that being too quiet does not suit everyone. I don't like too much hollering and horn blowing, as hounds can concentrate better without noise. A little horn when they are running however, adds to it, and helps keep hounds up together if any are adrift. People do like to hear you jollying your hounds. They need to know where you are of course, and they like to be told what has happened - whether a covert was blank or a fox has gone to ground." Communication is the keynote for a successful Huntsman, and certainly enlivens the day for all concerned.

Badminton - By 'Royal Command'

In 1967, the tenth Duke of Beaufort, universally known as 'Master' decided to relinquish the horn which he had carried for some 47 Seasons, and sought a professional to succeed him. Driving himself to the Eridge country in his car MFH1, he went to see Brian and invited him to take this, the most prestigious post in Hunt Service. To be thus invited to succeed the man dubbed the Greatest Huntsman of All Time was tantamount to a Royal Command. Indeed the late Duke's pedigree proved him more 'royal' than the Royal Family, being a true Plantaganet. To be the recipient of such a request was a great honour, but could with hindsight so easily have proved a poison chalice. That Brian showed good sport, and produced hounds to the highest standard imaginable, in the face of such pressure is to his eternal credit. John Cooke succeeded Brian at the Eridge, his reaction on hearing where Brian was going, "By gum, you're a brave man. Have you seen them up there ?" referring to the huge fields then often 250-300 in number.

Brian and hounds moving off from a meet at Badminton House. On his left is David Boulter then second whipper-in, on the right Denis Brown, long serving first whipper-in. (Jim Meads)

Brian proudly recalls his first morning's cubhunting from Hinnegar Lodge in Badminton Park . "Hounds hunted well in Bull Park and caught a fox on top. Hacking home I asked, 'Do you think I made too much noise Your Grace ?' I felt he didn't quite know what to say, as the job had been done, noise or not !" The two men could not have been more different in their style of hunting hounds. Having been encouraged to make plenty of noise in the Eridge woods, Brian found his methods under scrutiny from the mounted Field as much as anyone. Many of the farmers and subscribers at that time would never have hunted with anyone but the late Duke, and he does feel that they were inevitably his greatest critics, scrutinising his every move. He feels strongly that he would like to have whipped in to the late Duke, so that he could have emulated his methods, rather than learning from his own mistakes the hard way. He also feels he would have learnt a huge amount, "Perhaps some of it would have rubbed off! He knew more about hunting than most. Imagine hunting nine days in a week, six mornings and three evenings. I know I made mistakes to start with, but things got better as time went on." That Brian knew the whole pack, numbering 63½ couple just five and a half days after his arrival at Badminton on 2nd May 1967 impressed the Duke greatly. He was a man who took a keen interest in his hounds, and visited the Kennels frequently, sometimes with guests, but more often than not just to see hounds and find out how they were getting on. He never missed visiting Kennels on a Sunday. As anyone who has been involved with hounds will know, young hounds re-

turned from walk change from week to week, "He took so much interest in them, they might have been schoolchildren," recalls Brian. His knowledge of the country, and the habits of foxes were also invaluable. Tree foxes have always been a fact of hunting life at Badminton, where the thick boles of limes or dead ivy covered trees provide snug sleeping quarters for foxes. Brian recalls one day when hounds were hunting in the Park, then populated by sheep and cattle. Hounds had a line to a tree, but threw up in the foil, "His Grace suggested we look in the tree. Seven foxes were in there !"

The Hunting Season at Badminton was a long one. Cubhunting began as soon as the harvest allowed in August, and hounds hunted through to May 1st. The Horse Trials were held around the third week in April, and Brian hacked across the Park to meets in the hill country. The trade stands provided great temptation for the hounds, and one day, as they crossed the main A46, a driver stopped to tell them two couple of hounds were left the Badminton side of this busy road Whippers-in Denis Brown and Gilmour Lewis slipped back to look for the hounds, whilst Brian racked his brains to work out where the hounds could have got away from them. He began to wonder, on what now seemed a long hack to Hillsley, whether he had counted the right number. Word had already reached the meet about the missing hounds when he arrived, and the Duke did not look pleased. When Brian's horse trod on another hound, matters were made worse, "Oh dear, oh dear. He can't get them all to the meet and then he treads on the rest !" Keeper Mervyn Barratt was dispatched to help in the search, "Right oh, Your Grace, what are their names ?", he asked, unwisely, "Names ! Names !", the Duke exploded, "I don't know their names. Even these silly buggers don't know their names!" Tempers mellowed on this warm Spring day, and later the mystery was unravelled. Hounds had been in the Wash Box at the Kennels, where the door opens *inwards*. The Kennelman had let hounds follow him out, not realising the door had closed before the last two couple could get out. When he returned and discovered them, he let them out hoping they would catch up, instead of which they hit off the line of Col Guinness's horse in the Avenue, and followed that instead. It was a salutary lesson in the importance of continually counting hounds, and caused much amusement later, if not at the time !

An establishment like Badminton requires good team work to run smoothly. Brian's first whippers-in were David Goring, and Bernard Dobson who did two years apiece, followed by Denis Brown who stayed for 16 seasons, forging a long and successful partnership.

In 1974 Major Gerald Gundry MFH gave up hunting the doghounds, so Brian's days hunting hounds were doubled. He continued hunting hounds four days a week until a year after the late Duke died, and Captain Ian Farquhar MFH arrived to hunt hounds in 1985, as an amateur. Brian stayed on as First whipper-in and Kennel Huntsman, finally retiring in 1989.

Showing Success
Brian had an early aptitude for showing hounds, as proven with his first Peterborough Champion Eridge Freedom '60. He firmly believes that showing is a knack, "Major Field-Marsham used to say I mesmerised them!" That he made it look effortless is indisputable. He feels he was lucky to have such a wealth of lovely hounds in his care at Badminton, "They were wonderful hounds. So level, especially the

Brian Gupwell and the late Duke of Beaufort at Peterborough in 1976 with Champion Duke of Beaufort's Culprit,'75 (Crowner '69–Canopy '70) (Jim Meads)

95

bitches." As well as showing Champions at every major Hound Show, he went on to show 15 Peterborough Champions from Badminton. His total of 16 Peterborough Championships is a record unlikely to be equalled. The tension at Peterborough is tangible, and timing critical, as if you show in the last class before the Championship and are in the shake up, there is little time to get hounds in to the ring, particularly for those at the beginning of the alphabet, as packs are called in alphabetical order. Things can become rather strained at this 'white knuckle' stage, none taking things more seriously than the late Duke, who was also a stickler for punctuality. Brian recounts with amusement that during one nail biting Peterborough, he was late getting in to the ring for the Championship class. The late Duke, seated with the then Mr David Somerset MFH, (now Duke) and HRH the Prince of Wales, was becoming agitated, "I don't know where he's got to. I'll sack him !", he spluttered in the heat of the moment. The Prince protested that a man could not be sacked for being late in a showing class, "Yes he can. I've sacked huntsmen before in July he'll have to go." Thankfully Brian appeared, the Championship was won and naturally all such thoughts evaporated. The Prince of Wales of course had his first day's hunting from Badminton, with Brian hunting hounds in 1975. Current Kennel-Huntsman Charles Wheeler benefited greatly from Brian's showing expertise, "I was lucky enough to learn a tremendous amount from him", says Charles who adopted a similarly quiet style of showing hounds when he took over in 1989.

Brian receiving a prize from HRH the Prince of Wales, President at Peterborough 1978.
(Jim Meads)

Standards

Brian always had hounds looking exceptionally fit and well. People forget these days that although hounds might have longer days in the field, they do not hack to and from meets like they used to. It is therefore very difficult to judge whether they are fitter, or have more stamina than in years gone by. Busy roads preclude much hacking now, but it was normal for hounds to hack miles to the meet, and home again after a day's hunting, "They did much more road work. We would think nothing of hack-

96

ing to Foxley Green for a meet." (This would be a good nine miles from Kennels.) A hack to North Wraxall in the Spring would be nearly 12 miles away. Good hunts were enjoyed by the huge Fields, whose smart Blue and Buff livery was a hard won privilege. They were an impressive sight indeed in the days when gentlemen eschewed safety for the glamour of the silk hat, and hunting caps were remarked upon for their rarity. In this well foxed country hounds always caught plenty of foxes, one hundred brace per season considered the average. Brian relives one hunt which anyone who knows the country today would still relish. Though its point is six miles, I estimate that hounds would have covered nearer thirteen as they ran. They found at Pinkney, running to Pool Leaze. The fox turned back over the road to

Brian Gupwell and the Duke of Beaufort's Hounds on exercise at Tresham (Kay Gardner)

Ladyswood. This country was all grass then, and well fenced with hedges, so there was plenty to entertain the riders. They ran hard past Widleys, where the Field jumped into and out of the road over the hedge side of the Farm, not the low wall, crossing the Sherston Luckington road, running with Luckington village now well on the left. They ran to Sopworth crossroads where their fox was seen and turned sharp left, running in a straight line towards Badminton House. He ran to the left of the House and on over Cape Farm (more formidable hedges) to the railway at Acton Turville. He ran down the side of the railway without crossing it. Hounds would now have been in the stone wall country between Acton Turville and Tormarton. Their fox was eventually marked to ground in Grickstone, beyond Lyegrove and just beside the main A46. Brian had changed on to a third horse to keep with them during this hunt. The late Duke rode his good grey Finisterre from start to finish.

Favourites - and the Crowner '69 link

With so many good hounds it is hard to pick a few special ones. Crowner '69 (Heythrop Craftsman '62-Warfare '65), an exceptional stallionhound and Peterborough champion was a great favourite of Brian's who was widely used. This had been an exceptional litter, his sister Crumpet completing the Championship double with him at Peterborough in 1971. The New Forest Medyg '69 brothers Monmouth '77, another Peterborough Champion, paid the rare compliment of being used as a stallionhound in his first season, and his tri-colour brother Morgan '77, also stand out. Morgan was the most wonderfully athletic hound, and his 'party trick' on open days was to jump high in the air, no twist or turn being too difficult for him in pursuit of a biscuit. These brothers were out of Crimson '72, a daughter of Crystal '69, another Crowner litter sister.

Tigress '78 (Cracker '72-Treacle '75) lost an eye after being kicked. Her sire was Crimson's litter brother, "She was a real favourite." So much so that Brian's mother had a stick made with Tigress carved on the top of it. The lovely Wamba '78 (Puckeridge Grasper '75-Wagtail '73) was always destined for second place in the Show Ring, but she is fondly remembered, "I was also very fond of a bitch called Penance '66 (Palmer '59-Dainty '60), who could take a line down any road." Another good litter included Bonnylass '78 (Bedford '74-Tally '75). Yet again, Crowner '69 was Tally's sire. I well remember Brian's pride when Bonnylass caught a fox single handed in the very swollen River Avon below Hyam in December 1980.

Retirement

Brian continues to hunt, usually two days a week, and maintains a keen interest in hounds. In Summer he is to be found at innumerable Puppy Shows. His enthusiasm is unbowed. Sitting in the kitchen of his cottage at Badminton, looking out across the Park he says matter-of-factly, "I decided to ride where I would see a fox this morning. It looked the sort of morning to see one, so I went to a likely place." It is a comment which speaks volumes, and that he found his fox goes without saying.

97

L Ian Hedley Esq MFH with a presentation marking his 40th year in office

98

L Ian Hedley Esq MFH

On a grey and drizzly morning I travelled through the open and sometimes bleak Northumberland land scape to visit Mr L Ian Hedley at the family farm where hounds are kennelled. They sang well when I arrived, peering over the walls at me to get a better view. I had stayed at a nearby farmhouse bed and breakfast run by keen Morpeth follower Mrs Susan Ainsley. She could remember feeding leftovers from cricket teas to the Border hounds as a child, when they were still kennelled at Riverdale. Mr Hedley's son Michael still keeps around 600 Cheviot ewes, and the Hedley flock is well known. The morning was considerably cheered by Mr Hedley's reminiscences related to me without hesitation or prompting in great clarity of detail by this exceptionally bright-eyed octogenarian.

Early Days and World War I

As a boy of just two, Ian Hedley can remember being taken to watch soldiers with horses and gun carriages coming up to train at Redesdale during World War I.

When just five years old he had a Shetland pony called Blackbird, "He could turn on a sixpence if he didn't want to do something and go straight up on his hind legs." His 'saddle' was just a hessian sack, and the term, 'grip with your knees', took on very real meaning. At this time Jake Robson kept just four couple of hounds at Coldtown. Throughout the 1920s he hunted regularly every Saturday and recalls hunting on the first Saturday in December, after a Hunt Ball which had gone on until 6am.

Farm Manager Aged 18

Then, in the 1930s things were very difficult, money was short and the spectre of war loomed once more, "I had the farm to manage from the age of 18 as Father was old and infirm. I also became in-volved with the War Agricultural Committee, so didn't hunt much at all." His future wife Pat, who he had known since 1933, was in the WRVS and cooked daily at the Submariners Base, Wellesley Naval School Blyth, for all the men and Officers. She then went into the Red Cross in 1940, and was working at Hallington Hall where around 50 wounded soldiers were cared for. The injured were taken to the purpose-built Hexham Hospital on Tuesdays and Fridays. Pat was to see all the troops safely in to their Ford Vehicles for the return journey to Hallington Hall. She was then free to meet Ian in Hexham. The pair would enjoy fish and chips at the County Hotel, and spend the rest of the day to-gether. They married on September 8th 1945.

From Tenant Farmer to Master of Foxhounds

Once World War II was over, Jake Robson junior began to hunt hounds. His joint master died and he carried on for two years, still being joint master until March 1952. Michael Walton then hunted hounds for one year. A meeting was held at the Fox and Hounds, "The pub was crammed full. I was hunting a good horse by now, and they decided they wanted me to hunt the hounds. I said, 'I can't. I'm a tenant of the Duke of Northumberland and cannot do it without permission.' Well, I hadn't the cheek to approach the Duke myself, but the following day, being Monday, was rent day, so I decided to tell the Agent, Colonel Clark. The following Sunday morning I was gardening and my wife came out to say, 'The Duke's on the phone. What have you done wrong ?' Well, being the Duke, he wanted to know everything, why the Robsons and Dodds were giving up and so on. He was a very straight man and everybody loved him." Mr Hedley told the Duke all he knew and at the end of it he said, "Well, Hedley. The Border Foxhounds must not go down. You must take them on, and I will give you all the support I can. I want you to bring them back to their former glory."

Starting Out

So it was that the hounds came to Overacres. There were just 8½ couple, and the Hunt had very little money. Mr Hedley would put them in a tractor and trailer, hacking on to the meet himself. Soon they were catching a lot of foxes in this very well-foxed country.

The Boxing Day Meet was held at the Percy Arms. By three o'clock no fox had been found and the master was becoming very despondent. He decided to just draw a bit of a moss* and hack home, "Well, a fox got up from this moss and we had an hour and a half round, and round, and round. He holed not far from where we had found just as it was getting dark. There was a shepherd called Dunn. I said, 'If we're to do anything we must have a torch a spade and a terrier.' He replied, 'Master, have you ever known a Dunn done ?' and produced the lot. The terrier was a comical little thing, more Dandie Dinmont than anything. Anyway, it marked in this place and we got the fox." They then hacked five miles home down onto the A696 and hacked three miles along it, meeting just one car.

New Year Tragedy

A meet was held on the first Monday in January, after three hard nights of frost, but the rough ground was still huntable. The keeper at Hareshaw said he knew where there was a fox, "We unboxed at the keeper's and set off about quarter of a mile. There had been a shower of light fluffy snow, which still lay on the heather. They put this fox up and flew straight down to the North Tyne. The fox crossed the ice. I lost seven hounds. As I arrived the slow current just took them under the ice. It was the most ghastly sight." So ghastly that he is still visibly moved by it today. They managed to get two out, and eight hounds had gone on. Mr Hedley sent whipper-in John Dixon after them, urging him to do all he could to get that fox. The fox holed and Dixon put his sharp little terrier Sandy in, and he was duly accounted for. That left the pack down to just ten hounds. True to his word that he would give whatever help he could the Duke of Northumberland gave Mr Hedley four first season hounds, Roly Harker MFH Jedforest gave him another three, Colonel Cookson of the Morpeth also gave him two, "We hunted on. The Percy hounds had good noses, though slower than ours, but they made the pack up and we finished the Season having caught 48 foxes."

Building Up

Of the ten original Border hounds, one bitch, Lovely '47 and her daughter went back to Coniston Barmaid, reputedly the best hound there has ever been in the Lakes, "Lovely was well named. She was beautiful and well, if she viewed a fox he might as well turn round and come back to her !"

In 1954, Mr Hedley had twelve young hounds, "They were full of energy and we had some of our hardest days, I used to try and get them in a big bracken bed or covert." As these matured, they would become the nucleus of a good pack. Initially Mr Hedley used his own doghounds and one from the Liddesdale with success. That Season hounds caught 78 foxes. That year Frank Walton gave up the Coquetdale. One day, Arthur Elliot also called and asked Mr Hedley to take back Kale Water on the Scottish side as well as the whole of Coquet. This entailed calling a special meeting, as hounds would now have to increase from two to three days a week. The pack went from strength to strength, and seven of Mr Walton's hounds were taken in which helped to swell numbers for the extra days required.

The Jedforest Link

An annual joint meet with the Jed Forest at Penny Muir was greatly enjoyed. Farmer Mr Bob Tyzer was a great supporter and there would be perhaps thirty cars on the hill, and 60 riders, "I told Roly, 'I want a day off', and always let him hunt hounds. He was very, very generous." Hounds never caught less than four foxes from that meet, one day catching four by half past one. One of these was at Swanlaws, "Roly Harker saw a shepherd by a gate, 'Eee, where d'you think we'll find a fox?' He was really country, Roly. The shepherd told him there had been cubs in the Turnip field. He put hounds in,

Mr Hedley explained that a moss is a place where a special kind of grass grows. If sheep can pull it up in the Spring of the year, the nutriment in the long scallion-like roots keeps them strong. The shepherds call it 'on mossing.'

and soon the music started. with Roly's famous 'Have a care'. As he left Roly Harker tried to tip the Shepherd, 'Eee man that was grand' but he would not take anything." There were 32-34 couple of hounds, "By George when they got in to a rush bed or bracken bog there was some music. "At the end of the day Mr Hedley would just hang back, and his hounds would part from the others as they reached the wagon. At Mr Harker's box there would be fruit loaf, ginger loaf, tea and of course a 'dram' or two. This continued until Roly Harker's death. Years before the Border had traditionally held joint meets with the Liddesdale, two Robson brothers having married two Dodd sisters, the Liddesdale masters being another branch of the Dodd family, and the Douglas family.

When one of the Elliots approached Mr Hedley to take back Beaumont Water, loaned to the College Valley in 1924, he declined. Sir Alfred Goodson was a good friend and he had no wish to upset him. He also wanted to spend time with his wife and sons, already limited by the amount of country they had taken on. Runs in to Beaumont Water were not uncommon from the Kale Water side though, or from Coquet.

Border Foxhounds (Andrew Stirling)

Breeding and a Lovely Line

Now, the Border really were a pack in their own right, well in to their own breeding programme. After using their own and Liddesdale dogs at the outset, Mr Hedley tried College Valley and Blencathra stallionhounds with great success. One hound he got from the Blencathra, Dancer proved a real star. "Blencathra Dancer was a lovely hound. He had a wonderful temperament and got on well with all the other hounds in Kennels from the outset." It was impossible however to keep him in Kennels, "I would leave him in on hunting days, and how he knew where we were, in strange country I will never know, but he always joined us. We never even saw how he got out. He left some very good hounds. He was out of Border Melody '54, who was out of Lovely '47 when in her seventh or eighth season, and by a Liddesdale dog."

A line I had heard revered by many in the North is that going back to Border Stormer, one of the original Border hounds at Coldtown. He was a brilliant hound who caught so many foxes alone that the rest of the pack worried him.

101

'Prince'

Round Bellingham there is some wooded country, the rest of the country being moorland. It can be very boggy, and an added hazard are the shell holes around Coquet and the Ranges.

As hounds improved, support grew. When Mr Hedley began as master a field of eight would have been big. There is very little jumping, though he would sometimes leave the rest standing on his good horse Prince. Prince became something of a legend in Northumberland. He was the result of a chance liaison between a Clydesdale mare and a stallion named Tiger, whose own dam was a half Dales mare. He was as fast as he was surefooted, "He had amazing agility for such a heavy horse. Reliable to a degree and with the heart of a lion." He ate three buckets of oats a day, and retired after ten years when he never missed his turn, doing at least 50 days a Season.

The Joy of December

Most of all this passionate hound man enjoyed the December meets, when travelling dog foxes provided long points, "If scent was good, dear me, they just left you when they really got going." One day as hounds were being unboxed, there was a holloa. Hounds shot to it and holed their fox in a shrubbery at Wark. The lady of the house appeared and refused to allow a terrier to be put in. This was an absolutely straight 12 miles away. Two of the car followers fetched the wagon, boxed hounds and horses back to Otterburn, and hunting resumed in the intended draw !

On another occasion a fox went from Hindhope straight to Coquet Head. Mr Hedley thought he would go to the forestry and went there. Then he heard them on Thirl Moor, a big 1500ft hill getting further away. He stayed on top of the hill, "You can skirt a hill quicker than going down it, that's the great se-

102

cret of hill hunting." A sharp eyed Field member saw the fox come over to Blind Burn farm and up Eel Rigg. Hounds flew round Rigg Farm and caught him in Kale Water itself. They were seven hounds short, and there was no sign of them by 6pm, "I hoped they would come back as it was 34 miles to go back by road. They never came. They had split on Thirl Moor, taken another fox on, straight down Coquet in to the Reed and killed half a mile from Elsdon Burn. When I got home I was asked, 'Where have you been, hounds have been home since half past two'! There they were, waiting for us at home."

Dancer Junior's Tally

Another similar run took place when they split on Eel Rigg. Five hounds went on. The rest took more or less the same course, "One hound went on, and on, and on." He was Dancer Junior, son of the aforementioned Blencathra Dancer, "Two days later he landed home. Around his neck was a cotton tally - the tough linen thread and brown paper used on sheep dip pails. It said, 'This hound killed a fox on the doorstep of Uswayford Hall -

Mr L Ian Hedley and the late Johnny Richardson enjoy a good 'natter' at Rydal

Tom Wilkinson.' That was near Alwinton, about 18 miles on." Michael Hedley still has the tally.

Seven Foxes and 154 Scones

"On the second Monday in October we met at Barrow Burn, after the Show. We had quite good hunting, and hounds caught four foxes by 1.30pm. I said to the farmer, George Murray, Eliza and daughter Mary, 'I can't go home yet with all these people here.' Somehow, between 1.30pm and 1.45pm the many helpers had given 154 people tea and scones - a continuous chain of washing cups, and buttering scones. George said, 'Just go up on Barrow Law.' Sure enough up jumped a fox, careering about the fields a bit and broke away. The car people went round. Hounds coursed their fox along the top and killed him. George said, 'Just come back round Shorthope Rush bog. ' Up jumped another fox. They flew two miles round the hillside towards the cars, back up hill where he holed, and bolted. He ran down hill again, and that was that. They were just coming back and another one banged out of the hole. That was another half an hour. We boxed up at 3.30pm, having added seven foxes to the tally, everyone highly delighted."

A Countryman's Knowledge

George Murray's neighbour was Alec Rutherford on Battle Shiel. Alec had lost four black faced hoggs in one month in. He said a fox was responsible. George said it was not a fox. To settle it, they called hounds in, "Alec is a real gentle countryman who spent a lot of time just watching." Hounds were unboxed at Barrow Burn, hacking over the hill to Battle Shiel. First Mr Hedley drew a little bracken bed, and hounds quickly caught a fox, 'Master', said Alec, 'that's not him.' There was a hole on the steep hillside. We put Sandy in. Hounds sat listening. In moments a big fox popped out and in three great spans was down that hill, and up the other side before hounds could move. I looked at Alec, he looked at me, 'Master, *that's* him !' We ran that fox for an hour and a half in some of the roughest country, to Whiteburn Shank, through the Heigh to Kidland Forest, Bloody Bush Edge, back in by Milkhope to Kidlandlee School, then on high out on Alwinton Hill, where he holed above the village. Incredibly, Alec was there within five minutes with his spade, 'How did you know Alec ?' 'I just guessed that's where he'd come if he was pushed, Master.' It was a big place and nine other holes were blocked before Sandy was put in. The end was very swift. That was one of the biggest, fattest foxes I have ever hunted. Hounds' blood was really up and though I wanted the mask, Darkwood as usual made off with it. By the time I rescued this huge mask it was not worth saving ! I gave Alec the

brush and wonder if he still has it now - he is 94 ! He is one of the finest countrymen you could ever wish to meet. There was never another hogg worried. "

To Their Former Glory - A Picture

The Coquet foxes were renowned at that time 1950s to 1960s for their size, and would take pignetting fences in their stride. A picture in Mr Hedley's living room commemorates another special hunt, "On October 18th we met at Whitelea Farm. As soon as I let the ramp down they were away. Over the Scotch Egg, right round. We rode round the old cart drove. It was the most amazing place, coal mines, a lime kiln and lime quarry from the nineteenth century for burning and slaking lime. This fox tried many holes, swinging right handed over the Kielder Edge. We could get no further with the horses because of the big moss haggs and boggy ground. The shepherd, Andrew Hedley was very

fond of foxes, which he always referred to as, 'Ma foxes.' He said, 'Mr Hedley, it's one of ma foxes. I think he'll come back.' He went right round the Edge, a terrific distance almost to the Reservoir at Catcleugh. Hounds turned right by the Reservoir as we were making our way back, and almost met us. They killed the most wonderful big dog fox, short of the Rummell - two acres of loose stone." Andrew suggested they try some holes, and sure enough another fox was soon afoot, and was hunted for three quarters of an hour, "We just stood watching them up and down, round and about, until they

A study of some Border Foxhounds (Andrew Stirling)

caught him." Andrew Hedley said, 'You've killed two of ma foxes, and that's enough for one day, so let's see what Doug Thomson's got over the top.' " He then led the way, there being only one way through the bogs he knew so well. Hounds began to speak, "Guilty knew every hole in the Border country. Here was what we called the Long Hole, over 500 yards of peat where the ground falls in. She cheeked that fox all the way up, giving tongue so that he couldn't get in." He then ran down to the Burns, out to Jed Heads where the Jed Water rises right by Southdene Manse back to them, "We never moved all through that hunt, which was a very fine one to watch and they caught him quite close by." One more fox was accounted for before 2.30pm, and Andrew suggested they go back, "Let's see if old Ralph's got anything in the kist." The picture shows Mr Hedley coming off the West side of Carter back to Whitelea, now covered in forestry. Hounds and horses waited in the byre as they had tea. Old Ralph did indeed find a full bottle of whisky in the kist, where he kept his dog meal, "Those hounds had done all that hunting alone and it really was wonderful. Hounds are like a flock of sheep - when they are down, you have to have a clean sweep, and it takes about ten years to get them right. Now, I could truly say to the Duke that I had achieved what I set out to do. The Border hounds were back to their former glory."

Master of Foxhounds Honoured By the RSPCA

Hounds met at Ridley Cairn for the last meet of the Season on Thursday 14th April 1961. John Dixon hunted them, and came home five hounds and two terriers short. On Friday someone telephoned to say they were trapped in a nasty place on Barrow Hill. When Mr Hedley went to look he found a very bad place, all of 80 feet long, "The only movement you had to get in was six to nine inches up and down. Hounds were twelve feet down, and had killed their fox. It was the most ghastly place and smelled of sour, rotten peat." Realising he could do nothing that day he fetched some flesh for them. The next day he returned with two fencing rails, with which he made a 'hen walk' with strips of wood every foot. He stapled a rope to the bottom, and managed to lever it in to the crevice, "Straight away I called hounds, and they came up, the little

L Ian Hedley MFH Esq on Prince

terriers between them. The mess in that crevice was so great I had to carry the terriers up as they were stuck. The hounds had a good roll and were as right as rain." After a mile's walk back to the farmhouse, he was in a state of exhaustion, "Never have I been more thankful for a cup of tea, provided by Mrs Hedley - a distant relation." He changed footwear, had a good 'dram' and drove home, utterly sore all over from easing himself on tiptoe through the narrow place. His Barbour and oilskins could never be cleaned and had to be burnt. They never discovered what the big black hole full of this awful gummy mess was. The rescue made the News that night, "Eee I'll never get over that smell. It was shocking. Some of the foxes we killed there had that terrible smell on them. They must have been able to jump up to get out I imagine." Mr Hedley was presented with an award, along with those who helped him, Joe Robson and Fred Snaith, for his bravery in the rescue by the RSPCA .

The Bad Storm -1962 and a Boxing Day to Remember

1962 proved a very difficult year. Only odd days' hunting were had, "On November 17th two hill shepherds set off home from the market at Rothbury. They perished."

On Boxing Day the 'phone rang incessantly until he could stand it no more, and agreed to meet at the Percy Arms, where an expectant crowd had gathered, "There was ice and snow. I quickly put hounds into Tower Wood and they caught two foxes by 12.30pm. I thought I ought to put on a bit of a show and went to a moss. A fox banged up and we had a tremendous hunt north for four miles then he crossed the River through Ash Trees and Blakeup, Garret Shiels to West Tofts, Hareshaw and dropped down to the Brigg. He went over the A68 at Coldtown, crossed the Reed at Earhaugh and up the road to the Nick Quarry. The wind was blowing with flakes of snow in it. Conditions had held me up and I had to rely on the car people, who had seen hounds on Hareshaw. I got down the A68 to past Coldtown, crossed the River Rede at the Blackburn Lyn Bridge, up to the Fellside road to Hartside. Here hounds came back to me, Darkwood, as usual, carrying the mask. It was one of the most wonderful hunts we've ever had. In icy conditions, hounds did it all on their own." This hunt had been a good 16 miles. Just Mr Hedley, Jack Famelton and his two daughters were left. He told them he would trot fast home, "Don't heed the hounds, they will follow on." In the yard he jumped off Prince, ran in and swapped his hunting cap for a deerstalker. He then took Prince up to the hill, where a cow was due to calve. He could see the calf's feet, and trotted her down to the byre. He did not even dare wait to collect his deerstalker which blew off up on the hill. After a quick change and a meal he saw

105

the Fameltons into their wagon and checked the cow, who had calved without difficulty. The Famel-tons only just made it the 13 miles home. Hounds were never out again that Season, as the hill sheep were very weak. It was 23rd May before the deerstalker came to light !

The Blind Burn Eight

One day at Blind Burn hounds got among a litter and split. Eight hounds disappeared on one of these, and were waiting at the wagon at the end of the day. What they had done remained a mystery, but not for long. Three weeks later, hunting lower down, hounds holed a fox. As John Dixon and Mr Hedley rode down they found a hole, a great pile of soil dug out and three dead foxes. This discovery by pure chance solved the mystery of what those eight hounds had done.

The country was peopled with folk who understood hounds. One day at Coquet they were again eight hounds short. These were spotted by a shepherd called Smith and his sister working in the lambing pens in Spring. They were living in the West Percy country in the Ingram Valley walking many puppies, and taking numerous prizes. Hounds caught their fox there, and they tied it to a piece of string to entice them in to a building. Their quick thinking saving Mr Hedley a trip of 54 miles by road.

Hill Hunting Secrets

There seem to be two secrets to successful hunting in this open hill country. The first, as already discussed is to ride the hill tops as long as possible. The second, Mr Hedley believes is to teach hounds to go away from their Huntsman to a holloa, "As soon as I heard a holloa I would take my hat off and gallop on cheering, "Hike holloa !" I got them so as they would really fly to it, as old Jake Robson had them in the old days. I remember when I went to Kale Water first, after the Hunt Ball to pick up a cheque for the money raised - about £600. I thought I couldn't just take the money, and must put in some meets. I called them the Two Silent Hunts. Whenever people saw a fox they stood waving hankies. Well, my hounds weren't used to that." I thanked them all for their support afterwards and said,

Michael Hedley Esq. MFH and his father L Ian Hedley Esq. MFH (Jim Meads)

'I come here to do two things. To give you people good sport and to catch foxes. For Heaven's sake if hounds aren't hunting, and a fox is astir holloa, and keep hollering. Take my hounds away from me, and I'll certainly send them to you'." When Roly Harker heard this he challenged Mr Hedley. His method may not be orthodox, but is logical, "If I'm on top of a hill, and someone sees a fox at the bottom, scent will be gone by the time I get there. Hounds will be there in a moment if they go on." Thus he justified his words to Mr Harker, and no more was said, "We got on like a house on fire."

Michael Hedley Esq MFH judging with Martin Scott Esq (Terry Crate)

Following On

Michael Hedley has now done 27 seasons as Joint Master and Huntsman, only the fourth man to hunt hounds since the pack was founded. He never whipped in to his father but has always been keen. When he left school he was feeding hounds, and the pups back from walk knew him so well they would follow him rather than Mr Hedley Senior, "My wife Pat was unwell, and this is a young man's job really. I let him have a go, and he's been going ever since and made a very good job of it. He is a far better PR man than me." Sadly Mrs Hedley died after many years battling uncomplainingly against cancer.

Two of Mr Hedley's four grandchildren hunt, "Michael and Carol are terrific. They have good young committees. They have tremendous support going." When a regular follower died of leukaemia £1100 was raised and a further £3500 from the sale of calendars. The Edinburgh Air Ambulance has also benefited from a substantial donation.

Maintaining the Glory

Mr Hedley is still senior master, and with his son Michael hunting hounds little has changed. John Dixon is still whipping in, though these days takes a less active role. Michael Hedley still breeds along the same Fell lines, though he has introduced a Dumfriesshire cross bitch, who came as a whelp from the College Valley, "She has a wonderful nose on forestry roads or tarmac and can take the whole pack on." He too has the deep love of hounds so obvious in his father, "I am about to draft some hounds. It's a very difficult time, saying Goodbye, even when you know they will be looked after."

The country has altered little, just the odd field of barley, and some forestry in the Coquet Valley. Foxes do tend to run in to this more, where in the past they would have kept going. The area around the ranges now the second largest army training area in the country covers some 58,000 acres. Michael has noticed that the explosion in the badger population is pushing foxes out of much of their previous habitat. The terriers which would have followed the horses before, now have the luxury of motorised transport, and 'bleeper' collars which saves a lot of time. The pack has its own wagon too, rather than relying on hired transport which had to be summoned at the end of the day in the past. Many now follow on quadbikes, which are also used to hunt hounds on some of the forestry days.

Mr Ian Hedley stresses to me that it is as true now, as then, that the Border Foxhounds' very existence and continued success is owed in no small way to those wonderful countrymen, the hill shepherds. Hounds are now fed on a special dry Hound Feed mixed with powdered milk and codliver oil, "By Jove, they look good on it", says Mr Hedley Senior, with a pride in the Border pack that still runs deep eighty years on.

Charlie Johnson who started as the Bicester's Terrier boy aged 14
(Jim Meads)

108

Charlie Johnson

There can be few with as many famous family connections in the world of Hunt Service as Charlie Johnson. His grandfather on his mother's side was Arthur Thatcher, whose brother Bert Thatcher hunted the Zetland. His son Pat hunted the Zetland too for a time but when his father died it upset him so much that he no longer wanted to be in the Zetland country. Charlie's grandmother was a Goodall. There is also a connection with Harry Judd who hunted the Lanark and Renfrewshire. He had two daughters, one married Will Webster (Jim and Clarrie's grandfather), the other married Charlie Johnson's Great Uncle, Bert Thatcher, "Charlie Travers who hunted the Cotswold was related to us somehow too," muses Charlie Johnson, "Then of course mother's Uncle, Charles Isaacs, who hunted the Fernie, married a Goodall girl as well. . ." It is a pedigree to confound even Martin Scott ! Suffice to say Charlie Johnson's career choice was not a surprise to anyone.

Beginnings at the Bicester

Charlie's father, Clarence Johnson was born at the Ludlow Kennels, where his own father hunted hounds. After whipping in at the Lanark and Renfrewshire, and Fernie, Clarence came to hunt the Bicester in 1923. At school young Charlie thought of little but hunting, and was heartened when he heard that Fred Holland, huntsman to the Old Berks managed to get one day a week off school for his son. Clarence wrote to Charlie's School Governors but the Headmaster threatened to resign if they gave in. He had to be content with having the odd day off to go hunting, until he was old enough to leave, "I never wanted to do anything else. Hunting takes over your life, and that's that." Aged just 14 he began his career with the Bicester as Terrier Boy, dressed in full hunt livery, and mounted, carrying the terrier in a leather bag for two Seasons. In the second of these Mr Budgett MFH said he could work in Kennels during the Summer and whip in whenever required as well. This was a good grounding, "Father was very quick." Kennel work was very hard in the 1920s and 30s, with so much of it being repetitive manual labour. There were many staff however, virtually all the men who lived in the village being employed in Kennel or Stable. The Stables and Kennels were full to capacity, as was another stable in the village. Everything was done on a grand scale with even the Hunt second horsemen in livery.

The Stuff of Dreams

Hunting was at its zenith between the wars and special trains were laid on known as Hunt Specials. Two would set out from Bicester and Brackley to Woodford each Saturday full of subscribers, second horsemen and horses. Hounds had their own van on the Bicester Special. First horses returned to the Station to be cared for after changing. When hounds hacked back at the end of the day Clarence Johnson signalled his arrival with a touch of the horn. The second horses were fed gruel, rugged up and loaded for the homeward journey, whilst Charlie was despatched to the butcher's shop to buy four pieces of pork pie to sustain the staff on the way home. The Station Master's whistle was accompanied by a cry of, 'Hunt Specials First, Hunt Specials First !' This conjures up the most magic of scenes, Charlie describes it all in great detail, "I can still see those trains now, with all the steam." One day his father boarded the train with the Hunt Secretary, "That was a good day Johnson", he remarked, "a Field of five hundred and three hundred second horsemen." A dull thud may now be heard as hunt secretaries all over the country collapse at the sheer imagination of such a cavalry charge. Even a Beaufort Saturday crowd pales in to insignificance. The pictures painted in the mind by Charlie's reminiscences are vivid, sumptuous and all together mind blowing in a way undreamt of by today's modern world. By the time they returned around 7 pm hounds and horses would be stiff and tired, but there was still a four mile hack back to the Kennels.

A local farmer had a standing order of a tray of whisky for the hunt staff which they downed in one outside the pub near the Station, anxious to keep horses and hounds on the move.

Two Great Huntsmen Swap Sons

In 1931 he then spent five Seasons as second whipper-in to Joe Wright Senior at the Cheshire, whilst Wright's son took on the same role with Clarence Johnson at the Bicester. Charlie hunted five or six days a week with Joe Wright hunting hounds until he retired, "Joe Wright, he really was quick. You had to be with so much grass and those huge Fields. It was very similar to the Wynnstay. We had to have three horses apiece on Fridays after Christmas, or they wouldn't have stood it." Charlie was required in Kennels seven days a week with one night off, and one half Sunday off per month. He recalls getting onto his bicycle one night after 5 o'clock, "Where you going boy?" Wright enquired, "Northwich, Sir", "No you aren't. I want those hounds sulphuring tonight." Wright was very particular in the field too, "You couldn't point your whip to where a fox went. You had to go with him and show him quietly so that he was seen to make a good cast." Summer too was a very busy time. There were hound days, rather like Puppy Shows, when visiting masters would come and look at the hounds, and mull over breeding plans. These were often held twice a week and entailed a lot of extra work. Any servants who came would have lunch in the Huntsman's house. Even swilling down was a major operation as water had to be pumped by hand. Then Major Casey came as master from Lord Harrington's, hunting hounds one or two days a week, with Tom Peaker from the Worcestershire engaged as Huntsman for one Season, hunting hounds four days. He then left to act as Stud Groom to his brother at the Fernie.

War Changes the World Forever

When war broke out, Charlie joined the Cheshire Yeomanry and went to Palestine with horses still in use. Invalided out he returned in 1942 to Cheshire, with Arthur Redfern from the Middleton then

Charlie Johnson leads the Bicester Hounds away from a meet.
(Jim Meads)

Charlie Johnson and the Bicester Hounds.
(Jim Meads)

hunting hounds. In 1944 Colonel Field-Marsham and Colonel Buxton retired from the Bicester. A Committee took on the running of the Hunt, and the doghounds were kennelled in the north of the country. Mrs Mostyn and Mr Dewar Harrison approached Charlie and asked if he would come back to help out. Charlie spent the next three Seasons whipping in to his father until he retired. He had in fact already been hunting hounds a lot of the time with his father helping out, so was more than ready, after a long and thorough apprenticeship, to take over when he did retire.

Life at the Top

"It was nothing unusual for a young man to spend 12 or 14 years whipping in then. You had to do your time, but when you got to the top it really was something. Yes, it was hard. Work was hard and you had to put up with being cursed from morning to night." Charlie officially became Huntsman in 1947, and married Sheila.

Saturday Fields continued to top 300 in the northern end which was still all grass, "We never crossed a ploughed field, and all the fences were cut and laid stake and binders. The Grafton was just the same. I take my hat off to them all even being able to hunt the country now with the terrible roads. " Charlie greatly enjoyed regular trips to hunt with the Duke of Beaufort's, where Lady Ampthill used to provide a horse for him at Castle Combe. Without hesitation he names the late Duke as simply the greatest Huntsman ever, "There'll never be another Huntsman like him, certainly not as an amateur. I saw him in Lower Woods one day. Hounds had divided, and he got them up together so quietly and quickly with just a word, 'Come on old bitches,' and they were with him. That was what he was like with hounds. they were his, completely. It was wonderful to see. I paraded hounds once at the White City and he came in with Colonel Mike Ansell. One of the marvellous little badger pied bitches he let me have flew to him, and was all over him. He was just as pleased to see her ! He just had a way with them." The Bicester only hunted Mondays as a bye day after the war and joint master Lord

Beattie would also hunt with the Quorn, Charlie often accompanying him to see George Barker in action. Charlie tells me, "No-one could have had better masters than I did."

The Bicester Hounds

When Clarence Johnson took over at the Bicester they were a very good pack of hounds. Colonel Lonsdale had been there for many years using Warwickshire blood a lot. Then joint master Lord Chesham used Beaufort blood a lot, along with Brocklesby and Berkeley, "Then we started using Mr Ikey Bell's bloodlines. He was always here. My father used to go down to the South and West Wilts Kennels a lot. We used South and West Wilts Godfrey '28 (Kilkenny Gory '21- Carlow Goosecap '22). Then he used the Brecon Paragon '23 (Mr Curre's Danger '15-Pamela '21), Curre and David Davies lines. That was how the Welsh blood first came to the Bicester Kennels."

Pulling Together

"After the war we used mostly Beaufort and Heythrop dogs. The Duke's were the best we had, definitely." Good hounds were scarce after the war, and the Duke gave Charlie Prattler '53, and some bitches to breed from. He also had some pups from Captain Ronnie Wallace. "Duke of Beaufort's Prattler was a very good old dog. Major Gundry told me all that line were very low scenting, and particularly good at road hunting. He hated electric fencing and would see it round kale long before the others. " There was a tremendous spirit of everyone helping each other to keep going at what could otherwise have been a very difficult time. It was now that the Johnsons first became involved with the Old Berkeley Beagles. "John Robinson's father Fred had Thurlows Hound Feed and let Charlie have extra feed. In return I walked a litter of puppies for the beagles, to help them out", explains Mrs Johnson."Then we got pies too. John Brazil had Brazils pie place and once a week we went down to collect all the unsold pies and hundreds of hard boiled eggs. Jim Bennett went there too. It all helped out. Some of the farmers let us have tail barley as well for the hounds. Pre-war it had all been oatmeal puddings, but times were harder now", Charlie adds.

Charlie maintained a high standard at Stratton Audley, and showed excellent sport. Sadly a recurring back problem led him to retiring early in 1964, "I just couldn't go on. I went to everyone - Harley Street, Stoke Mandeville, but they couldn't do anything." He took a bad fall, and was warned that another could have dire consequences. Not wishing to be inactive, the Johnsons set up a boarding kennel, which became almost too successful, dogs arriving from Wales and Cornwall, some owners even flying their lucky pets from Cheshire. The house and kennels Mr Dewar Harrison let them have at Shelswell was becoming a bit much, and when they heard the Lodge was available they were delighted.

Reflections

Charlie feels that it was the war that put paid to the long established families of Hunt Servants. Certainly there are not the whole families of brothers, cousins and intermarriages that seem to have prevailed pre-war. there were more men employed in kennels too then, so more opportunities. He is proud to have served in the Cheshire Yeomanry, but equally proud of his family's record in Hunt service, and to the Bicester hunt especially, "My great great grandfather Stephen Goodall hunted the Bicester hounds for Sir Thomas Mostyn, when they were kennelled at Bainton. " He gives me a tour of his splendid collection of paintings, photographs and memorabilia, including one of Sir Thomas Mostyn's famous hound, Lady 1810, with her whelps. Unfortunately, though in very good order for a man in his late 80s, his back does not allow him to attend Puppy Shows, but Charlie keeps in touch with his colleagues. His contemporary, Albert Buckle had been to see him the previous day, and his successor Bryan Pheasey lives in the same village. Mrs Johnson would not allow me to leave without another piece of home made cake for the journey home. A reminder of the genuine hospitality and unique cameraderie which binds hunting folk of all ages, though they may be strangers, who at once become friends.

112

Sir Thomas Mostyn's (Bicester) 'Lady' 1810

113

David Jones blowing for hounds at the end of the morning .
(Kay Gardner)

114

David Jones

The majority of people would be familiar with David Jones as the man frequently photographed with a Welsh Foxhound Champion at Builth Wells. Others know him as a famous breeder and judge of terriers. In 1997 his picture appeared regularly as leader of the North Welsh March to London for the Hyde Park Rally. Then his no-nonsense forthright defence of the sport earned him many plaudits. It was during that time I first got to know him when I joined the marchers on the section between Eastnor Castle near Ledbury, to London itself. As a leader, he is without rival, and his early morning rallying of the 'troops' as they faced yet another gruelling day I am certain kept many of them going. I noticed that he lost no opportunity to quietly praise and encourage. His handling of endless media enquiries when even he must have been feeling a trifle jaded was unbelievable. In 1999 I finally managed to get a day's hunting with David in some fairly rugged country. The meet was early, and on foot. It was a typically hot August morning. I quickly understood why he covered the ground so easily en route for London. As hounds disappeared down one steep valley side and up the other he would appear just behind them as if by magic. We had left for the meet around 3am, and the cry of those hounds echoing through the valleys made it all worthwhile. Just to prove our insanity we also went to a meet of the Radnor and West Hereford at 6pm that evening ! Before that however, David led us back to the Kennels where he showed us the hounds, before producing a wonderful cooked breakfast in this idyllic spot. The course of his life could have been very different however as I was to learn.

Following the Sennybridge Farmers' Hunt

David Jones was brought up in Merthyr Tydfil, its countryside ravaged by coal mines and steel works. He followed the Sennybridge with his father as a boy, and hunting was to become an integral part of his life. David's greatest influence as a Huntsman was Leighton Price, who hunted the Sennybridge Farmers hounds, which he followed so keenly in his teens, "Leight was a great character - what you might call a bit of a case really ! He had hunted as a schoolboy whipping in to the Pantysgallog hounds. He had then gone in to farming and returned to hunting later in life. We had great fun and they were as good a pack of hounds as you would see. One Season they never lost a single fox, they caught every one. In open ground they would catch a fox before he could reach the forestry."

Young Plumber Meets Lost Hound. Result ? The Taf Fechan Hunt is Formed

David trained as a plumber, and one day a woman brought a hound from the local pound to his father's workshops to try and trace where it had come from. Having no luck, David kept the hound, which was to become the foundation of a new pack. With Gerwyn Thomas, and the late Peter Thomas, who were not related to each other, David Jones formed the Taf Fechan Hunt. Their country had not been hunted for over 25 years, and one of the biggest problems was fitting in all the meets, "Hunting had been missing for so long the farmers were competing to see who could put on the best spread for us !" It cannot have been easy country to hunt with its forestry, open cast tips and rocks. They were able to get on to the Brecon Beacons though, as these were not hunted by anyone else at that time, "It was a huge country really. To see hounds outside the Town Hall in Merthyr on Boxing Day, a real Labour stronghold, well it was something, really it was." For five Seasons David continued to work as a plumber whilst caring for and hunting the Taf Fechan pack. Here, he met his wife Sue, a Merthyr girl, though her grandmother had lived on a farm. Her life, she said, would never be quite the same again !

From Plumber to Professional Huntsman at the David Davies

From a seemingly unorthodox beginning, David was offered the job of professional Huntsman to the

Principality's premier pack, the David Davies in 1973. Plumbing's loss soon became Hunting's gain. In central Wales, the David Davies' country consists of Vale country and hills verging on the mountainous. These sustain strong foxes which must be caught as this is prime sheep country. To this end a Lambing call system is operated. Hounds are hunted from a horse on Saturdays, and on foot during the week due to the roughness of the terrain. The Welsh hounds need all their independence here. Even this fairly wild country has changed and it is now impossible to cross the main road as traffic has increased. Shooting, as elsewhere has increased over the years, "When I first came the hills were covered in fern, gorse and grass, now much of that has been ploughed. Grants have increased farm roads and the Vale is harder to hunt near Newtown as the town itself is growing." David's recipe for successful hunting is simple, and he sums up with just one word, "Determination."

David Jones laden down by silverware at Builth (Terry Crate)

A Few Amusing Anecdotes

One true story often told is of a day just before David arrived here, when Lord Davies was hunting hounds. He was out by Gwga Lake, a wild, rushy bit of country, "Hounds ran on and on, and the master lost them for about four hours. Miles and miles he walked, eventually meeting an old boy in his eighties. He asked if the old boy had seen hounds, 'Yes' , he replied, 'Flying over the hill. They jumped the wall, and a black bitch was hard behind their fox.' 'Good', said the master, 'How long ago ?' The old boy replied, 'A week last Wednesday' !"

One well known character in the David Davies country was Mrs McLaughlin, "She was a well to do lady, but hunting through and through and did the terriers. People in those days really *knew* their hunting. She had a little van called Bluey. One day as I was going up a hill, I passed Bluey, towing a brand new Land Rover. This puzzled me so I asked Mrs McLaughlin what had happened, 'Oh' she said, 'The brakes had gone so I was just loosing it down the hill.' Another time I saw her drive straight in to a stationery car, 'Oh,' she cried, 'Look what we've done to each other'!'

David Jones with Welsh Foxhound Doghound Champion Breiddon '95 (Taurus '88-Bluebell '90) at Builth Wells 2000 (Jim Meads)

Hounds

Fell blood has proved beneficial, with Eskdale and Ennerdale Bendigo used in the late 1970s. Interestingly though, the straight Welsh/Fell cross did not succeed, "The Fell and Welsh have now been kept separate. They run up well together, as they were both bred to hunt similar countries. Some of the Welsh hounds are actually faster than the Fell hounds we have. " Asked about particularly influential hounds, David has no hesitation, "There was a man called Peter Lindsay who hunted the Pennine, who died in a car crash as a young man. We had two of their pups. Pennine Nettle (Pennine Talisman '73—Percy Milvain Nightie '72). Talisman was a brother to Token '73, who was the dam of the famous Blencathra Glider '76. Token and Talisman's dam was Magic '67. Percy (Milvain) Nightie '72 had the

116

David Jones and the David Davies Hounds (Kay Gardner)

best nose I have ever seen in a hound. It is a line of tremendous fox sense." Another great success here was a Stallionhound called Eskdale and Ennerdale Champion, "That's a superb line. He bred me Nancy, Nimrod and Needles out of Pennine Nettle. It is a line we still have today and the five Season hounds look like second Season hounds. They have great drive, and the older they get, the more intelligent they become." There is no substitute for the wisdom of older hounds, which makes longevity such an important asset to any pack.

Size - Does it Matter ?

I asked David what he felt about the size of a hound, and whether the large or small ones coped best in hilly terrain, as I had noticed both big and small hounds in this pack. Once more he refers to Leighton Price, "Leighton was a great hound man. He had a big black dog called Driver '51 who was tremendous to hunt, as well as some little Welsh hounds like Tapster, another very good dog. Brian Price hunted the Brecon at that time and always had something good, whether hounds or terriers. One day they were hunting together on a big hill at the edge of the Beacons. The fox climbed a very steep place following the zig-zag of a watercourse. Leighton bet Brian a fiver that Tapster would get to the top first, ahead of Driver. Driver went well in to the lead and half way up, Brian was counting his money. Then Tapster flew past, followed by all the rest until Driver was last ! To me, that shows the disadvantage of a bigger hound, who has more to carry."

A Tale From the Riverbank

The most astonishing thing David has seen a hound do was in the Otterhunting field however, "It was amazing, I think. Ray Williams had a hound called New Forest Manton. We were at Newcastle Owen and hounds had been hunting some six hours. They ran from a huge pool into a shallow. Ray took them back to the pool but they and could take it no further. There was some rough water in a corner and Manton disappeared completely underwater. In, and out he went, and as he came out he looked

117

David Jones in typical country (Kay Gardner)

up at Ray and went 'Oww!' Three or four times he went right under and did the same thing. He was quite literally telling Ray, 'That's where he is.' It was quite incredible to me, to see a hound 'telling' the Huntsman something like that."

David Davies Hounds Provide a New Outcross

The value of a Welsh outcross has benefited many Kennels this side of Offa's Dyke since World War II. Its merits or otherwise have been hotly debated ever since, with hounds such as New Forest Medyg '69 , a son of the hitherto unknown Plas Machynlleth Miller '63 proving hugely influential. Captain Ian Farquhar introduced more Welsh blood when at the Bicester via Vale of Clettwr Falcon '73 and his sister Fairy. On arriving at Badminton, he was able to build on this, as well as the existing Brecon Petrel '32 and New Forest Medyg '69 bloodlines. Recently he decided to try another Welsh outcross, and this time went to the David Davies, to use their Builth champion Benjamin '94, (Barrister '89-Brecon Sheba '86) Captain Farquhar may not be prejudiced against the 'woolly' Welsh hounds, but when presented with silky smooth English bitches, Benjamin proved decidedly fussy. He rejected their libidinous advances and refused to have anything to do with them. This was to the advantage of his brother Bouncer '94, who perhaps did not get so many chances then, and was not nearly so fussy ! "It was very funny really ! Anyway Bouncer was used, and is a superb dog in his work. I would say that 90% of the hounds shown at Builth next year will be by Bouncer. They are from the original 'B' line that was here when I came. They were not the best looking hounds then, but had good feet and shoulders and were marvellous to hunt. They were really tough, hard hounds."

Globetrotting with Terriers

David Jones' other great passion is breeding terriers, and his lines are now world famous. He has sent dogs all over the world, and travelled widely himself to judge them. He has many terriers in America and has been out there to see them hunt, "I've done everything from hunting bears in America to being bitten by a 'coon in Canada !" This month he is off to judge in Canada again.

118

Marching to Further Hunting's Cause

David Jones rallies his troops on the March to London (Kay Gardner)

Like many of us, David believes more should have been done to explain hunting's role to the wider world in the past, "The children of twenty years ago are today's teachers. That was the big mistake." His commitment to hunting's future remains solid, and he is a worthy champion of the cause. To this end David Jones' face became more widely known to the general public in 1997 when he was asked to lead the North Welsh March from Machynlleth to London, "I had never met Mark Miller-Mundy, but he rang me, as Nigel Peel had passed on my number. The first idea was for each hunt to march and hand over in the next country, like a relay. I agreed to organise Wales as I believed we really had to do something. We called a meeting, and it was suggested we should walk all the way." The first sign that this was the right approach came during the first day's marching. David had been telling someone about red kites when one appeared, following the marchers and swooping low to fly parallel to them for some distance. One of the most interesting things about the March, which I had joined for a week, was the lack of any hostility towards us. Even as we crossed motorway bridges lorry drivers would hoot and flash, giving us the 'thumbs up'. In towns, even as we neared the capital I never saw one protester. David agrees, "There was no hostility. I really do not believe the general public want to see hunting banned. I led a March last year to Cardiff, and wondered if we would find any hostility in the Valleys, which are such a Labour stronghold. It was just the opposite, we had total support al the way." The March to London had been an incredible experience, and David proved a powerful and charismatic leader, "It was like taking an army with you, and there was a great feeling of camaraderie." It was also gruelling, the North Welsh Marchers averaging 28 miles per day, most of it in high temperatures and humidity. The size of some blisters had to be seen to be believed. Sore shins and even stress fractures received treatment along the way. There were many memorable welcomes, but entering the packed Square in Stow on the Wold was easily the most moving. When Brecon Huntsman Ian Hawkins led the singing of John Peel there was not a dry eye to be seen, "Stow Square was incredible, it had a passion you just would not beat anywhere. I believe every person has a day when something really becomes dear to them. That was the day."

The Future

That passionate belief sustains David Jones' view of the future, "What kind of world puts the needs of animals before those of little children ? It has all become too much." He recently received a call from someone who was trying to help Lithuania set up packs of hounds, as they recognised it was a good way of boosting the rural economy, "It comes to something when the government in Lithuania recognise the benefits of Foxhunting more than our own ! Hunting is part of our history, but it is part of our future too."

The Pytchley's longest serving Huntsman, Peter Jones.
(Jim Meads)

120

Peter Jones

My instructions for finding the Pytchley Hunt Kennels were succinct and accurate, as might be expected of a man who has spent the last 30 years here, "What time do you want to come m'dear? Let me check the calendar. No problem." I had little difficulty in recognising the Kennels with its houses of glowing red brick and Georgian windows. The surrounding lawns and drive were immaculate, as if vaccuumed and polished. Peter's wife Mon provided tea and sandwiches as her husband told me about the career which has led to him becoming the Pytchley's longest serving Huntsman.

Fernie Born and Bred

Before the War Peter's father was in the Stables at the Fernie. When he returned after the War he whipped in to Bert Peaker for three seasons, and two for Walter Gupwell who succeeded Bert Peaker as Huntsman. He then went as Stud Groom to Hunt Secretary Mr Watson, where he remained for 42 Seasons, "I was born and bred in the Fernie Kennels. When I was a little lad, father had a friend called Charlie Warrener who used to make lovely sticks, his father was Stud Groom at Lowther. Charlie's voice to me always was the Pytchley, and he was a big friend of Stanley Barker. Father knew Stanley well when he was whipping in and as Stud Groom, Charlie's father knew him too, so I spent a fair bit of time in his company as a little lad. I never had the opportunity to hunt with him. I always thought when I was at school that if I could just ride second horse to Stanley Barker I would have achieved something. I never in my wildest dreams imagined I would come here and hunt hounds longer than him."

Starting Out at Home

Peter's career started in 1958 at the Fernie, at the same time as Bruce Durno, working in Kennels during the summer and stables in winter, "Walter Gupwell was a great influence on me and he was the one who really got me going." On just the first morning's bicycle exercise Peter witnessed the worst incident he has seen in over 40 years of Hunt Service. There were railway sidings at Welham. They stopped with hounds for a light engine to pass. The house was between them and the line, so no-one had a clear view of the line, "It was very unfortunate. The old dear who was the gate lady opened the far gate when the train had gone, then ours. I put hounds close up behind Walter, as you would to cross over the line. As he moved off, the Grimsby fish train came straight through the middle of the hounds at 60 mph. I thought Walter would be killed, as it knocked the bike clean out of his hands. It was very upsetting, as we could do nothing. We lost 6½ couple of hounds but we were lucky it wasn't worse. Walter could easily have been killed. I didn't quite get nightmares about it but it was very unpleasant and hurt me really hard."

Moving On, and Marriage

After two Seasons with his home pack he went to the South Notts in 1960 to whip in to Fred Sallis who had been at the Fernie when he was a boy. Here he met his wife Monica whose father farmed. They have now been married 39 years, "I couldn't do the job without her and she knows as many farmers as me. She works damned hard, and hunts two days a week." He then went to the Woodland Pytchley whipping in to Joe Wright for two Seasons until he retired, "He was the one I learned most from. He was a great bloke, and in those two Seasons I learned such a lot. He was always very calm. I think he was a very underestimated Huntsman." One pet hate Peter has is when people see a hare and say hounds are on that, when they haven't been standing there two minutes. "I learnt that from Joe Wright. One day I saw a similar situation, and hounds caught their fox. Joe said, 'There's that hare.' Hares rarely move until hounds are right by them. Old Charlie's gone by then, and

the hare will often run the same line. You have to trust your hounds. Nine times out of ten that is better than information." By co-incidence, Peter points out that the three who influenced him most had all been Middleton men, Walter Gupwell, Stanley Barker and Joe Wright. Peter then came to the Pytchley in 1968 to whip in to Bert Maiden for a further two Seasons. This was the first time a whipper-in had been single handed. Instead of having two whippers in Michael King was employed as second kennelman to new Kennelman John Jackson.

Peter Jones blowing the Pytchley hounds away at the start of a hunt. (Jim Meads)

Back to the Pytchley - as Huntsman, and Help From Stanley Barker

Next, Peter spent one Season whipping in to Joe Miller at the Grafton, with a view to hunting hounds when he retired. However, Peter was then asked if he would come back as Huntsman to the Pytchley , which he did in 1971, "I really looked up to Stanley Barker, though I'd only hunted a few times with him in the car. He was ever so good to me when I started here as Huntsman, such a help. To think this was the man I had idolised as a kid ! I thought the world of him." Peter had another advantage on his side, "Fortunately, as a young lad I had six months working with an agricultural contractor. I worked for some of these farmers, so I knew a lot of them especially on the Saturday side. Living in the area I was in Young Farmers. I obviously got to know the country and a lot more farmers when I whipped in. My first few Seasons I hardly ever missed the market at Market Harborough on a Tuesday. There are always some pro-hunting ones and some that don't hunt, but don't mind seeing hounds. We would sit down have a laugh and a cup of tea. That couple of hours a week helped me a lot. If you sit down with the farmers you find out what their problems are." As well as good relations with farmers, Peter enjoys a good working relationship with the local shooting community, "There is quite a bit of shooting. The Cottesbrooke Estate shoot, but we hunt it just the same. I shoot in a syndicate . We enjoy some good days, and invite farmers to shoot with us. Nearly everyone without exception would say if hounds are really running don't stop them, but I would never draw when they are shooting. There's no point falling out, we are all good friends."

122

A Changing Country

The country has changed even in the thirty Seasons Peter has been here. The arrival of the A14 about four years ago means they cannot run from the Naseby side to the Cottesbrooke side any more on a Saturday. Several coverts were also lost in its construction, "That has been the biggest setback since I have been here. I never saw the best of it as the M1 came in 1959 when Stanley was still here." Daventry has expanded tremendously, "Places we had seen hounds running quite recently are all houses now." The boundaries of Northampton too creep ever outwards, "We used to hunt all round South Lodge and Ecton when I first came. Its all housing estates now, we used to go there once a month. We haven't had to cut down, though it has left quite a few draws out. There used to be kale around Northampton, that's all under houses and roads now. The A45 didn't bother us too much because we didn't get down that Earls Barton side. I've had hounds run down there twice. I asked Stanley once when it happened in the 1970s, how many times he'd been there, and he said, 'Never'! We found a brace on an old brook line, came away with one, crossed the Wellingborough-Northampton road by Earls Barton and ran back into Doddington. It wasn't so busy then. You wouldn't get there now because of the A45. In the Saturday country there are some nice pockets of grass around East Haddon, Winwick, Cottesbrook and around Thornby on Miss Barlow's Estate. In the Wednesday country there is a large portion of grass still around Everdon, Fawsley and Charwelton towards Staverton. Joe Adams and his super family have grass headlands all around their large acreage which makes it so easy to get around. There are quite a lot of jumping places now or wicket gates. Admittedly, there are fewer places to have a cut and thrust these days."

Good Fortune in Masterships

Since first being employed as Huntsman to the Pytchley Hounds by Lord Wimborne and Mr Rice in 1971, Peter feels he has been very fortunate in the masterships he has had here, "I have had two horses every day and have always been well mounted. There have been many changes of mastership, but each time a team has been put together, 90 % of the time from the Pytchley country itself. In these thirty Seasons I have not had a cross word with any master. We discussed everything together." There was great excitement in the Pytchley country when during Mr Dick Saunders' term in mastership, he won the Grand National on Grittar. Mon has always hunted. Peter's son Nick was in Hunt Service hunting the Vale of Aylesbury for four seasons, but now runs a successful horse ambulance business. Daughter Tricia also hunts, as does her husband Stuart. Two grandchildren Sam and Victoria ('Tottie') have nice show ponies , and hunt regularly with the Meynell as well as the Pytchley. Tricia's daughter Harriet, although only three, has already been out a few times on her Shetland pony. Peter does all the earthstopping cards and farmers' cards, "The farming relationship is very good. On hunting days the masters leave the draw up to me." Continuity has been maintained among the hounds as Peter has been breeding them ever since he arrived, " I didn't come in to do it, it was a nightmare at first !"

The Pytchley Hounds - and Breeding Them

Peter believes that the key to good Kennel management is routine. To this end he takes hounds on bicycle exercise for an hour every day, unusually even when they are hunting, "I think it is better for them, and it is no different to the days when they were hacked on to all the meets."

I asked him about the hounds, "There are so many I could mention, you wouldn't have room for them all !" The biggest influence in the Kennels since he took over has been a dog called Fernie Forester '66 (Heythrop Falcon '60-Satin '63) lent to him by Colonel Murray-Smith, "He was a super dog in his work. All my 'Fs' go back to him. Bruce won something at the Great Yorkshire with him. I hunted him the first Season I came and gave him some bitches the next Spring. Then we borrowed him again. In the end Colonel Murray-Smith gave him to me. Pat Langrish used him at the North Staffs." Another doghound bred by Peter who stands out was Coaster '73 (Coiner '68 - Crazy '70). Since coming here he has done all the hound breeding himself, and says that if it is a mess he only has himself to blame! "I never planned it that way, it just happened. It was a bit of a nightmare to start with." He has now more than got to grips with it however, and clearly enjoys being able to breed the type of hound he wants to hunt, "I had two super little sisters Pleasure and Pliable '86 (Quorn Playfair '72-Pardon '72), two of the nicest I have bred, who produced some very good pups, and an old brood bitch called Plumage '90 (Cotswold Grappler '85-Pliable '86), who has been a great influence breeding five litters.

Another good line we had was from a dog Bert Maiden bred called Lexicon '71 (Atherstone Ledger '65- Beauty '65), who was a very good dog in his work. He left us some good stock." Peter regards the Kennel's 'F' lines, 'L' lines and those out of Pleasure and Pliable '86 highly, "More recently we used two Limerick dogs, Limerick Timothy and Limerick Purser, who was only a first Season dog when Tom Normington and I saw them in Ireland. Limerick Purser is still here and the Oakley have borrowed him. I like the Old English lines, I'm not into woolly coated ones." Cotswold and VWH Stallionhounds have been used very successfully, "Looking back through the pedigrees to Stanley Barker's time the most predominant sires were Portman Freeman '51(North Cotswold Landlord '44-Frolic '47), Portman Grossman '52 (Duke of Beaufort's Grimston '49-Lollipop '49), and Portman Playfair '51 (South Dorset Salesman '44-West Waterford Playful '48). In a round about sort of way I've come back to that now through using the VWH Stallionhounds. We've gone from the 1950s to now and back again through Sidney's. We've used VWH Dancer '91 (Exmoor Daresbury '87-Hannah '88), VWH Guinness '92 (Portman Genius '87-Hannah '88), and VWH Gardner '95 (Portman Galway '91-Grayling '90). I had a day with the Cotswold and was very impressed with their music. We'd used so much of our Ledger and Forester I had to start looking elsewhere. So we went out to the Cotswold, which the VWH have used as well of course." He took a chance and used Cotswold Glencoyne '84 (Blencathra Glider '76-Clematis '81) on a bitch, the first time a Fell line had been introduced, "They were very, very good, but I only had that one litter. Sidney had a dog called Baronet '88 (Cotswold Glencoyne '84-Barmaid '84), so I used him as well to bring in some more of the Glencoyne blood. We got some nice ones by him too, and they've all gone very well. The Meath in Ireland had a lot of my drafts and Nimrod Champion at the Ledbury used to send some there as well. From that Baronet line they had one called Batchelor, and Mrs Borwick MFH says he has done very well." Hound Shows do not appeal to Peter Jones, "We've only been to Peterborough four times. Showing leaves me cold. I feel it's all hype. Stanley Barker said to me, 'Hunting's your bread and butter. Showing's just a bit extra.' We've won classes and been placed there. I think you have to be very enthusiastic to do it. I always tried my best but it's not my forte. I'd sooner hunt six days a week!"

Why Moderate Days are More Fun

Saturday Fields regularly number over one hundred riders, and Mondays have become almost as popular. I asked Peter how he copes with the pressure of having an expectant Field behind him, and what qualities a Huntsman needs most. He has a very sensible attitude, "What happens behind my ears I block off. I rarely know what happens to the people behind me. I wouldn't have a clue who's out half the time. It's one thing that's never ever worried me. Even though two of the best Huntsmen of the century Frank Freeman and Stanley Barker were here, that goes through your mind when you first start of course, it never worried me. Stanley was brilliant. He loved riding back to Kennels with me, and gave me a lot of advice I respected him so much and I think it sunk in. As a Huntsman you have to make a lot of split second decisions. Sometimes you are right, sometimes wrong. I do expect a whipper-in to be very sharp. If I want hounds, I want them now." He claps his hands sharply to illustrate the point, "That's one thing that was dinned in to me when I was whipping in. You only really understand it when you start hunting hounds. The further a fox gets away from you the less scent you have to work with. On a good scenting day, any fool could hunt them ! On the bad days the grey matter has to get working - whether to cast right or left, when you can push on. I was always taught not to cart hounds about. People worry too much about the Field wanting to jump. If they want to have a jolly that's fine. If hounds are hunting in covert and another fox is hollered away while they are still speaking I will not lift my hounds to put them on to the other fox. Not if they are still doing their job in covert. It is no good thinking the other fox might be better. Just let them get on with their job."

From a Huntsman's point of view the trickier scenting days can be the most fascinating. "I get more excitement when you can keep touching the line on a moderate day and just keep going on, than on a day when there's a screaming scent. There is more chance to watch your hounds work and see them as individuals. Joe Wright said that some days hounds can just get switched in to a fox, and that is right. Some days you see a hound not really working as well, another day he's right up there doing his bit. They are individuals just like human beings. You have some hounds you know you can always rely on 100%. That's the thing on moderate days. You can watch them work and learn a lot more about them than when they are a field ahead screaming on. You learn more when you are working together. You push them on a bit two or three fields, and they feather again. I get more pleasure on a moderate day as you are with them all the time. When you are breeding them as well,

124

it makes it easier to see where you have gone wrong. We all get over-excited sometimes. You are always keen to catch your fox, but you learn by experience." A good Huntsman must be dedicated to the job first and foremost, to always give his best. Stanley Barker said to me, 'You can only do your best, if your best is not good enough you can do no more.' I listened and watched as I whipped in, picking up little bits off one and another, put them all together, and the easy ways of doing things. When I came here, early on in my second Season, Stanley hollered a fox away by the railway line. Scent was good in covert. We could see this fox, but as soon as hounds got out in the open they couldn't own it at all. I said, 'Now what will I do ?', he answered, 'I had a lot of days like this, and you'll have a lot more before you finish. Just don't cart 'em about boy.' We just tickled on, as we'd seen where he went and kept them going for twenty minutes, but it was hard work."

Proper Earthstopping - the Key to Good Hunts

Though hounds have hunted very close to their adjacent packs several times they have never joined up. There have been numerous hunts in to the Warwickshire, Grafton, and Fernie countries, "Two seasons ago hounds ran from Kilworth Sticks. Farmer John Matthews said, 'The Fernie are coming to Money Spinney at 1 o'clock.' I said, 'The way we're going we'll be there by 12.30!' We crossed the lane and hounds checked after two more fields, so I stopped them short of Money Spinney." He believes trust in hounds is paramount to getting things right, "If somebody gives good information when you have to get hounds away from a busy road fair enough. You must have full confidence in hounds all the time. No-one's infallible and any Huntsman makes mistakes." Peter explains, "We don't dig foxes, I can hardly remember the last time we did. Stanley once caught a record 110 brace. In the best Season since I came, my second, hounds caught 56 1/2 brace. All but two brace were caught above ground. We average 46 brace a Season." He is a great believer in good, old-fashioned earthstopping, "I'm lucky enough to have some super lads. The Emery family Trevor, Robert his son, Sarah his daughter, Billy his brother, John his cousin and a lad called Colin Roberts. They work so hard stopping and enable me to do what I do. They are fantastic. They put in hours and hours of work to keep foxes above ground, which means my hounds can always find foxes." He feels fortunate that the country is laid out for hunting with many small coverts, so there is not much hanging about, "Naseby Covert is not good scenting. If they check and one's gone you can pick them up as its such a bad scenting covert. Yet Long Hole just three fields away is always a good scenting covert. Old Poors Gorse is not good scenting, yet we had a good hunt this year. Hounds rattled round pushed him out and flew. Only seven of us got away with them, to the back of Kettering. That was 12 miles, and they really did go all the time. It is a country where they can really go in the right conditions."

From a meet at Misterton Hall he had one of his best hunts with John Kennelly whipping in. Hounds found at Thornborough and ran to the Raspberries and back to Thornborough. Two brace of foxes were in front of them. They stuck to their hunted fox running into Fernie country to Gilmorton, "They *did* go, you couldn't touch them ! Three quarters of the hunt was in Fernie country. From Gilmorton they ran through Walton Holt, to ground in some earths near Welford. Tony Barratt was Stud Groom then, I saw him on the road and shouted to him to get me another horse. I ran the last four fields on my feet and just left this little mare on the lane, she was cooked. Old Johnny Wrathall and his son were either side of me as we came down to Walton Holt. He said, 'This *is* foxhunting' I replied, 'Well we haven't seen much of 'em have we boys?' It was all you could do to keep with them. It was all of sixteen miles as they ran in one hour twenty minutes. We found again after that and had another forty minutes into Stanford Park. Just two hunts in one day. It was a hell of a scenting day." They had another good hunt near here, "We met at Kilworth Sticks and ran right up to Fleckney. Two and a half brace went away. We ran to Walton Holt, to Knapton Vale, straight up to Jane Ball, and swung right handed for Mowsley. Hounds had been to Laughton and back before I'd got there ! Then back through John Ball, across to Jane Ball, then into the back of Arnesby village crossing the old A50. On we went to Fleckney and Sadington. We changed horses at Shearsby Bath in the Fernie country and hacked back through Walton Village." In a bit of old rough grass a fox jumped up, "They were away again. Those were the only two hunts we had that day. They ran like stink again."

He recalls another exceptional day, "I'm very bad at looking at my watch, as I'm too busy thinking about other things ! We found on a farmer called David Holdey's in a little spinney. This time I did look at my watch. It was twenty past twelve, and I had been thinking about working towards second

horses as we'd had a busy morning. This fox went to the water tower at Preston Capes. Hounds ran back for Woodford Halse and the further they went the faster they went. They went to the right of Woodford Halse and there was only the whipper-in with me. The Field now realised we were out of sight by a long way, and a lot of them got in their boxes. There was a super farmer called John North and his son Philip following. To this day I don't know where they appeared from, as they were on the horizon ! I said, 'Where the hell did you come from ?' They just smiled and said, 'Ah we're Bicester men, we know our way round.' We were in Bicester country by now. Hounds checked at West Farndon. Denny Green was on the road there and hadn't seen anything. I went on down the road, and kept going. We were lucky as that fox must have run the road for 400 yards. Just as they got to a gateway, whoosh!, away they went. They ran to Redhill in the Bicester country, towards Chipping Warden across the road. A few people caught up with us now. On they went to a place called Lower Boddington. It was ten past three when we finished there. A farmer called Bill Adams had a farm at Charwelton and hunted with us. Just ten days before he told me he had bought another farm and said, 'It's all grass and you're always welcome.' I had laughed as it was a good five miles inside the Bicester boundary. It was unbelievable, here we now were on his Springfield Farm at Lower Boddington !" That hunt had a point of ten miles, nearer twice that as hounds ran.

Peter Jones leads the Prince of Wales across plough during a hunt. (Jim Meads)

Neck Broken, but Nerve Undented

On February 17th 1999 Peter Jones had a fall. The fencing man took him home and he took his own coat and boots off, "I was in so much pain from my neck to my hands I was a bit dubious of taking my stock off. I've never known pain like it." Initial X-rays at Northampton General revealed nothing, "Mr Gregor Kerr hunts with us, rides a bit in point-to-points, and is one of the head blokes there. He usually hunts with us on Wednesdays, but was operating that day, so I didn't see him when I went to the hospital either." By Friday morning the pain was just as bad so Mon rang the Chiropractor, "Going by what Mon told her, she rang Gregor and said, 'I'm not touching him it's too serious'." He got Peter straight in to that hospital and X-rayed him with his neck bent, "When he said to me, 'Lie down Peter and *don't* move', I did start to worry." He explained that they would operate right away, "I knew then it really was serious." Peter had been walking around for the last three days with a broken neck. The possible consequences of this hardly bear thinking about, "Gregor told me I was very lucky. I could easily have ended up in a wheelchair, or been a goner." After more scans and tests Gregor dispatched him by ambulance to the surgeon he had worked under, Mr Wilson Macdonald, in Oxford,

"He was so straightforward and told me exactly what he was going to do. The Sister asked how I had done it, and I waited for a reaction. It turned out she hunted with the Cleveland ! " When he woke up on Saturday he instinctively wiggled his fingers, and moved his shoulders. The only pain was in his hip, where a bone graft had been taken. He now also had a plate and two bolts in his neck. Though he was out of the saddle for eleven weeks, he was walking hounds out just three weeks later, "I never worried afterwards, these things happen in life. It never deterred me from going across country. Of course it makes you think, but it's just one of those unfortunate things."

Sixth Sense ?

After Peter's fall that day, hounds had stopped hunting and showed no interest in continuing. It was decided to take them home, but they refused to do that too, and sat at the roadside singing. Nothing would budge them and they had to be collected by lorry. Perhaps some sixth sense told them that he had been badly injured, even though he was unaware of the severe nature of his injury for several days ?

Top Pytchley, Top Man

Though remaining in the same country Peter has never tired of it, "Though I was a Fernie born lad this was the only place I ever wanted to go in my life. This was known as Top Pytchley. It was the only place I ever wanted to come. I think it's worked out all right." This is something of an understatement, for Peter is now entering his thirtieth season to become the Pytchley's longest serving Huntsman, overtaking the record of his idol Stanley Barker. He has well surpassed his childhood ambition to be second horseman. We travelled in convoy to the Warwickshire Puppy Show that afternoon and I sat with Peter and his wife Mon, John Cooke and his wife Shirley. "He's not in your book is he ? Well you can count me out!", says one, "You should have seen me thirty years ago", proclaims another, "If his missus had seen him thirty years ago she'd never have married him !", mutters another to derisory laughter. Dissecting the judging is obligatory, "Look at it's shoulders !" There followed sage nodding. "Never mind that one's shoulders, look at the other one's hocks." There followed denial about who tipped which hound to win, "Ah but I didn't *mean* that one." More derisory laughter, "Anyway they've chucked the best one out." Someone adds as a nice light bitch comes in, "Now that's what I call a body. If she was blonde and seventeen everyone would be after her !" More important than any technicality however they pay the great compliment that all the hounds look well and happy, which means more than all the good shoulders and well let down hocks in the world. This good humoured banter between the Hunt Servants and Denny Green typified for me the character of these ordinary men who accomplish extraordinary things. Like Peter Jones, the little boy who dreamed of working for Stanley Barker, who went on to wear that famous Pytchley collar for longer than his idol, broken neck notwithstanding.

Burton Huntsman Jim Lang
(Jim Meads)

128

Jim Lang

Jim Lang's father was Stud Groom to the Four Burrow in Cornwall. He remembers as a child leaning over their gate to ask Mr Percival Williams MFH how the day had gone, "You could say I was born and bred to the job really." At just 15 he went to work in the Stables with his father, and rode second horse to Mr John Williams MFH. Hunting with the Four Burrow was great fun, "Mr Percival was the salt of the earth, and Mr John was a good man too. They did it because they enjoyed it. I certainly learned a lot." The country could be hair-raising to cross, with its rivers, becks, and banks, "Some were so deep you had to run down one side, jump across the bottom and up the other side. Mr Percival always named his horses according to where he had bought them. He had one called Exeter he'd got from Exeter Market. Whenever he came to a really bad place he would get off, and send Exeter over first, 'Goooo on !' Then he would shout, 'Whoa!' climb over and remount. It was better than anything in a circus. They always had their horses ever so fit. They hacked a lot, and were often home before me. They were very good at finding horses, picking just the right type, and keeping them fit." Small wonder that Percival's granddaughter Venetia is such a successful National Hunt trainer. For Jim, all this was a good grounding, and after eight Seasons he moved away from his native Cornwall.

The Meynell - Brave and Professional

His first post at whipper-in was at the Meynell in 1962, where he was second whipper-in to Mr Dermot Kelly MFH for two Seasons. John Cooke was Kennel Huntsman for the first year, followed by Johnny O'Shea. Jim had only been out of Cornwall two or three times, "People didn't travel so much then. And all good Cornishmen do things 'dreckly'! I made quite a mistake one day. After hunting, Mr Kelly came to the Kennels to thank us. I told him how much I had enjoyed the day, jumping so many fences. He took me to one side and told me not to say that, 'People pay good money in subscriptions to pay for their hunting not for you to enjoy the jumping.' I knew then I had said the wrong thing. It made me understand the need to be professional." Jim's proficiency across country was fully tested now in country that could hardly have been more different from what he had been used to in Cornwall. "The Meynell country is as good as you would get anywhere. It took some riding, as there were some big hairy places, and few hunt jumps. There was no cut-throat riding though, and everyone was glad to see you had survived at the end of the hunt!" Jim clearly enjoyed those two Seasons enormously, and it more than equipped him for his next step up the ladder, as second whipper-in to the Quorn in 1964.

To the Quorn and Jack Littleworth's Influence

He enjoyed riding the Quorn country too but found it easier to ride than the Meynell. Michael Farrin was first whipper-in then, with Jack Littleworth hunting hounds. It was not only Littleworth's skills as a Huntsman he admired, "He was a marvellous horseman, even the most awkward horse would go well across country for him. He was gifted." Jim recalls his habit of whistling, "He was always whistling away", a trait of Littleworth's nephew, Sidney Bailey. Jim's humour is never far from the surface, "Perhaps they were brought up on 'Trill'!" More seriously he adds that Littleworth was a great influence on him as a Huntsman, "He was quiet, and always seemed in charge of the situation. No matter how many were out the pressure never seemed to get to him." Then he jokes,"Not that I saw a lot of him mind, he had passed me most of the time !"

Humour and Entertainment, from Whipper-in to Huntsman

As our conversation progressed, it was no surprise when Jim told me he believes that a Huntsman needs a sense of humour most of all ! "You must talk to everybody, no matter who they are.

129

Mr Percival Williams impressed on me, 'Jimmy, talk to everybody. That roadsweeper might tell you where he saw a fox.' You should make a point of speaking to everyone you meet. If you jolly people along they will help you more. I know I've not got the sweetest of tempers but I try to jolly things along, then everyone enjoys the day more, including the car followers who are part and parcel of the scene. I have a job to do of course, but it should be entertaining."

With his bubbling humour Jim Lang is clearly a man who enjoys life. Ready to move on he came to the Burton in 1967 to whip in to Jack King. After one Season he was put on as Huntsman. That he has remained since is clear proof that the arrangement is mutually agreeable.

Changes in Agriculture

The country is open and arable with vast flat fields. "Once the drilling is done at the end of October then it is like hunting on grass for the hounds. They can really go - there's nothing to stop 'em ! If it is dry they might struggle and can only go as fast as their noses, but they do work hard. If it is really wet they scream on and it is desperate." As farming methods have changed however he feels it is far easier for hounds now than it was 15 or 20 years ago," Then it was ploughed in really deep. It was hell, and made the going hard work even for hounds. No, now it is dragged, quickly ploughed and sown with winter crops it is much better. The plough is not continuous now, you get odd fields in between." Though this is not a jumping country the obstacles can be daunting, "We have big ditches full with water and I can't swim an inch !"

Inevitably, this has led to changes in the hound-breeding policy, "We don't have the heavy thick legged plough hounds any more. When I first came they were big old hounds full of Brocklesby and Belvoir blood. They hunted all right. Our first introduction to a lighter type came from Captain Clarke at the Cottesmore. He gave us a dog called Blizzard '76, his brother Bloater won a lot at hound shows. Blizzard was known as the Ugly Brother - he was big and white. Mr Lockwood Senior was not too keen to change at first, then Blizzard did well enough to be given two or three bitches." Interestingly the pack are now predominantly light coloured too, "Blizzard gets the blame for that. Car Followers' hounds I call the white ones." Jim has his own explanation for the change though, "Well, some old Huntsmen go deaf. I've already started wearing glasses, so we had to have hounds I could see. Thank goodness we don't get too much snow . . ."

Blizzard in a Tight Spot and the Hazards of Ditches

Blizzard had a narrow escape one season. Hounds were hunting in hard frost. They hunted their fox to Norton Place, "The Lake was icy and the fox ran across it. Blizzard tried to follow, but the ice broke under his weight." Stuart Coley was whipping in to Jim then, and with the help of Vet Mr Sutherland they got him out. Stuart had gone across a telegraph pole so got very cold and wet, "Mrs Duguid, a former nurse offered to take him in for a bath and change of clothes. He coloured up and would not go. It later turned out he was too embarrassed as he was wearing his girlfriend's tights !"

"One of our retired senior masters was rather portly. He had a great friend of similar size. We'd had a tremendous amount of rain and there was a notorious ditch out by Foldingworth. Hounds found and ran straight towards it. Tony Wing was whipping-in to me at the time and we got over all right. Just a field further on the fox was headed, so we came back. As we approached the ditch we could see that the master's horse had stumbled in with him, then we saw that the same thing had happened to the other gentleman, whose top hat floated past us ! One of the farmers turned to me and said, 'Oh no, all the land between Wickenby and Snarford will be flooded if those two have gone in' !"

Sticking to Lines that Suit the Country and the Adaptable Fox

"We have used Cottesmore dogs since, and the Wheatland seem to do us well. Myles Salmond was my amateur whipper-in so he knows what we need. I am not keen on the Welsh hounds. We have some second generation Heythrop and Exmoor blood, mainly from the Quorn where Michael Farrin used them. Some of his seemed to 'click' with ours, but we've nothing direct. We do not need big hounds, and the lighter ones can cope better when the going does get heavy. We have few hedges, and those have small gaps in them. Big hounds lose a lot of time if they cannot get through a small place. We visited the Wheatland country once, and it took our hounds about three hours to get used to the pig netting. We don't have anything like that here so they were not used to coping with it. The

Cottesmore sires do seem to suit us, as they are used to plough. I am a great believer that 'andsome is as 'andsome does when it comes to hounds. Over the years we have stuck to the lines that seem to suit the country."

Apart from tho changes in farming, the Burton country has changed little over the years. Foxes seem to have adapted. One positive change as far as they are concerned is the increase in potato fields. Jim believes these, with their 'banks' between rows have provided a substitute for the shelter once provided by hedges. "They like to sit in them, out of the wind. I suppose

Jim Lang and the Burton Hounds. (Jim Meads)

they find voles, moles and suchlike. It is a good example of how nature adapts." The country has many game shoots, which can make arranging pre-Christmas fixtures complicated as only a handful of farms do not have shoots. A shooting man once told Jim he could not see the point of all the expense involved in hunting. He said he could not see the point of employing four people and keeping eight horses when a 10p cartridge would kill a fox. Jim's answer was simple enough. He pointed out that buying cartridges, employing a keeper and beaters seemed pretty pointless when you could rear your pheasants and wring their necks when you wanted to eat them!

Huntsmen - a Protected Species ?

Spending so many years in one place has done nothing to dampen Jim's enthusiasm, "It's a way of life. There's still something new every day, and you just take what comes. Someone who hadn't seen me for a while said the other day 'Jim, you're as grey as a badger.' I said, 'That's all right, they're protected!' You have to keep a sense of humour in this job, definitely. It keeps you toddling along."

It seems that few things really rattle this Cornishman, though he does own to two pet hates, "I wish, when hounds are hunting people wouldn't holloa fresh foxes when you are trying to get them settled. I am an easy going sort of bloke really. One thing I really do not like is to hear a whipper-in getting a rollicking in front of everyone. I have had it done to me ! You are far better just telling him to buck his ideas up, and explaining it in the lorry on your way home. I have learnt to bite my tongue and scowl ! My better half often says, 'Why do you always look at me when things go wrong ?' She's a good 'un, Julie. We have been together eleven years now, and have a daughter Helen." He could not afford to upset Julie too much as she is the Hunt's Stud Groom responsible for providing his horses, "She runs the stables so well, and turns the horses out really fit." No Huntsman can do his job properly without good horses and this is one area Jim has never had cause to complain about, "Here I've only had to say I wanted a horse and it has been bought. However fit and well you are in yourself you risk your life every day, and good horses are so important. It has been one real piece of luck for me in Hunt Service that I have always been well mounted."

Making the Best of What Life Has to Offer

Jim is clearly a happy man with no regrets about his chosen career, "I could have gone in to racing, but I liked my mother's Cornish pasties too much. Anyway, I was more interested in the hunting side. This is a good, healthy life. It is harder now for the youngsters coming in. I have seen a lot of people come and go. It's very true that if you go to a hunting man's funeral the Church will always be packed. I have been lucky to have a roof over my head, a supportive family and security. Things can change week by week in life, so that is worth a lot. I have had a lot of offers to move away but the people here have kept their word and stuck by me, and the Hunt has gone from strength to strength. I believe in making the best of what you have got." It seems a pretty good philosophy to me.

131

Tim Langley and the Berkeley Hounds
(Nigel Broom)

132

Tim Langley

In my native Gloucestershire, Tim Langley is something of a legend, having worn the famous tawny coat of the Berkeley for 30 seasons. He showed consistent good sport with this flying pack in the Vale. My own early memories of him were in the Berkeley hill country, which borders that of the Duke of Beaufort's in the beautiful Ozleworth valley, where both my great grandfathers lived out their working lives. I could walk to nearby Berkeley meets, and sometimes the two packs would meet very close to each other. I well remember on one such occasion, hounds joined up in that valley to hunt the same fox, some 60 couple hunting with spine tingling cry before marking him to ground at the top of a bank. The sight of the two liveried huntsmen riding down the hillside with that huge pack, which then divided to follow them home in late Spring sunshine is one that will be with me for ever. My first mounted day, aged eleven, was behind Tim Langley, from a meet in Wotton-under-Edge. It poured with rain most of the day, but when hounds found and Tim 's horn rang through the woods it was worth anything. We hacked home from Dursley in thunder, lightening and hail, my boots full of water. Over twenty years after that memorable day I travelled to Berkeley to learn more about this familiar figure.

Boyhood - From Ascot to Horse Guards via Windsor

Surprisingly Tim is not from a hunting background, although his father had always ridden, and came in to regular contact with farmers in his job, managing a firm of corn merchants. Tim was born close to Ascot, and watching hounds hack home began the hunting bug. His father would take him to see the colourful pageantry of Ascot Races, and horses were part of life from an early age. He was educated at a grammar school in Windsor, "They tried to make me play rugby on Wednesdays and Saturday afternoons, which wasn't any good !" , he laughs knowingly. It is hard to believe now that in those days it would have been possible to hunt every day but Thursday in that area. The Garth country was very good in those days, all the bit around Ascot huntable, and hounds would meet in Windsor Great Park. "It's amazing to think of it now. I think I must have sent most of my schoolmasters to an early grave !" He was naturally bright enough to get on however, and it becomes quickly obvious that he is an intelligent and well-read man, "Siegfried Sassoon was a marvellous writer you know, I read a lot of his work early on." At 15 he applied to the Enfield Chase who were looking for a second horseman, and got the job. After nearly two Seasons he took on the same role at the Old Surrey and Burstow, where he was employed by Brian Gupwell's grandfather, who was Stud Groom there at the time, "We were proper second horsemen in those days. Not going out in a box." After just three months he got the chance to go as second whipper in to the Berks and Bucks Staghounds, hunted by Tom Newman's son, Sam. Just one season later he joined the South Oxfordshire as second whipper-in. War was imminent, "I tried to join the army, but they didn't want me, so I stayed until May 1st." Taking another post at the Hambledon, just a few weeks later he joined up, and that pack did not hunt for the rest of the War. Like so many Hunt Servants he joined the Royal Horse Guards, and passed out of their riding school just before armoured cars replaced horses. Whilst stationed in Brighton, he felt unwell. The Medical Officer said he had a high temperature but could find nothing else wrong. He dismissed it as little more than a chill, "Some silly old Colonel from RMC said that my throat had cleared up nicely. My left arm and right leg were going dead." This was later dismissed as sciatica. It turned out that the 'chill' was polio. The Regiment went to France just after D Day, and Tim was unable to re-join them.

A Man Returns to Start Again

So after seven years in the army, he returned to Hunt Service, becoming second whipper-in at the VWH (Cricklade) where an amateur, Stephen Player was hunting them, and Raglan Snell was Ken-

133

Tim Langley and the Berkeley hounds on the banks of the River Severn. (Jim Meads)

nel Huntsman. A mastership change at the end of that Season found him on the move once more, this time to the Old Surrey and Burstow as 1st Whipper-in. He had known their Huntsman Jack Champion in the Army, "The Old Surrey and Burstow was not an easy country to hunt and Jack Champion showed great sport there. He was very talented, not predictable in character, and could make a good hunt from an unpromising start." This was a time of fun, and though a comparatively small Kennel, it boasted six kennel staff before the War and three after. Two packs hunted on Saturdays in this country, now so diminished that it has been joined to that of the West Kent.

Marriage and a Difficult Move

Tim now wanted to marry Della Ash whom he met whilst with the VWH . With no married accommodation available he looked for another post, and went to the Wynnstay, where he stayed for two Seasons. By this time Tim had amassed a great deal of practical experience. The boy who had gone to war had come back a man, eager to resume his career and get on. The Wynnstay post may have suited his new marriage, and given him insight into that grand riding country, but after seven years of army discipline, the strict regime of Jack Simister went against the grain. He had also tasted a life of fun with the buoyant Jack Champion, and Simister's way was very different. The two men were like chalk and cheese, "He never overlooked a thing and everything had to be done exactly by the book, right down to which hand your whip was in, or which way your horse's head was looking. I learned a great deal, but cannot say I enjoyed my two years there. I began to dread going hunting."

There were few light moments, but one worth recording for its novelty relates to the collection of hound excrement to be used in tanning leather. Stored in barrels, the contents, known (ironically) as 'puer' were somewhat explosive in hot weather. When they delivered the barrels to Ruabon railway station, porters could be seen scattering with lilting Welsh cries of "Shi-it! Shi-it!"

Added to Tim's unhappiness in the field, their cottage was pretty squalid, and now with a young daughter he decided he really must find another position, or perhaps even give up hunt service.

134

A Train Ride to Paradise

From the moment Tim arrived for interview in Berkeley, he felt at home. Its wonderfully historic atmosphere struck him at once. Harry Scott and his wife were welcoming, and Captain Berkeley seemed courteous and fair. He was delighted to be offered the post of first whipper-in. After so many short term moves, he never imagined he would stay for 30 Seasons.

Harry Scott was a very easy going man to work for, "It was a piece of cake after Jack Simister !" Tim appreciates that Simister's disciplined ways probably made his future easier, and will always be grateful for that. Harry was quite a character. When the Otterhounds met nearby, he took the kennel staff out on bicycles, insisting on stopping at every pub. Wobbling home, he and Tim ended up in a ditch, Harry muttering all the way back as they pushed their mangled steeds, "I told you those cotter pins were loose." When he retired Tim was asked to stay on as Kennel Huntsman. Mr Berkeley's father was about to be joined by Captain Bell, who would hunt hounds, it was thought perhaps for a couple of seasons, when Tim would take over. As it turned out Captain Bell stayed for 12 years, "We had some great hunts. I remember once we found in Lasborough and ran to Cherry Orchard in Badminton Park. A seven mile point and over twelve as they ran." Tim's patience paid off, and duly taken on as Huntsman at the age of 46 he enjoyed some marvellous sport, after this extraordinarily late start, "People moved about a lot more then, and some stayed Kennel Huntsmen all their lives. I must admit I was starting to worry !" He certainly made up for lost time, Mr Berkeley recalling how difficult it was to get him to go home.

Thirty years in One Country

The Berkeley country has diminished in size over the years, and Tim saw many changes, "It's so much smaller now than when I first came. There were no motorways then, no Severn Bridge, hardly any plough, and no wire. It really was lovely. I liked the people so much, and the Field were mostly farmers then. I'm very pleased to see so many people hunting nowadays, but they will never know what it was like then, however much they enjoy it now." Traffic, as elsewhere has changed the routines enormously over the years, "We used to ride on to all meets, leaving Kennels at ten past nine for a meet at Arlingham. It's sad but unavoidable." He recalls riding home through the town of Dursley as the Listers workers pedalled home on their bicycles, "Hounds were very much an accepted part of the community then. People were used to seeing them about, and loved seeing hounds come through the villages." It is not unreasonable to suppose that this could well be one reason why hunting is more misunderstood these days. "The hounds themselves had far less foot problems then. Their feet were so hard they picked up fewer thorns." Once, riding a horse of Captain Bell's he felt rather unsure of its abilities. The last thing he remembered as he set it at a fence was calling to Joy Williams, 'Pick up the bits.' They took the fence out by the roots, and Tim was taken to hospital, "I had broken my neck", he muses, as if recalling a bruise. After the War there was not much money about, and many of Tim's horses cost £40 or less, and had to do a whole day, including hacking on in the morning, and home again often in the dark. Tim recalls, "One day we caught a fox in the dark at Arlingham. We had to ride the eleven or twelve miles home, and Harry liked to stop at the odd farm on the way. When we got back, the Stud Groom, Jack Lambert was not best pleased, 'Where the hell have you been ?', he spluttered, 'Only owls and whores are out this time of night' !"

Tim's first Season as Huntsman was marred by the Foot and Mouth Epidemic, "What a way to start !" I was very lucky on the whole though as we hardly ever lost a day due to bad weather." The famous Berkeley rhines were jumpable then, not dug out deep by JCBs as they are now, and caused a fair amount of grief. Tim remembers one day after the Hunt Ball. During a good hunt near Hill, there was a holloa. Hounds did not run in to the village, and Robert Harraway rushed to open a gate for him, knocking him straight in to a rhine, "I was soaked ! We never crossed a ploughed field all day. It was a great hunt. He got to ground in Aust Cliff." An eight mile point in 75 minutes to blow the cobwebs away.

Routine and Change

Tim has never used bicycles for exercise, preferring ponies, "Bicycles don't go well across country you know." He partly blames Jack Simister for this aversion, as he would take them through terrible places on bicycles. There are more practical reasons however. Virtually all the Vale country can be negotiated by ponies, and thus avoid the roads, especially the morning traffic to the nearby Power

Station. He always went out at 6am, back to feed at 8.30am. He instigated a tradition of Hound Exercise Breakfasts, calling on local farmers and friends, which proved great fun. He is not a believer in 'letting hounds down' in summer, and allowing them to put on weight. "They don't need rest like horses. The more you occupy hounds the better. Exercise little and often, I say." In the heat of summer, hounds could swim in the River, and it was not unusual for their Huntsman to join them. He liked to feed hounds cooked flesh all week, and raw after hunting. "I always felt it was easier to regulate feeding on the trough, bringing in the shy ones first, then the bulk, followed by the gross feeders last of all." The whole flesh collection and disposal system has changed beyond recognition now, "We would see 60 or 80 sheep a day and spend half our time skinning."

One break with accepted routine was Tim's dislike of coupling puppies to old hounds when they came back from walk. Apart from the work involved, he did not like to see the old hounds pulled about. It is a very personal view, and he relied on the young hounds' dependence on their Huntsman. This requires both confidence and trust, and that his method worked speaks volumes about his rapport with hounds. He was very particular about hounds' beds, "Bare concrete beds! Unheard of in my early day. We had insulated concrete bases of course." Threshed straw was quite different, not full of dust like the modern stuff, "We had ours sent specially from Lincolnshire. There is nothing worse for hounds' coats, and wind than dusty straw." He recalls getting into terrible hot water in Harry Scott's time. There were two thatched cottages at Ham, and the Agent had some thatching straw unloaded to repair the roofs. Tim saw it and immediately earmarked it for hound bedding, "Well, it was far too good for thatching. Poor old Harry got in to terrible trouble, and he knew nothing of what I was up to !"

Tim felt fortunate in having the services of Jim Roberts as his kennelman for 18 seasons. A real hound man, he too now lives at Ham.

Work Hard, Play Hard

Unfortunately Tim and Della's marriage broke up in 1965, but they parted friends and shared the growing up of their two daughters. The social life in and around Berkeley was entered into with just as much enthusiasm as the hunting itself. Parties were numerous, no-one enjoying the revelry and practical jokes more than the Huntsman. Tim's days as a single man were soon to end, for in 1978 an attractive young airline stewardess took his eye. First he knocked a drink over her. Then he stood on his head at a party, where he crashed into the coffee tray and she had to administer first aid. An unorthodox start. Alison however forgave her suitor. Reminded by her mother that she was 34 years old, Tim's response was typical, "No ! I've never been out with anyone *that* old." That Season Tim suffered a horrible fall during the first morning's cubhunting. His horse, Concorde, took exception to some brambles and came over backwards on top of him. He blew for whipper-in Chris Maiden. Tim was put on to a gate, and insisted he was perfectly all right. Getting up he crashed back to the floor. His femur was broken. Former Master and local Veterinary surgeon Barclay Watson took him to Frenchay where he was operated on. The surgeon warned he may need a new hip soon. Someone quipped, 'Concorde - 3½ hours New York, Frenchay 25 minutes.' After a long convalescence , and no hunting for the rest of that Season, he undoubtedly sensed that the end of his career was in sight. His more happy association with the world of aviation, in the form of Alison was to ease the pain of this realisation. The cub hunting had gone well, and Tim's confidence was on the up. In the latter half of the season however his leg became painful, and he headed his 1980 diary: "Thoughts on Doing Things for the Last Time." A brief and happy interlude was provided by the huge lawn meet held in celebration of the late Duke of Beaufort's 80th Birthday, attended by thousands. This was a joint meet with the Berkeley, and having known the Duke for so long, and his Huntsman Brian Gupwell being a great friend, Tim felt very proud to be involved.

Blowing for Home

In the Summer he tried many different treatments for his leg, including a course of acupuncture suggested by joint master Mrs John Daniell, but nothing eased the pain. His hip was crumbling, and during cubhunting he quietly went to see Mr Berkeley to tell him he could not continue. He urged Tim to wait until after the Opening Meet. Tim married Alison on October 31st, and the support she gave him proved incalculable. The Opening Meet would indeed be his last. On December 20th Tim had one of his best hunts ever from Hill Woods to Shepperdine on the banks of the Severn, past Rockhampton

Tim Langley and the Berkeley Hounds at a meet in Wortley, March 1979, which had to be put back an hour because of frost (Kay Gardner).

through Eastwood over the Thornbury road to ground at the Hacket. This had been a virtually non stop fourteen miles. Just before New Year, he suffered another fall, this time breaking his right foot. He was unable to return to the saddle until February. Some years before Brenda and Harold Lyes lent him a horn after his became buckled. The time had come to return the horn to its owners. After two more crunching falls, and in absolute agony, Tim gave in gracefully. He only hunted hounds once more that season as the Prince of Wales was visiting. He stuffed himself full of painkillers, borrowed the horn again and kept going in dreadful weather until 2.30 pm when he handed over to whipper-in Chris Maiden. He felt disappointed to end on this note, as the Prince had enjoyed some very good days with the Berkeley until now. Just one month later, Tim Langley's hip was replaced. He missed his hounds dreadfully, and knows that feeling will never pass. It was five years before he could face going to a meet on Ham Green. The hip recovered sufficiently for him to ride again and he enjoyed some good days with other packs. He even hunted hounds once when Chris was laid up. The foxes however had not read the script, and one escaped by sitting on a sandbank in the middle of the River, seemingly laughing. Keeping fit to ride after his catalogue of injuries proved difficult and he was finally forced to give this up too.

The author renews acquaintance with Mrs Sally Woodhouse's 'Zebedee' six years after they shared an eventful day with the Berkeley, from Ellerncroft Wotton-under-Edge, hunted by Tim Langley

That Certain Something

Tim has very definite ideas about what makes a good Huntsman, "There are many good Huntsmen, but the truly *great* ones have what I can only call flair. A Huntsman should be able to ad lib a bit, not too much or he will make a fool of his hounds, and you mustn't do that, ever. Any dam' fool can show sport on a good scenting day, but the secret's showing it on a bad scenting day, and that's where the ad libbing comes in. Taking the odd chance. A sense of *urgency*, that's what it amounts to. Without it you may as well stay at home You must pick up your hounds and say 'Come on, we *are* going to do it.' It is *so* important for a huntsman to communicate what he is doing to his hounds. They will get wild if they don't know what's going on. Then his Field master, and not least his whipper-in. That is most important. The late Duke of Beaufort was a first rate Huntsman, terribly good. He knew all his hounds so well. I was in the army with him. When we lost the horses he was made 'Mechanical Officer' ! I've still got my driving licence, signed by him. Going back to the hounds, a Huntsman must never have favourites, though he will obviously think more of some than others. They are just like schoolchildren, and pick up so much from you." One hound he does recall with great fondness was Crowner '73 (Tottenham '67-Crotchet '69). He was a very wise hound, and if the others ran heel way would stop

138

with a look of utter disdain. He can forgive a Huntsman being a bit hot headed, for that bit of 'fire' should be part of his make up, but he must not let it show too much. He detests those who curse their whippers-in the Field, "I cursed plenty of other people, but would always talk to a whipper-in quietly when we got back, or were walking out. A good whipper-in is such an asset. You have to concentrate on your hounds, and he can help by finding a way out of a field, and that sort of thing." He subscribes to Mr Jorrocks' theory about scent and women both being as difficult as each other. I, of course, cannot agree.

A Few Amusing Anecdotes

Captain Bell once gave Tim a list of cub hunting meets verbally. Tim duly arrived with hounds in the hamlet of Wortley at the appointed hour. It was ominously quiet so Tim walked to a nearby house. "It turned out to be Lady Manners' place. I asked her for a copy of the local paper, 'What the devil do you want that for ?, she asked, 'To check the meets', I replied. The meet was actually at Symonds Hall (the other side of the valley) and we made it by the skin of our teeth."

There are many amusing incidents, "Hunting is so full of humour. The late Colonel Turner was a real officer and gentleman who did not suffer fools gladly. He acted as master in the south of the country. One day at Tytherington I set off at a huge post and rails. My horse demolished them. He rode up, and I braced myself for a rocket. Instead he handed me ten shillings, 'I'm far too old for jumping fences of that order. Thank you' he said, and carried on."

Once on returning from the Hunt Ball Tim telephoned the operator to request an alarm call at 6am. He thought it most odd when somewhat puzzled she replied, "But it's already 5.30 am, Sir . . ."

No Regrets

The twinkle and humour are still there, tinged with a little sadness that he will miss his hounds forever. Brian Gupwell remains the kind of friend he can have great disagreements with. The two have shared a good many escapades over the years, Brian having started at Badminton the Season Tim took over as Huntsman at Berkeley.

Tim enjoys life at Ham with Alison, who is still in her job, "I'm sorry she isn't here, but she had to go to New York", he explains, as coolly as if she were shopping in Bristol. He is still a voracious reader of books and poetry, and enjoys classical music, "I like messing about with wood. Not very good at it, but I enjoy it." Whilst he likes to see the garden looking its best he claims not to enjoy the work required to ensure this. Occasionally he goes out hunting by car and catches up with his old friends, "Most of my friends now are dead, or at least looking that way !" , he laughs. Always a brave rider, he would love to have been a jump jockey. Intelligent and well spoken, there would probably have been a host of academic careers open to him too, "I don't have any regrets. Wouldn't change a thing. I only resent one thing, and that's getting old and decrepit." Yet so much of 'age' is attitude, and with his tremendous sense of fun, the young Tim Langley is never very far from the surface.

Ian Langrish with the Garth & South Berks Hounds at Englefield.
(Jim Meads)

140

Ian Langrish

Ian Langrish is another familiar hunting face of the 70s and 80s. Now retired and living on Sir William Benyon's Estate, Ian is Warden of the woods he knows so well from his days hunting hounds. He offered to meet me a few miles from his home, and lead me through the maze of lanes that criss-cross the extensive beech woods, "Can't have you driving about all night up there !" My first glimpse of him came on one of these lanes. Several cars had stopped as a large branch had been brought down by a lorry. Ian was clearing the way with his chain saw. He clearly enjoys his custodial role. The Benyon's sons Richard and Edward used to help him out at the Kennels as children, "I'd see Lady Benyon winding all the car windows down when they'd been helping me in the flesh house !"

Part of Life

Brought up in the village of Kilmeston between Petersfield and Winchester, halfway between the HH and Hursley Hambledon Kennels, hounds were always a part of life for Ian Langrish and his brother, Pat. Their father followed hounds a bit, and they were always made welcome. Mr and Mrs Goschen, who had their own pack also nurtured their early interest. Jack Kealey was a tremendous early influence on both boys, "He was never downcast, even when things went wrong. He was always the same, jolly and would do anything to help anyone. He had a lovely voice, and to hear him blow the horn was something to cherish."

On first leaving school Ian worked on Lord Ivor Spencer Churchill's farm. He sent him on an Agricultural Engineering course at Southampton University College. When he had finished that, Ian did his National Service, "I spent the best part of a year in Egypt which put me off going abroad for the rest of my life !" On his return, he resumed work on the farm, but needed an operation on his nose, and was not allowed to work for eight weeks, "During that period I had a motorbike to get backwards and forwards to work on. I wasn't allowed to work after the operation, but no-one said I couldn't hunt !" So he spent eight weeks following hounds on his motorbike.

Only One Thing for it

When Lord Ivor died, the farm was to be sold, so Ian went to the neighbouring farm. This worked out very well, as he volunteered to work every Sunday, so that he could hunt on Saturdays. He then took Wednesdays as holiday. By now his motorbike had been replaced by a horse, and he was encouraged by Huntsman Jack Kealy and Masters Mr and Mrs Muirhead. Some Sundays, especially in the Summer, he was not required at work, so would go and help in the Kennels, often with his brother Pat, "Jack did all he could to encourage us, as did Colonel and Mrs Mitchell who had taken over the mastership. Two days' hunting a week just wasn't enough for me any more. I knew there was only one thing for it, to go in to Hunt Service." Ian began scouring '*Horse and Hound*' for vacancies, and applied to the Cattistock, who wanted a whipper-in for 1961, "I thought nothing ventured, nothing gained, and with the Mitchells help, I got the job."

Whipper-in at the Cattistock - Hard Work and Fun

So, Ian found himself whipping in to Joe Roberts. the joint masters at that time were Colonel Jack Spencer and Mr Hammock (now Sir Stephen), "I was completely green really. There were three of us in Kennels, with a lot of work, but they were two happy years. They were a nice lot of people down there. The first year I was there Colonel Spencer thought it would be good for all the staff to join in the Carnival. Kennelman Dave Furmage was a great big chap, and John Biggs the Stud Groom was tiny. They went as Lady Chatterley and her lover. Dave had a wig and a dress on. Joe and I went as

rag and bone men in torn up clothes and old top hats. We were all to go to a dance in our fancy dress that night, except Joe and I were the only ones who stayed in our costumes ! It was non-stop for us then, as everyone wanted to dance with us."

First Taste of Film Action

Tom Jones was filmed here, "We were all in that, It was rather hectic, we all had to go to the location, and Joe Roberts sent me off to be made up. He came out in long boots with big bun of hair under a tricorn hat. The hounds didn't recognise him at first !" Ian describes Joe Roberts as very strict during working hours, but great fun afterwards, "I learned an awful lot from him." In the last Season of Colonel Spencer's mastership there was heavy snow, "We were completely snowed in at the Kennels, which was great fun, but hard work as Colonel Spencer made us go hunting on foot. We had a lot of fun doing that." At the end of this mastership, in 1963, Ian had to move on.

Ashford Valley Interlude

Moving down to Kent to whip in at the Ashford Valley proved less fun. Only Huntsman Gerry Wilson and Ian were in Kennels, and the two men could hardly have been more different. When Ian handed in his notice, the Hunt Chairman tried to persuade him to stay another Season, and they would put him on as Huntsman, "I had hunted them a few times when Gerry was laid up, but did not feel I had enough experience. I was tempted though, as they were very nice people down there, and they tried hard to keep me." He stuck to his guns however, and decided to move on. One morning Gerry Wilson called him in to the 'phone. Jack Champion was on the other end, asking if he would go on trial for a day to the Old Surrey and Burstow. Ian agreed to go, "The masters then were Colonel Sir Ralph Clarke, Sir Derek Greenaway and Mr Lambert." As is often the case, things did not go quite according to plan, "A hare had got up, and some hounds had gone in to the next field. There was a lovely set of rails. . ." 'Was' soon became the operative word, for Ian's horse took them out by the roots, "I came an awful purler, right in front of everybody. The horse just never took off at all. I later learned it was well-known for it !" This ignominy did not detract from Ian's abilities however, and he was offered the job. Not wishing to rush in to anything, he promised to let Jack know at an inter Hunt darts match. This proved easier said than done, as it was crowded and rather hectic. The next day Ian telephoned Jack, and told him he had decided not to accept, "Well, there was an explosion on the other end, beginning with, 'Now you look here, I want you to come. . .' He wasn't going to give up like that." Holding the receiver at arm's length by now, Ian was soon persuaded to change his mind.

Luxurious Start at the Old Surrey and Burstow

Arriving on May 1st 1964, Ian was told that his accommodation had not yet been completed. "One of the reasons I turned it down at first was that going there as a single man I would have to do all my own washing, cleaning and cooking. I wasn't very good at that ! Any rate, they said they'd get a lady in to cook and do the washing. She was already living in a cottage there, but they hadn't finished decorating the Bothy where I was to live." Far from having to slum it, for that first week Ian was shown to a local hotel. "I lived in luxury, reporting in at the desk each evening, they had dinner ready by the time I'd had a bath and changed. Then I went back to my room to watch colour TV. Every morning a girl knocked on my door with a cup of tea !" Few whippers-in can have had such service, not legitimately at any rate ! The living arrangements back at the Bothy proved successful however, and he remained here for seven seasons.

Champion, a Kennelman of the Old School, and Jorrocks

Jack Champion liked everyone to have a good day when he was hunting hounds. His Kennelman Frank Reece had been with him for many years, "He was one of the old school. I'd only been there a few days trying to learn hounds' names, people's names and so on, and was doing the lame doghounds with Frank. He had a stutter and started to say something to me. I pointed out a hound and said, 'This fella's lame Frank.' Before he could finish what he was saying, this hound nailed me. Poor Frank was trying to say 'D,d,d,d don't touch him.' By the time he'd said it, it was too late !"

The Film of *Jorrocks* was made here, "One of the actors needed a quiet horse, and the Huntsman had a really good quiet one. When this actor got on, he took off round and round the field ! It all finished up all right in the end."

142

Long serving Old Surrey & Burstow Huntsman Jack Champion.
(Jim Meads)

A Lucky Escape

One day Jack's horse went lame, so he took Ian's, "I returned to the box with it, and got a message to say the other horse had gone lame too, so he'd got on another, and wanted me to pick my horse up as well. When Jack first took my horse, hounds were running on Major Lewison Gourde's place, at Titsey Hill. When they finished, Jack asked me if I had any hounds, as they were two couple short. I hadn't, and knew they'd been all on when I left. Our terrier man, Charlie Canfield and myself went out, and couldn't find them anywhere. The police were informed, and we went out again the next morning at 6.30 am. Charlie cycled seven miles to Kennels every day, and was never late once. We stayed out all day trying to find these hounds. On the Tuesday night it snowed heavily, and we couldn't hunt Wednesday, so Charlie and I set off again with our sandwiches and coffee. We went for miles, with no sign at all. On Thursday morning we were just off again, and Mr Champion came out to say Major Lewison Gourde had rung. Apparently he'd lost a terrier years before in an old ice house in the hill, which had been boarded up." Ian and Charlie decided it had to be worth a look, and were running out of ideas, so went straight there. Sure enough, when they got there, the boards had rotted. Armed with torches. ropes and ladders they went in, "It was quite a long passage in, pitch dark. There was a sheer 20 foot drop in to big round room bricked all around. Sure enough, there were the missing hounds in the bottom. They had heard us and were going berserk. They'd been there since Monday with no food or water." As Ian went down the ladder, they jumped up, and he was able to catch them easily. Further investigation revealed their fox beneath the floor, and as he had been confined in a small place all that time they shot him. "It was very worrying at the time, they were two couple of our best bitches. Luckily they got over it all right."

Brothers Determined to Reach the Top

As Ian whipped in to Jack Champion, he learned that his brother Pat was to whip in to Bruce Durno at the Fernie, "I was flabbergasted. My first reaction when mother told me was, 'But he can't ride !' He'd only hacked my horse home from hunting before. Anyway, he did really well." The brothers had decided long before that if they were to go in to Hunt Service, they wanted to reach the top. Both did, as Pat went on to hunt the Tynedale, "He was much more musical than I ever was. He hunted the Fernie when Bruce was laid up, and when he blew that horn, you could hear Jack Kealey."

Time to Move On - a Season with the South Wold

Whilst at the Old Surrey and Burstow Ian met wife Sue, whose father was Stud Groom to Sir Ralph Clarke. They were married in 1968, and lived with her parents for the first year whilst a house was done up for them, and their son Robert was born. Ian now felt ready to move on again, but this proved easier said than done. The Postal Strike meant communication was almost non-existent. eventually he heard that the South Wold wanted a whipper-in.

Ian went as whipper in to Guy Sanderson at the South Wold. At the end of the first Season he went to the Eglinton, and Ian was offered the job of Kennel Huntsman by Mr and Mrs Pinney. "I liked it there very much as from a hunting point of view there were no main roads or railways, though it was not that well foxed. Sue didn't like it there as it was rather exposed, and the wind was always blowing, so I decided it would be better to move on again." The Garth and South Berks were looking for a Kennel Huntsman, so Ian applied to Captain Campbell, in 1971 for what was to prove his final move.

Settling at the Garth and South Berks for 23 Seasons

Ian spent the first four years as Kennel Huntsman whipping in to Captain Campbell. When he left, Mr Black offered him the job of Huntsman, which he gladly took, and remained until his retirement in 1995.

Great Hounds

As a litter, the mottled Grumpy and his sisters Granule, Graceful, and Grapevine '72 (Granby '69-Pastry '66) were pretty special, "They always gave 101%. Many a time they would come back from hunting, and had worked so hard they would just have a drink and go straight to bed, too tired to feed." One day hounds met at Checkendon, "I didn't really want to go, it was so windy. We were in the beech woods, and you couldn't hear yourself speak. In no time at all two couple were missing, and no-one had seen or heard them." Eventually hounds were boxed up as conditions were so bad. "I parked on a corner of a huge beech wood blowing and calling." After some time one hound appeared. "I was so pleased to see him. I put him back in, he stunk of fox. Another one came, just the same, followed by a third some time later." Last of all to appear was Granule, "She was way down in the woods. I jumped out of the lorry and ran down to make a fuss of her." Instead of going back to the lorry, Granule went on ahead of Ian, seeming to lead him in to the woods. "I kept going behind her more than half a mile in to the woods. Then she cut off through some bracken. I followed on again. There by a tree was a dead fox, still warm, which had been in a place there. They had dug down about two feet to him, and she obviously wanted to show me what they had been doing ! I still have the mask of that fox, in memory of Granule." That litter's sire Granby '69 was by Old Berks Grammer '61, who produced so many good working hounds, whilst their dam Pastry '66 was by Duke of Beaufort's Palmer '59, regarded by many as the greatest hound bred at Badminton, possessing great character, fox sense and nose. Both sharing Portman blood, notably through Portman Playfair '51 (South Dorset Salesman '44-West Waterford Playful '48), who appears in Old Berks Grammar's bottom line and his sister Pleasant '51 in Duke of Beaufort's Palmer's top line this was obviously a very happy nick. The dominant mottle this line so often produces was passed on through their descendants, who went on to win the two couple class at Ardingly - Dazzle and Dainty '76 (Grumpy '72 - Dahlia '71) Hester '75 (Heythrop Herald '71-Graceful '72) and Waitress '76 (Grumpy '72-Wanton '63), all very highly thought of by their Huntsman. Sadly they missed Peterborough as one of them went lame.

Another litter of six bitches and two dogs also proved outstanding, "Mrs Frome whelped the bitch, Pleasant '69 keeping two bitches, Mrs Ward and Mrs Purser walked the rest." They took the bitches Footpath, Folly, Fortune, and Forecast '74 (Heythrop Footman '71-Pleasant '69) straight to Peterborough in 1975. "They were all as alike as peas in a pod. We took the other two, Fountain and Foxglove in case any went lame at the last minute. This litter like Dazzle and Dainty '76 also had lines to Old Berks Playmate '64, "They showed themselves brilliantly." No-one was more delighted than Mick Fox, who held hounds for Ian, "He used to help at Kennels a lot. He had his own horse and was asked to wear a scarlet coat and help whip-in. He drove the local dust cart, and could hardly speak when we won !" Many people shared the pack's delight, "Colonel Rodney Palmer was master and Huntsman here for years and bred super hounds, with Victor Clarke as his Kennel Huntsman. He couldn't wait to come over to Kennels and congratulate us."

144

Ian Langrish with Hunt Supporters.
(Jim Meads)

"Waterman '82 was a good white dog. I hunted him for just over ten seasons." Latterly Ian was particularly fond of a dog called Saddler '84, by Duke of Beaufort's Saddler '79 (Limerick Seaman '76-Pansy '77), who did very well at the South of England Show. Yet again Duke of Beaufort's Palmer '59 is prominent in that pedigree. Farmer, by Bicester Farmer '76 (Fresham '73-Vale of Clettwr Fairy '73) is another who merits a mention. Both Saddler and Farmer were regarded very good dogs in their work by Ian Langrish.

During his last Season, Ian took hounds to the Old Surrey and Burstow country. As they ran out of a shaw (a long narrow wood) he noticed that Cobbler, his sister Countess and all her progeny were in the lead.

The Country

Though roads can be busy down here, some good hound work can be enjoyed, "It is heavily wooded which wouldn't be to everyone's liking. If you want to hear a pack in full cry, the beech woods are the place to go, especially if you're used to open county. You've heard nothing until you hear them really going in those beech woods. It really is something." Hearing can prove deceptive though, "In my first Season they were really roaring in there one day. The next thing I knew, they were gone. Somehow the noise seems to go up and down in the canopy of the trees, and doesn't seem to carry if they go over a ridge. I lost them that once, but they had a hard job to lose me after that ! "One of the greatest compliments was paid by Ted Hill, former Huntsman of the Barlow," His brother in law hunted with us, so Ted came down several times, and I had a lot of respect for him. One day, he was up with me and said, 'Now that's what I call music. You can really hear all the different notes.' They did have a lovely cry. I judged Ted's last Puppy Show with Willy Poole. Four days he kept me there !"

Faith Justified

This heavily wooded country has an abundance of deer - roe, fallow and muntjac, "I could hunt hounds all day and never actually see their fox. You really had to trust them 100%. One day a whipper-in told me they were on deer, and showed me where the deer had gone, up a path and left-handed. Hounds ran that line, but swung right-handed. A few seconds later we heard a holloa. It would have done more harm than good to stop them." As so often happens the deer and fox had taken the same line for some distance, "I'm not saying they never hunted deer, but if you weren't sure it was far better to say nothing to them." On another occasion the Field were positioned to line the railway. As they rode across, they disturbed some deer, which ran in to the covert Ian was about to draw. Showing tremendous faith in his hounds, he put them straight in behind the deer. "They started speaking within a few minutes, and as I blew and cheered them on I'm sure the field thought we were on the deer." Ian's faith was justified however, "Farmer's daughter Fran Harnett was down by the road, she had a beautiful holloa, and when I heard her, I knew we were all right. Hounds went away on their fox, no problem."

Huntsman and Hounds Pay Tribute to a Special Master

Ian found it particularly rewarding to see hounds hunting so truly, "The fact that I not only hunted them, but bred them added another dimension really. It was quite something." During his time as Huntsman Ian was totally responsible for the hound breeding, though Mr Maunder, who was master for eight Seasons took a great interest in that side of things. His mastership is remembered with great affection, "Mr Maunder was a farmer who became MFH and was super, especially with the farmers. Nothing got the better of him, and he could twist people round his little finger." Mr Maunder's daughter had been married in the USA and had a Blessing in the local church when she returned. Mr Maunder asked Ian to blow the couple 'away' from the church, "I hated doing that in cold blood, you never feel quite right. I wouldn't have cared if a thousand people were out hunting, but this made me nervous. Anyway I couldn't say no. The happy couple were sitting on a straw bale on a flat-bed trap, drawn by a pony. As soon as the pony went round the corner, Mr Maunder signalled, and I blew. The next thing I saw was people running up the street. The pony had taken off left handed, through a narrow gap between two rather expensive cars. The trap had hit both cars, the pony was now facing backwards in the shafts and the happy couple were in a bruised and bleeding heap on the road. Luckily the bride thought it was hysterical. I was so embarrassed, but Mr Maunder soon smoothed things over."

When Supporters' Club Chairman Jimmy Bushnall rang Ian to tell him Mr Maunder had been unwell, he was keen to do anything to help, "He suggested taking some hounds over one evening. Their place had always been open house and I was all for it, picking out all the hounds he had walked - nearly half the pack. We went over to his place with them in the lorry, and had a wonderful evening in the yard with Mr and Mrs Maunder. The hounds really enjoyed themselves too." Within three weeks, Mr Maunder had died. His wife asked Ian to blow the coffin 'away' from the church, which he did by swiftly donning overalls and climbing right up amongst the bells, "I hadn't known if I would manage it or not as he was more of a friend than a master. Such a super chap. I was so glad we took those hounds over when we did."

A Star at Night, and on the Carpet

Ian appeared in yet another film here, *First Night,* filmed in Stratfield Saye, starring Richard Gere and Sean Connery, "We went over there after work every night for a week." He was also in a commercial for carpets, which was shown in the North of the country, "We did that at Winkfield, Guy Luck and myself. He had to go in and sit on a settee with a glass of whisky. Then, when a girl came in, I had to get up and embrace her in the middle of the room. Guy thought he had the best part with his whisky until the girl came in, then his mouth dropped !"

Ian was asked to serve on the Executive Committee of the Hunt Servants' Benefit Society. Sometimes the late Duke of Beaufort would be in the Chair, "I used to go up there and have the odd day with Sir David Black who kept his horses with the late Jack Windell." Jack Windell was a famous and well loved tenant farmer, who lived in Badminton, "We had breakfast there before hunting. One day I thanked the Duke when we finished and Major Dallas, the Hunt Secretary said I should come up the following week for the Duke's 83rd birthday. I worked on Mr Maunder, and we took three horses up.

Ian Langrish takes the Garth & South Berks Hounds to parade
at the CLA Game Fair, Stratfield Saye in 1989 (Kay Gardner)

Late in the day we ended up in the Park. His Grace had told me, and Chris Maiden who was also out to go up with Brian Gupwell. At the end of the day, he said it had been like watching a set of traffic lights all day! It had been marvellous to see him out in front popping over walls at that age. He was some man."

One in Quarter of a Million

Ian believes firmly that the role of the Huntsman has adapted well in modern times, but urges thoughtfulness for those who now fulfill the role, "As a Huntsman, you must respect other people's points of view. I was very lucky to have a good team behind me, a supportive wife and three sons. I think there is a lot more give and take nowadays. The time when a Huntsman only had to look at someone to make them jump has gone. I enjoyed my hunting and meeting all the people that came out. I enjoyed talking to the keepers, farmers and followers. I hope they enjoyed it all as much as I did. I was never brilliant with my horn, or voice, but I always did my best. You have to enjoy what you do. Once you lose that you want to call it a day, or things will go badly wrong. " He hates to hear Huntsmen swearing and losing their temper, particularly with staff, "If you've got something to say to your whipper-in, let it be between the two of you alone. If you respect other people that way, they will have more respect for you." He especially liked Children's Meets, "I really enjoyed it when the children were sent on with me to see what went on. I was always helped and encouraged and have always said that's how I wanted to treat other people. 'Do as you would be done by' is a great motto." He always tried to show thought for children who were in difficulties, perhaps on a strong pony, "The way I look at it there are about 200 Huntsmen in this country, out of fifty million, and I was lucky to be one of them. I really appreciated my time in Hunt Service, and made a lot of friends all over the country."

When Ian retired he received a letter from the Chairman of the local Parish Council thanking him for his 'control and cheery friendliness when walking out the hounds, and the courtesy and consideration with which he carried out his duties as Huntsman.' Proof enough that as one in quarter of a million men he has been a tremendous ambassador for our sport and for his profession.

147

Stan Luckhurst at the end of his last season with the West Kent.
(Terry Crate)

148

Stan Luckhurst

Talking to Stan Luckhurst for the first time feels like speaking to an old friend. He has that easy manner of conversation shared by so many professional Hunt Servants of his generation. My first impression is of a happy-go-lucky man, not easily ruffled, with a ready smile. His passion for hunting is spoken softly in the kind of gentle voice that could be listened to all day. He still enjoys hunting in his native Kent, which unusually, he never left during the course of a career which spanned fifty years.

Horse Mad Boy to Second Horseman at the Ashford Valley

Born in the Ashford Valley country in Pluckley, reputedly Britain's most haunted village, Stan Luckhurst left school at the age of 14 in 1949, "I had always been mad on horses. My father was a waggoner on the farm, so horses were in my blood." Stan went straight to the Ashford Valley where after a Season in the Stables he rode second horse to Huntsman Bert Taylor. Mr Chester Beatty was sole master at this time. This all went very well until Stan was called up at 18 to do his National Service.

King's Troop, Royal Horse Artillery

Like so many Hunt Servants Stan went into the Kings Troop, Royal Horse Artillery. His compulsory two years were so enjoyable that he signed up for an extra year, "Colonel Frank Weldon, who became so famous for winning Badminton on Kilbarry was my Commanding Officer. He was a really nice guy, very fair. Lord Allenby hunted with the Ashford Valley. I remember one day I had done a gate and was getting on a horse from the offside. I didn't realise he was getting on the nearside and we met in the middle !" He was none too pleased at the time. "He must have told Colonel Gaselee about this young whipper-snapper though, because he wrote to me to say they were looking for a whipper-in at the West Kent. Of course I had to write back and say I was staying in the King's Troop for another year." All was not lost however, for at the end of that year, in 1955 Colonel Gaselee wrote again to say that there was a vacancy for a Kennelman.

Kennelman to the West Kent

So Bombardier Luckhurst arrived at the West Kent, unaware that he would be here for the rest of his working life. Colonel Gaselee hunted hounds, with Harry Lenthall as Kennel-Huntsman, Douglas Hunt, whipped in, and he too served in the King's Troop Royal Horse Artillery later going on to hunt the Hursley Hambledon. After two Seasons Stan was promoted, "I then took on as Second whipper-in and Stud Groom. I had twelve horses to look after ! We hacked everywhere from the Kennels which were at Hamptons then near Plaxtol, Tonbridge. That meant leaving at 3.30am some mornings to get to places like Ash for 5.30am. There was no traffic then and we would ride through Ightham, Wrotham, and Borough Green, for two hours. The hounds would be taken on by trailer."

A Famous Racing Family in the Hunting World

The Gaselees are best known in the Racing world. Colonel Gaselee's son is trainer Nick, and his daughter Virginia married another famous trainer, Peter Walwyn. The whole family hunted, Colonel Gaselee's wife riding sidesaddle, "Colonel Gaselee was a hell of a good master. He hunted hounds, and did it very much his own way. I always remember one Season hounds hadn't caught many foxes. We were up at Martin's Hill and after a nice hunt they caught their fox on top. When I caught up he was off his horse with the hounds getting quite excited that they had caught this fox. Suddenly he stopped cheering and shouted, 'Stand still !' I wonder what I had done and asked, "What's the

149

matter ?' His false teeth had shot out amongst all these hounds breaking their fox up ! We searched about and found them all right." Colonel Gaselee had a very laid back approach and would sometimes go quiet without explanation. One hot autumn morning this happened and everyone thought he must have gone. Stan went to look and found him sitting in the covert, "He was just sitting there quietly with his leg up cracking hazelnuts on his saddle, with the hounds lying in the sun around him."

Continuing up the Ladder as Masterships Change

That Stan remained with the West Kent was more by accident than design, "Every time I thought I ought to move on, another job came up here. I was happy there, so just kept moving on up where I was." Although he remained with the same pack, their Kennels actually moved around the country, "We were like nomads ! We went to Hamptons with Colonel Gaselee from 1955-66. From Hamptons we moved over to Mr Richard Thorpe's place, when he took over." Mr Thorpe's mastership was another very successful one. He had taken over on condition that Stan hunted hounds, "That's how I started hunting hounds with Mr Thorpe. He was a very good master and provided really good horses. We had new Kennels then at his Home Farm, near Tonbridge."

West Kent Payment '72 Makes History in 1973

Mr Thorpe bred cattle very successfully so had a good eye for pedigrees, "He had that knack for it and bred some lovely hounds." It was during his mastership that the West Kent's Payment '72 made

West Kent Payment '72 with Huntsman Stan Luckhurst at Peterborough after winning the Championship in 1973 (Jim Meads)

history for the pack by winning the Peterborough Bitch Championship in 1973. She won the Championship at Ardingly the following year. Payment was impeccably bred. Her sire Eridge Painter '66 was by the pre-potent Duke of Beaufort's Palmer '59, out of a bitch Eridge Woeful '64 who was daughter of the Eridge's own Peterborough Champion, Freedom '60 and by Duke of Beaufort's Woldsman '60. His litter sister Woeful '60 had won the Peterborough Championship unentered. Payment's own dam Chantress '66 was a granddaughter of Heythrop Choirboy '56. It is a pedigree packed with Peterborough Champions and hounds of the highest quality from the Beaufort and Portman Kennels. Martin Scott who was judging that year with Captain Ronnie Wallace recalls, "It was thoroughly well-deserved. A tumultuous roar went up when the result was announced, reflecting the popularity of this win."

A Terrific Achievement in 1977

This was to be a particularly memorable period. Payment went on to breed them some lovely hounds, including Agent '77 (Cottesmore Actor '71-Payment '72) who was best unentered doghound at Peterborough in 1977. His brother Actor '77 was third in the class. The pair were second in the unentered couples class. In the entered couples Maestro and Major '75 (Warcry '73-Magpie '71) were third. Of the bitches, Likely (Heythrop Lindsay '73-Welfare '73) was second in the unentered class, with another of Payment's progeny Purley '75 (Heythrop Cupid '72-Payment '72) third in the brood bitch class, "To me, that was our best year. It was lovely to win the Championship with Payment of course but in 1977 we did very well. The Duke of Beaufort's won the most, then the Heythrop and then us. That meant an awful lot. You think about the size of those packs, and the number of hounds they have. They would breed more puppies each year than I had hounds in the Kennel. For a two day a week pack like ours to take all those prizes, we'd done jolly well."

There was great camaraderie between the Huntsmen in the South, "Brian Gupwell, he was at the Eridge of course, and a very good guy, followed by John Cooke. Then Ray Goddard was at the Southdown, where Cookie finished up, I went to an invitation meet with Cookie once in the snow. We

were *covered* in snow like two little snowmen !" John Cooke recalled that April meet in the Eridge country, " It came down thick so we were smothered in snow !" He told me that Stan is one of those rare souls who never speaks ill of anyone, and never has a bad word said about him, "We were always running in to each other's country, and getting up to mischief. Stan is one of those people things happen to. The number of times I've heard him chuckle, 'Well, it just happened.' We had a lot of tussles in the ring at Ardingly, but never a cross word. We had a really good gang down there then with the likes of Jack Clarke and Jack Champion." Payment's sire Eridge Painter '66 was one of John's hounds, "Stan came down intending to put the bitch to Painter's brother Palmer, who

Stan Luckhurst and the West Kent Hounds on a misty morning. (Jim Meads)

had been used a lot. I said, 'If I were you, I would go for his brother, Painter '66. They were very, very good dogs. Painter '66 got hit by a car and looked for all the world dead. In three weeks he was hunting again, he was so tough. When the West Kent won that Championship with Payment '72, I had a lovely thank you letter from Mr Thorpe MFH, saying, 'You had as much to do with this as anyone.' "

Pat Thatcher's Remedies

When it came to influences on his own career, Stan again looks to the South, " Bert Taylor at the Ashford Valley was a wonderful horseman. Pat Thatcher at the Tickham was so good with hounds. He always gave everyone a good hunt but was a great one for letting hounds hunt for themselves. He was a great influence on me. He knew so much about hounds. He passed on a lot of old-fashioned remedies to me for hounds - this was in the days before penicillin, don't forget."

Nothing Better

"A Huntsman must have a great deal of respect for his hounds. He should watch for things all the time and have a real sense of the country. Using his voice and his horn properly is so important. It's no good blowing fancy calls that neither the hounds or the Field can understand. Blowing out of covert and 'Gone Away' are the two most important horn calls. If they aren't clear then no-one will know what is going on. All Huntsmen should try to be level-headed. There's no point in getting up tight because you will convey it to the hounds, your horse and the people around you. Politeness is always important too." Few appreciate how much a Huntsman has to think about in the course of a day, "You are pitting your wits against the fox. If hounds over-shoot the line you must cast back and round until they pick it up again. It's jolly interesting, and there's nothing better." The day rarely ends for a Huntsman, even when hounds are back in Kennel, "You can have a super day, hounds lose their fox, and find again. That wonderful moment when the pack really does go. Yet all that can be spoilt if they lose him and you don't know why. If he goes to ground, or over a bad road fair enough. But if you lose him without knowing why, you can spoil the day for yourself. You get back home and keep thinking about it, if only I'd done this, or that."
Stan was also noted for his horsemanship, and really enjoyed parading his hounds whenever the opportunity arose, especially on his favourite horse Red, with whom he had a very close bond.

An Outstanding Season

Stan recalls one Season 1970-71 as being particularly good, "They say that you only get one like that every so many years. Scent was so good all through the autumn, winter and Spring. It was the best scenting season I've known, you just couldn't wait to get back out again !" The West Kent country consists of woods and hills with a lot of open country including the Hoo Peninsula beside the Thames, "There is still quite a bit of grass in places, and even where it's arable you can get round easily. The farmers were brilliant. They were a really good lot out on the Marsh, in fact there are a lot of good hunting people here." In common with the rest of the South of England increased traffic, fast roads and railways, as well as increased building have taken their toll, hence the pack's subsequent amalgamation.

151

Stan Luckhurst and part of his 'team.'
(Terry Crate)

Three Pony Clubs and 250 Children at the Meet

The West Kent sustained three Pony Club branches, "I remember one meet we had for them at St Clair's when 250 kids turned up. There was Mr Thorpe on his big old bay with kids overtaking him left right and centre ! We had a fair run from Wrotham to Farningham where hounds caught their fox under a chicken run. About 16 kids were up there with him still." That would be a point of around eight miles according to my map.

Hounds - the Individuals that Make a Team

Stan feels some people make a great mistake in breeding hounds to be all the same, "They are individuals. You can't really say this one is better than that one because they are all so different. That is why you should breed from different bitches so that they are not all from the same 'family'. They make up a team, some good to mark, some good scenting hounds, some with good cry." As individuals they are also highly intelligent, "We had a little bitch called Miniver who we drafted to the Royal Engineers Draghounds along with another four couple. I took them to Chatham, over forty miles away, in a closed trailer. Three days later I was walking hounds out in Colonel Gaselee's field on the Sunday afternoon, and Miniver came trotting up the road."

The Important Role Played by Old Berks Stallionhounds

Of those hounds he has had down the years many have played important roles, Payment and her offspring are remembered fondly as are some Stallionhounds, "Old Berks Tewkesbury '61 (a half brother to Old Berks Grammer '61) was a wonderful hound. He had such a good nose. He was given to me in the end. You would see him casting when hounds had lost their fox, and he would often be the first to take it on. It was interesting though because the others wouldn't take any notice of him at first, because he was a stranger. I suppose they didn't know they could trust him. He would look round as if to say 'Well, what's up with you lot ?' They accepted him once they realised they could trust him. One of Tewkesbury's sons, Thorough '70 was brilliant in his work."

Chorister '96 (Portman Calbeck '95– Greeting '93) also had a distinguished career, "One day, not long before I finished we were hunting down on the Marsh. They'd hunted like billy-oh all through the floods, and got away from us. They stopped at a flooded ditch, and they had been so close to their fox I thought they must have caught him. All of a sudden Chorister went right in under the water and pulled the dead fox out. He must have fallen into the ditch when they caught him, and old Chorister was the only one who went in underwater to get him out !"

Many of Stan's best hounds were by Old Berks Stallionhounds, "We used Old Berks Playfair '60 (Sailor '57-Pliable '56) on three bitches, and all those pups were very good." As Portman blood had already nicked well here through Payment, it is no surprise that those consistent Old Berks sires full of Major W W B Scott's best Portman lines, should be so successful.

Payment Lost, Partner Gained

Sadly their lovely Peterborough Champion Payment went missing, "I was out looking every bit of time I had, and would take four or five couple with me. She never did turn up." On one of his searches however, he found something unexpected, "One day I was out searching for Payment and I came across some girls on horses. They were leading one, and offered it to me." He rode along with them for a while, and they later rang to come over to the Kennels. Recently divorced, Stan was delighted, "This was the time of long leather boots and short skirts remember !" Stan's mucky overalls and wellies proved less impressive. One girl kept in touch however, Linda, and from that chance meeting they have now been together 21 years.

Another Mastership Change, Another Kennel Move

When Mr Thorpe's twelve year mastership came to an end, they were lucky to have Mr Tim Lyles come in to the mastership, "We moved the Kennels then to his Watergreen Farm. He was an absolute brick as a master. Even after he gave up we could still walk hounds out any number of ways on his land. That was marvellous for 18 years. He was very good as regards hounds, as I lived 3$1/2$ miles away from the Kennels then. He had hunted the Bolebroke Beagles for ten seasons. You wouldn't believe how much he did for us." This continued until 1999 when Stan retired, and the West Kent amalgamated with the Old Surrey and Burstow.

In Father's Footsteps, and Beyond

Stan's son Paul helped his father a lot in Kennels, and when he was 16 went to the Mid Devon where he worked under a very good hound man, Bernard Parker, who I was lucky enough to see hunt hounds brilliantly in our hill country just before he retired, "Some Canadian masters used to come and hunt with the Mid Devon, and wanted Paul to go out there when he was only 18, which I felt was far too young. He waited until he was about 21 and has been out there in Hamilton now for 14 years. He absolutely loves it. I am going out to see him again next week."

Stan Luckhurst collecting hounds up together.
(Terry Crate)

Enjoying Every Second

Clearly Stan still has great enthusiasm for the sport and must miss hunting hounds dreadfully, "Yes, I do. I can honestly say I never woke up in the morning thinking, 'I don't want to go to work.' I enjoyed every second." I am left with the feeling that for Stan Luckhurst, Life is very much about enjoyment. Who could argue ?

153

Bert Maiden leads the Pytchley hounds away from a meet.
(Jim Meads)

154

Bert Maiden

There is something both amazing and humbling about the remarkable record in Hunt Service of the Maiden family. Many families can boast long involvement, but the Maidens can trace back eight successive generations of Huntsmen. A continuous chain going back three hundred years. All had noteworthy careers, none more so than the second Joe Maiden (whose father was also called Joe). He lived (1795-1864) to be 69, a very good age then, and completed 54 years in Hunt Service. All this despite surviving a gruesome accident when he fell in to the Kennel copper. His leg was so badly burned that he later lost it, and continued to hunt with a false leg. The crudity of surgery at this time must have made riding excruciating, yet he still scored an incredible 25 mile point whilst hunting the Cheshire! He hunted the Cheshire for fourteen years, and the gentlemen subscribers presented him with the not inconsiderable sum of £250 as his testimonial, and ended his hunting career at the North Staffordshire. His son Will whipped in to him, and sadly died in a fall with the HH. His other two sons both hunted hounds, Jim in Ireland and Harry the Belvoir. Bert's father, also Will hunted the Meynell.

Early Memories

Born in 1927 at the Meynell Kennels, Bert was one of nine children. The Kennels were away from the village, so the children very much did their own thing, "There was no other life really, but school and Kennels", says Bert cheerily, clearly content with his lot. During holidays and after school he liked nothing more than to help in Kennels, or with walking out, brother Jack being of a like mind. Young Bert had problems with his legs as a child, and one of his sisters would lead him to and from school at Sudbury on a pony. His earliest memories in the hunting field are of days with the Whaddon Chase. His father Will was Kennel Huntsman there to Sir Peter Farquhar and his Joint Master Lord Rosebery. From a Kennels meet his sister asked where she should take Bert on his pony, and Sir Peter told them to go to the top end of the covert half a field away. They were breathless with excitement when first the fox, followed by hounds and Sir Peter galloped past. Bert's pony bolted, and his new cap flew off. Lord Rosebery caught him, and later told Will that his son had been more concerned about losing his cap than any imminent danger ! He clearly lacked nothing in enthusiasm or courage in the Field, as on another occasion he tried to cross a flooded brook, and was swept away on his pony, one of his father's friends coming to rescue them. He showed me a cartoon done at the time of him on his intrepid pony captioned 'The Greatest Horseman in the Whaddon Chase.'

Father's Footsteps

Bert's father retired due to poor eyesight as Huntsman to the Whaddon Chase in 1938, taking the New Inn at Long Itchington, in the Warwickshire country. Yet during a 5½ mile point in his last Season, he had kept the fox in view all the way ! When War broke out just a year later, Warwickshire Huntsman George Gillson was called up and Captain Nicholls approached Will Maiden to see if he would fill the breach. His retirement short lived, thus began the inevitable career in Hunt Service for Bert Maiden. By the time George Gillson returned from the War, Will Maiden had given up all thoughts of retirement, moving on to the South Dorset. With regular staff back from war duties young Bert found himself without a job. Being small and light, he secured a position in Mr Sunny Hall's racing stables at Russley Park near Lambourn (where Taffy Salaman now trains) which can be seen from the M4. His first night away from home was so cold that he slept in his overcoat. The lure of Hunt Service was too great, and with his father now enjoying a new lease of life at the South Dorset, the opportunity arose the following year in 1946 for Bert to whip in to him again. He spent four Seasons there whipping in to his father, who showed no favouritism in the field to his son, but is described by him as "a different man off his horse, when we got home."

155

The White Collars of the Pytchley and Stanley Barker

Maiden finally did retire, aged sixty, in 1950, and in 1951 Bert secured the post of second whipper-in to the legendary Stanley Barker at the Pytchley. Barker himself had taken over from the revered Frank Freeman. Bert vividly remembers his first Opening Meet. It was so wet and dark riding to the first covert that they could have done with a lamp. Walter Gupwell was out and asked Bert not to leave him in case he got lost ! On Mondays and Saturdays hounds hacked to the meets, being boxed on Wednesdays. On only his second Monday, a hound went missing after first draw, and was no-where to be found. They hacked home and within one and a half miles of the Brixworth kennels, in the last of the light, a car drew up, and the driver said a hound was back at Great Harrowden near Wellingborough. This was ten miles back, and Bert was despatched with the horn to bring the hound back. Duly found in a pub yard, seen only by the streetlamp, Bert led him home arriving at 9pm. The Stud Groom was not best pleased (second whippers-in had no second horses) and the rather weary whipper-in said he had better sort it out with the Huntsman, as he was only doing what he was told to do!

Bert enjoyed his time working for Stanley Barker. There were five men working in the Kennels when he arrived. He recalls that Barker was very keen on painting everything with dazzling white Snow-cem. This was tricky to mix, and if not just right would dry out yellow. When he was away, they had the bright idea of painting over the existing Snowcem with whitewash. It looked very smart to begin with, but then began to peel, and the whole lot had to be re-done.

From a meet at Guilsborough Green during his first Season, six men were sent on point ahead of hounds moving off. The big Field went berserk on the new grass, and as he looked over his shoulder he was glad he had heeded Stanley Barker's words to, "Ride hard or they'll knock you down ! " Up to the War this was regarded the best four day a week country in England. With such a great family tradition in Hunt Service it feels unfair to ask which Huntsman Bert most admired. His father was un-

*Stanley Barker at the end of his last day hunting the Pytchley in 1960
with his whipper-in and successor Bert Maiden (Jim Meads)*

156

doubtedly a tremendous influence, and a great huntsman, but you could not begin to compare the countries he hunted to the Pytchley, "Stanley Barker was a great horseman, and hounds just loved him", Bert sums up with real admiration in his voice. Barker's skill with the horn, and melodious voice are the stuff of dreams. I was lucky to be given a rare copy of the record made at this time "Hunting by Ear" recently. It should be compulsory listening for all who aspire to hunt hounds. Bert was present when the recording was made, "It was done at the Kennels. The swishing water in the background was me !" He chuckles at this claim to fame. After two Seasons as second whipper-in, he was promoted to first whipper-in. His father felt he should move on and gain more experience. Bert however had other ideas. Barker was an easy man to work for, and he was determined to stay. Besides, he had already met the future Mrs Maiden, a London evacuee, and had no intention of leaving. Manpower was reduced to just one whipper-in, and Bert's brother Jack took over as Kennelman from Harry Childs. In those days, the Kennelman's job was more akin to that of a Kennel Huntsman nowadays, and he was second in command.

Bert and the Pytchley hounds settling in to their new Kennels in 1966 (Jim Meads)

Patience rewarded - Huntsman at Last

After this long and patient apprenticeship, Bert became Huntsman when Stanley Barker retired in 1960, after nine years whipping-in here. Colonel Lowther also retired from his 33 years of mastership at that time. Bert had already hunted hounds at Christmas when Stanley Barker uncharacteristically took two falls in a week, cracking his ribs after his horse put its foot in a rabbit hole. Major Borwick had whipped in to Bert then. He achieved a $5\frac{1}{2}$ mile point, twenty miles as hounds ran. They were still looking for hounds at 9pm in Aston Heath, outside Northampton that Boxing Day !

Still conscious however that he had a hard act to follow, the new Huntsman's nerves were not assuaged when in a break with recognised etiquette, Barker continued to hunt with the Pytchley. He came out every single day, as he was in charge of the Macdonald-Buchanan's horses at Cottesbrook Park. Unsurprisingly Bert recalls this as a very tense Season. It was not that Barker ever once interfered or criticised, he was just there. Having got through that first Season, literally under Barker's gaze as hounds left each covert, he began to relax. Proof that he was doing a good job, and continued to do so for eleven Seasons. Colonel Borwick, himself a respected hound judge, had consulted with Mr Ikey Bell over the hound breeding, and used some South and West Wilts blood.

Joint masters Miss Grant Lawson and Major Peter Borwick bred the hounds now. Miss Grant Lawson was from Yorkshire, and wanted to use York and Ainsty sires. They also went to the Heythrop and Warwickshire for Stallionhounds. Bert recalls that Miss Grant Lawson smoked Turkish cigarettes and had a very gruff voice in consequence. She was regularly called 'Sir' on the telephone, and luckily had a great sense of humour.

When Colonel Borwick died, hounds caught a fox in the churchyard where he was buried. Bert witnessed this, and the story is confirmed by Colonel Borwick's daughter, the Dowager Lady Hindlip, who spent many happy years hunting here. When her brother Major Peter also died, hounds ran over his grave in the same churchyard, "It didn't do much for the floral arrangements", she laughs.

157

North Staffordshire - 92 couple all on

In 1971, Bert went to the North Staffordshire. Mr Philip Hunter, also Master of the Cheshire Forest had all the hounds together. There were 92 couple there when Bert arrived. Many were draft hounds, so any ear marks found were a bonus when it came to identifying them all ! In his first Summer he recalls a disastrous hound parade on a very hot day. Mr Hunter gave him a polo pony to ride, which dumped him at every available opportunity. His assistants Chris, Pat Langrish, and Paul Bellamy (now Oakley Huntsman) were all on young horses. Mr Hunter was commentating, and blew down the microphone whereupon all but seven couple of hounds disappeared to all four corners of the Showground. Hounds were out five days a week. It was this move which settled Chris Maiden's future. He had been all set to break with tradition, and start a farming career in the Pytchley country. When he learned of the impending move however, he did not want to be left behind, so found himself whipping in to his father, who alternated hunting the Cheshire Forest with Mr Hunter on Tuesdays and Thursdays, both packs hunting on Saturdays.

Joe Maiden Makes His Presence Known

During his first Season as Huntsman here, where it may be recalled he was following in the illustrious footsteps of his ancestor Joe Maiden, Bert experienced a fascinating incident. He had not been hunting hounds long, it was during his first autumn. Hounds hunted a fox, and caught him in a churchyard. Bert got off his horse and went to make much of his hounds. Stooping to pick up the body of the fox, he came face to face with Old Joe Maiden's tombstone, where hounds had caught him. Only a hardened cynic could call this a co-incidence. Indeed his parents came to look at the grave afterwards, as they remembered it as having railings around it. This mystery was quickly solved - the railings had gone to help the War effort.

After two years Mr Hunter took his hounds back to Cheshire, and Bert remained for one more Season.

Pytchley Huntsman Bert Maiden receiving instructions from Lord Paget MFH at a meet
(Jim Meads)

Shanks' Pony

Now Bert made his most fundamental change. He gave up hunting hounds and went as Kennel Huntsman to the Cheshire Beagles, Dr Parkes being Master at that time. I asked him how he found the change from covering the country on a horse, to toiling after these little hounds on foot. He chuckles, "Well, I thought it was silly !" Once he developed an eye for the country and realised that you did not have to run everywhere though he really enjoyed the houndwork, "I got wiser." Chris meanwhile had gone to the North Shropshire. Bert made one last move to another pack, the Eton College. This enabled Mrs Maiden to be nearer her relations in London. His experience was invaluable to the schoolboy masters, and there could have been no-one better qualified to care for the beagles. The only downside to Eton was the travelling long distances to meets due to increased urbanisation. Both Mr James Vestey, now MFH Jedforest, and Mr Marcus Armitage, Grand National Winning amateur jockey, and now joint master of the Old Berkshire Foxhounds benefited from Bert's guidance. He proudly showed me a glass bowl presented to him when he retired in 1993. On moving here, the Maidens quickly became a familiar part

Chris Maiden and the Berkeley Hounds
(Terry Crate)

of the Berkeley community, though sadly Bert's wife died recently. He has taken obvious pride in Chris's career at Berkeley, living just a stone's throw now from those historic Kennels. Bert still likes popping down there, always ready to give a hand if needed, and Chris is a regular visitor to his cottage.

159

North Lonsdale Huntsman James Mallett
(Jim Meads)

160

James Mallett

As I dropped down through Hawkshead to Lake Windermere, there was a definite change in the type of country. I stayed in the picturesque village of Near Sawry, on the edge of Esthwaite Water, a noted beauty spot. I enjoyed excellent home cooking with Margaret Lambert, Joint Secretary of the North Lonsdale, whose home has a glass frontage overlooking Esthwaite Water, like a living cinema screen, teeming with bird life. She is delighted that someone is keen to find out about the North Lonsdale, so often in the shadow of the Fell Packs, to whom they are affiliated. As well as being keen Hunt followers Margaret and her husband keep trail hounds for this other traditional Fell sport. Huntsman Jimmy Mallett lives in this same picture book village, once home of Beatrix Potter, and I was able to walk to his house where he and wife Elizabeth are also full up with Bed and Breakfast guests. As a small boy Jimmy always kept terriers, which he later went on to breed, "Father was a townie, through and through from Birmingham, who was stationed here during the war. On mother's side, her grandfather was very keen, so I suppose that's how I got it."

"I spent most time as a lad hunting with Antony Chapman. The Eskdale and Ennerdale used to come to Langdale where we lived, when Art Irving was hunting them, then Edmund." Though he originally served his apprenticeship as a mechanic, and set up his own business, the lure of hunting proved too great, "I'd always preferred the outdoor life. I had hunted with the North Lonsdale for a number of years and when the Huntsman retired, I applied for the job." Now in his 24th season as Huntsman, "I had it all to learn. I'm still learning. There's always something different, so you never stop learning."

Hounds For a Difficult Country

Hounds are kennelled at Greenodd, and all hunting takes place on foot. The pack was founded in 1947 by local farmers, to hunt part of the Coniston country, which was too big for them to get round. Today some country is still shared with the Coniston. The North Lonsdale country is notoriously difficult to hunt. Heavily aforrestated, and full of deer, it is very different from the other countries in the Fells, "Even here things have changed a lot in the last 23 years. The Season is six weeks shorter now, as farmers down this end lamb in January. There's very little moor country now." I saw a big red deer on my way to see Jimmy, and it is not unusual for hounds to come across a hundred in two miles, so steadiness is of prime importance, "I often see more deer than sheep !" With the deer comes another problem, deer fencing. Made up of squares, bigger at the top then the bottom of the fence, hounds must learn to jump up, and through, "If they can smoot the fence where the fox has got through, they will." It is important not to take too many hounds out, as they all bunch at one place in a fence, and can hurt themselves as they become impatient to get through. If they spend too long looking for a place to get through and become scattered their fox gains a lot of time on them, "Twenty or twenty five hounds are enough. I've seen three hounds caught in a fence at once." The country is very well foxed so blank days are few and usually attributable to poor scenting conditions in the forestry. Foxes are difficult to catch on top, and the increase in badger setts is an added frustration.

The hounds kept here are all Fell types, with a lot of Blencathra and Ullswater blood. Jimmy used to keep about 30 in Kennel, but has increased this to 40. With the fencing causing a certain number of injuries, 40 is a more realistic number when hot bitches are taken in to account, and other unforeseen circumstances. This was a lesson learned the hard way, when through a variety of misfortunes 11 hounds were lost in one Season. That left a big hole, as all were under fourth season hounds. With some gifts from other packs, he got the pack built up again, but will never keep so few in future.

161

In this country, hounds must be able to work on their own, as they are often completely unsighted to their Huntsman, and in windy conditions out of earshot too, "Many a time I won't see them from start to finish. One wild day above Hawkshead I took some visitors out. Hounds put a fox off. They went round that big block by Windermere. We heard them go, and that was the last we heard. There was a howling gale and mist, and we couldn't find them at all. The car followers went all round this four mile block, and saw nothing, so I knew they must still be in there, and had perhaps put him to ground." As Jimmy walked on, hounds came back to him, "I knew there were some holes in the corner. Sure enough they'd caught their fox." Hounds had found, hunted, marked, bolted and caught their fox all completely unaided. They came back to Jimmy as if to say, 'Ok, we've done that, so what next ?'

A Hound Named Joss

"There's always character in Fell hounds. The ones I had from Johnny Richardson always had plenty." One, Joss, had already used up a number of lives when at the Blencathra, and only had one eye, "Johnny told me one day they were hunting out by Bassenthwaite. Someone was waiting at a bus stop, and when the bus arrived, Joss trotted up, and pushed in front of them. He hopped up in to the bus, and when it stopped at Keswick, he got off, and made his way back to the Kennels at Threlkeld !" He had been at walk on a farm in Langdale, and went missing for two days. Some walkers going from Langdale to Wasdale Head heard what they described as a dog barking, but muffled and they could not tell where it was. It so happened that the man they told was Edmund Porter MFH Eskdale and Ennerdale, who was working out there for the Summer. He walked up and found Joss in a borran marking a fox. On another occasion walkers again heard him in a borran. This time they thought it was someone calling for help and rang mountain rescue. So Joss arrived at the North Lonsdale with a colourful past. Jimmy recalls yet another of Joss's scrapes, "One Saturday he went missing. I searched high and low, when he didn't arrive the next day. Five days later a woman rang and asked if I had a hound missing. She said, 'We were watching the wrestling on Saturday and I got

Jimmy and the North Lonsdale hounds in rugged country (Jim Meads)

up to make some tea. It was pouring with rain and this hound pushed the door open. He shook himself, soaked us all, and lay down on the mat by the fire.'" Apart from popping outside to answer nature's calls, Joss had been living there happily all the time Jimmy was searching.

Hunting in an area where visitors roam can cause its own problems. One hound turned up in an animal sanctuary after an absence of nine weeks. Another was seen being bundled into a car and was never seen again. He was not the first to disappear without trace.

Welsh Link

An annual diversion is Jimmy's visit to Wales with hounds, in the second week of March. His great friend Tom Davies hunts the Dysynni and the two have helped each other out with hounds over the years. Last season Jimmy enjoyed joint meets with both the Dysynni and David Davies packs, "We've had some fantastic hunting there over the last seven or eight years." Through this association, some Welsh blood has been introduced to the North Lonsdale pack.

West Country Harriers Go North

Jimmy has no doubts as to the hounds required in this terrain. "They have to be mainly Fell bred." Something more experimental has also impressed the Huntsman, "If I had my time over again, I would like to breed a pack of hounds,

Fell crossed with West Country Harrier. I had a Taunton Vale Harrier from Johnny Richardson, and put her to a dog of ours. I've still got a lot of that line, as they are the best at hunting a wall top or road, or when scenting conditions are difficult. If you go back through these West Country Harrier pedigrees, a lot of them go back to College Valley lines, as do our Fell hounds, so it is not surprising that it works really. My predecessor had a trail hound called Sal '49, who was put to Blencathra Bellman '49 in 1956 and Blencathra Champion the following year so we've a fair few go back to her. She would be our foundation bitch really."

Hounds First and It's Good To Talk

Jimmy feels that a Huntsman needs different qualities in different areas, but some are universal. "To get on with everybody, that's important. Above all you have to be a dog man. I do believe the old saying that foxes are caught in Kennels. You must have hounds fit, particularly in rough country. I often say to my followers, 'I'm here to please my hounds first, farmers second, and you last'!"

Blencathra Huntsman the late Johnny Richardson who helped so many along the way (Jim Meads)

The experience he acquired in those early days with Antony Chapman and Art Irving influenced him greatly. "When I actually became Huntsman, no-one was more helpful that Johnny Richardson. He was a real gentleman. Sometimes, when things aren't going right you need someone to talk to and I could always talk to Johnny. He helped me a lot with the hound breeding as well." A Huntsman's life is not all a bed of roses and when things do not go right it can be a very lonely position, particularly when starting out, and learning along the way, " To be able to talk to someone like Johnny, who has a lifetime's experience was such a help."

One major blow was the hounds contracting a mystery illness. Again, no-one lent a more sympathetic ear than Richardson, "You are under a lot of pressure when the season is so short, and if you need to give hounds three weeks off, the pressure mounts." Extensive tests by vets and Glasgow University have failed to pin down the virus. Despite every imaginable test and post mortems no cause, or cure has been found. It is a problem which recurs every year, and must be soul destroying to a Huntsman. From being fit and healthy hounds become lethargic in a matter of hours, losing condition rapidly. Pneumonia is an added risk, and thankfully the tests have come up with a specific antibiotic to prevent this. No amount of steam cleaning, refurbishing and re-concreting yards has helped. Just one other pack in the country is known to have the same problem. Jimmy has put in a lot of work to try and find a solution over the years, but it continues to baffle all concerned, particularly as healthy pups have been whelped with no problems at all. Jimmy ranks a Huntsman's commitment to the job highly, and there can have been few harder tests than this.

Visitors Welcome

Jimmy's son has inherited his love of hunting. When Jimmy first followed the North Lonsdale on Saturdays he would take his two children in their pram. David whips in to his father, "It's a young man's job this, and he can get about well." He does this as well as shepherding his own flock and lambing 600 ewes.

The North Lonsdale are in good heart, and have an enthusiastic following. The Langdale Country Fair grows ever more successful, allied to all the usual fundraising efforts, "We are a small pack, with a small following. Yet visitors who come out always enjoy it, and often remark on how friendly we are. I like to see visitors out. Everyone is welcome here. Some areas are better viewing than others, but there is always good music in the forestry."

163

Stan Mattinson and the Coniston Hounds.
(Eric Kitchen)

 164

Stan Mattinson Esq MFH

For my first visit to the Lakes I chose Spring, just before the Easter rush. Looking at the tall dark Fells topped with an icing sugar dusting of snow, only the lambs belied the season. I stayed at Near Howe, Mungrisedale, recommended by Stan Mattinson where Gordon and Christine Weightman walk Blencathra hounds, and run a thriving guest house. Few winter visitors come for anything but hunting. It is a wonderful place to stay, relaxed, friendly and with stunning views all around. From here I would hunt with the famed Blencathra pack. These hounds are directly descended from two of John Peel's hounds, Briton and Cruel, purchased by Mr Crozier on his death, and used extensively by him during his mastership of the Blencathra. On Wednesday morning I set out for my first day with Fell hounds to the Borrowdale Hotel. The day began with a Hunt Coffee Morning. These are a regular feature, everyone pays £1 for coffee and biscuits and it proves a great way of getting to know fellow followers. There was a draw with prizes of hunting pictures, sticks and the like. A small auction raised more money in the packed room. Incredibly I met some friends of a friend, but such is the world of hunting. Hounds were boxed on a little way from the meet, and we followed in convoy. I was soon making my way up a fell side on peaty turf. Barry Todhunter took hounds to draw high above. Huntsman and hounds soon dwarfed by the surrounding country. The sheer scale of the landscape is awesome. The wind was chill and I sheltered behind a small fir covert. Hounds were well on, drawing high and right handed. I was contemplating whether to move on, when a local with a CB told me they would draw back. I waited. There was a holloa. A message crackled over that the fox is making for the road behind us. I turned to watch. A stick cracked in the covert, and a big dark fox flew the high stone wall right behind the man with the CB, who was looking uphill. I grabbed him by the shoulder, to his astonishment, manhandling him round ,"Eh up, Barry !", he spluttered into the crackling CB, "Yan lass 'as just seen't fox come over't 'wall." Two couple of hounds were ahead of the rest and we could hear them. They were only a couple of minutes behind, but in the cold drying wind scent proved very poor. I walked on, and watch them working below. The first couple of hounds sped on. I took a quick photograph, and Stan later confirmed that they were Shannon '98 and Gadfly '96. The other couple soon caught up. That fox was eventually marked in a bad borran the other side of the hill, where he had to be given best. This was a far better start than I had hoped for my first bit of Fell hunting, especially to get such a wonderful close view of that airborne fox. That afternoon I toured around the area, visiting Keswick, and going back to Caldbeck to visited the Church and John Peel's grave. The following day from the same venue the weather was really atrocious. Visibility was poor at times, and a relentless rain fell, which soon turned to slushy ice in the bitter north easterly wind. Hounds drew the rocks behind the hotel, and I found watching them picking their way over the high rock faces captivating, but we were able to see or hear very little for the rest of the day as the weather worsened. The country was as stunning as ever even in the gloom of rain, and I got a taste of the lovely Watendlath, Scafell Pike and the area around Rosthwaite. Hunting stopped before 2 o'clock, and soaked to the skin, I prepared to travel back to Threlkeld, where I would interview Stan Mattinson. We had met that morning as he was following with his wife Margery. This patient, eloquent man has a soft Cumberland accent, and a kind, open face. He apologised for the weather as if I might hold him personally responsible, "My she's a bonny la'al thing", he says of my terrier, who shows off to order.

Learning from Johnny Richardson

Born on a hill farm at Uldale, Stan's parents were keen hunting people, as were his grandparents on both sides. It was only natural that by the age of nine young Stan was already a regular follower of the Blencathra. In 1960 he was taken on as whipper-in to the late, and legendary Johnny Richardson. The old system of moving hounds around the country was adhered to. On a Monday they would

165

set out from the Kennels at Threlkeld and walk hounds to whichever valley they were going to hunt that week. They would then hunt three days in the appointed area, before returning, again on foot, to Kennels on Friday. "Johnny Richardson was a great character, and a great hound man. You couldn't wish for better. He was very quiet and unassuming really. Knowledgeable, but sensible." The key to learning from Richardson, was to observe, and learn by example. "If you kept your eyes and ears open, and were prepared to learn it was all there." Richardson's knowledge was sought after. "He was a born diplomat for hunting, that's for sure."

Stan continued whipping-in until 1973, and then concentrated on sheep farming for the next fourteen years.

The Blencathra Hounds and Some Successful Outcrosses

It was through Johnny that the Blencathra developed a close link with the College Valley. Johnny was a great friend of their Master, Sir Alfred Goodson, and naturally went to him whenever an outcross was required for his lovely Fell hounds. He first introduced College Valley blood between the late 1950s and early 1960s. Their Lawyer '51 proved a good nick, as did Playfair '58, and latterly Poacher '72. Interestingly Poacher went back to the noted low scenting line of Duke of Beaufort's Palmer '59, and Stan enthused about the Poacher progeny and their low scenting capability. Border blood proved another valuable outcross, and hounds from Mr Hedley MFH were eagerly accepted. "They did us a lot of good." Border Melody '64 was especially good. There is also a Welsh line in the Kennel. This came about because Mr Pyrse Williams MFH of the Eryri asked Johnny for a good Fell line. Johnny gave him a bitch called Ruby '66 who had a mixture of Blencathra and College Valley blood. Johnny said he would like a puppy back when Ruby was bred from. Mr Williams wanted to put her to a Welsh dog. At that time Plas Machynlleth Miller '63 was being used (sire of the famous New Forest Medyg '69). When Pyrse Williams asked the Plas Machynlleth master Harry Roberts if he could put Ruby to Miller, he recommended instead his brother Monitor, who was a better dog in his work. A doghound pup, Bellman '71 was duly returned to the Blencathra. Breeding Fell hounds has the added complication that the bitches only come in to season once a year.

Stan Mattinson and wife Margery with the Coniston hounds at Kentmere

Huntsman to the Coniston

When he saw that the Coniston wanted a Huntsman, he applied, and was delighted to succeed in 1988. He found hound breeding most interesting, and after his thirteen years at the Blencathra was given free rein in breeding the Coniston pack. At that time Mr Gregory MFH had introduced South country blood successfully, whereas Stan wanted to stick with traditional Fell blood. He introduced some Border blood and was able to use his intimate knowledge of the Blencathra hounds to good advantage in choosing Stallionhounds. Apart from a wooded area in the South of the country, the Blencathra and Coniston countries are virtually the same in type.

The Coniston still hold an astonishing six or seven Hunt Balls a season, whereas the Blencathra might opt for more modern entertainment, "They're all grand folk, but just enjoy different things like that."

Hunting the Fells

"Fell hounds are far more independent by nature. You don't need to take them to look for a fox, they'll go and find him. They'll go on until some pick up a line, then pack up together and away you go. It can be hard work, and is definitely a young man's job. You've to have hounds handy. You have to rely on them." In Stan's day there were no CB Radios. "You had to follow hounds and try to be in the right place if you possibly could. You had to be prepared to watch and see where the sheep were moving. Nine times out of ten you would be all right, but CB Radios have obviously made it a lot easier. Mind you a couple of useful chaps on the tops can signal to a Huntsman and save a lot of legwork." Lamb Worrying callouts can prove very taxing. "You'd often be out at four or five o'clock three or four days a week. Just because you started at five didn't mean it would be over in the first half hour either. You could be going until dinner time. Day in day out that can be really wearing. You have to do it, because that's what hounds are here for, to provide that service to the farmers. They welcome us, so that's how it has to be."

The Fell Hound Character

It is hard work for the hounds too, and he has a lot of respect for these highly intelligent animals. "They know their job well. You can hunt a fox one day out of the crags and maybe lose him. Next time you go there hounds will go to exactly the spot in the crag where they last found him." He feels that because they have to do so much of the work themselves they are even brighter than their cousins down South. The going can be dangerous at times in the rocks, and hounds can be working high above, whilst their Huntsman walks the sheep trods below. He can only recall two occasions when hounds got themselves stuck, "The fox is much more nimble than a hound, and can hop from ledge to ledge. If a hound risks jumping across they can miss their footing and get stuck or 'crag fast' as we call it. The Mountain Rescue Service is very good and have willingly rescued a number of hounds in the Fells over the years."

The weather can turn to make even familiar country treacherous. Thick fog can descend all too quickly or blizzard conditions reduce visibility and make the going hazardous. Stan recounts one tragic case around New Year 1961, "A young lad walked out from the village on to Saddleback. Snow and sleet was moving in as hounds left Kennels and grew steadily worse during the day. The boy was up on Saddleback Ridges with his terrier, and must have got lost in the blizzard. The Mountain Rescue Service tried hard to find him that night, but the blizzard hampered their efforts. The conditions were extremely bad. Next morning we went out, and Johnny brought an old hound called Bowfell '56. Johnny suggested going round to Sharp Edge, thinking the boy may have tried to get down there. Bowfell put his head up and scented the air. He took us straight to the boy who had sadly died from hypothermia. He had fallen over the edge and crawled in under the rock face with his terrier. It was terribly sad." This story also illustrates the nature of the Fellhound.

Bowfell '56 was particularly special, "On one occasion hounds marked in a place on Saddleback. About 300 yards away was a difficult place on Hall Fell side. Johnny bolted the fox with his terrier. He made a beeline for one of the ghylls, climbing towards the bad place. Hounds hunted him hard, except for Bowfell. He did not join in at all, but made straight for the bad place, where he headed the fox off, turned him back and caught him." Bowfell thought ahead to where that fox might go, and outwitted him.

The homing instinct is high in all hounds, but is even keener in the Fellhound. They can cross valleys into another hunting country, and still appear back at the meet, or even at Kennels. Stan definitely feels that they are that bit brighter because they must think for themselves all the time. " Of course they spend a lot of time at their walks, returning each year, and know their 'home' area particularly well from a young age. They are also very much a part of the family as far as their walkers are concerned. It all adds to their characters without a doubt."

Bitches are generally preferred by Stan for their speed, "In my opinion it takes a really good dog-hound to keep up with bitches in this country. You tend to get more effort from bitches than dogs too." At this point a knowing smile passes between myself and Mrs Mattinson !

One in a Million

Another hound that stands out in his mind from Johnny Richardson's day was a black and white bitch called Parry '54, "This bitch had come from Mr Bay de Courcy Parry, or 'Dalesman' as he was known. She was out of one of his bitches that Dalesman brought to a dog here. Johnny liked her dam, so Dalesman let him have this bitch pup, and Johnny named her after him. She became stone deaf, but never missed a trick, watching Johnny all the time." One day hounds really ran a very long way. "They just went and went. Now Parry was a very good bitch to mark. Anyway the others came back eventually, but there was no sign of Parry. Johnny had an idea where they'd gone to, and went to Bannerdale. Sure enough there was Parry, still marking." On another occasion when hounds had gone straight away she did something quite extraordinary, "Johnny was a stickler for going on after hounds. When they finally came back, they were all around him, old Parry last to arrive. So here she comes, giving mouth. She makes her way through the others, jumping up at Johnny. She then turned, and went back the way she had come. Johnny followed her into the next valley with the others. Parry had gone to where they had left their fox. She literally told Johnny, and fetched him. You get one in a million like that, or like Bowfell '56."

Hound Shows and the Social Aspect

Stan enjoyed the Hound Shows, getting hounds fit, and sharing the pride of their walkers if they won. At Fell Hound Shows, walkers hold their own hounds which adds to the excitement of the occasion for them. Rivallry is friendly, and the Shows are a great way for people from all over the Fells to meet up and have a good chinwag. All the Fell packs hold monthly draws and coffee mornings. Undoubtedly the amount of visitors early and late in the season provide a welcome extra boost. The Blencathra Sheepdog Trials are very popular, combined with hound and terrier shows, hound trailing and stick dressing.

The social aspect of hunting here is very special. As well as the aforementioned coffee mornings there are many 'Socials'. Hunting and its associated activities are very much a family thing, and it is not unusual to find several generations of one family present. Hunting is often followed by a 'Tattie Pot' and lively singing. It is something that really binds a community together. Visitors are always welcome to join in these occasions, "The people up here are really dedicated to their hunting." The Opening Hunt takes place in the second week of October. Sometimes non-hunting visitors, like those walking the Fells stop to see what is going on. Many are city dwellers, but are prepared to listen most of the time. Perhaps this is one advantage foot packs have over mounted packs where everyone is inevitably 'looking down on' passers by, "There is very little pomp and ceremony. It is quite a different way of hunting, as you have seen, but in the words of the song, 'The peasant from the cottage, the squire from the hall, all are welcome to follow'."

The Fell Fox in the 21st Century

"We love our hounds, we love our countryside, and yes, we even love our foxes. I've great respect for the fox." At first sight this difficult terrain may not appear well foxed. Stan explains that many foxes live in crags, where they simply would not be seen. They are also exceptionally well camouflaged, "They are not as timid now as they were. They see so many walkers and people about that they sit tight. Ten years ago if a fox heard hounds he'd be away. You hardly ever saw them come down into the fields. Now they can hunt almost up to a fox before he jumps up. They sometimes catch foxes like this, because they leave it too late to get clear of the pack." There are evidently a lot of mice and small rodents high in the Fells, often seen by Huntsmen as hounds draw, and he believes foxes rely

a lot on these as food, along with carrion.

Remember the Terriers
Though undoubtedly a more controversial aspect of the sport, nowhere is terrier work more vital than here, "If you had to leave a fox every time he got into a borran the farmers would think hunting was a waste of time. You really do need terriers to shift a fox from those places, its as simple as that." Many farmers are quite happy to have foxes left if they are not being a nuisance with stock. At lambing time however the whole object of the exercise is to account for foxes that are worrying lambs. Unlike lowland packs, farmers do not need to be visited by the Master, as fixtures are set from the start of the season so everyone knows where hounds will be well in advance. The only exception to this is when a farm changes hands, and a visit then is essential. There are no shooting fixtures to be planned around.

Stan is a real countryman, a sensible, reasonable man, who will explain hunting's case to anyone. One day a man approached him out hunting and said that hunting was far less efficient than his shotgun at dealing with the fox. Stan's reply was straight to the point, "Maybe, but every fox you wound will take several weeks to die of lead poisoning or gangrene. One fox wounded that way will suffer more in those few weeks than every fox I hunt in a Season." His point was taken and he explained to the man that hunting is the most selective way of taking foxes.

Stan Mattinson MFH with Barry Todhunter and the Blencathra Foxhounds on a wet morning at the Borrowdale Hotel, April 2000 (Kay Gardner)

Lamb Worrying and Nature's Ways
There is no better example of this than a lamb worrying call, when the specific fox that is causing the problem will be hunted. Barren vixens are often the most troublesome of all at lambing time, and will kill or maim many lambs, as if in spite. Stan's theory is that this viciousness may be caused by a hormone imbalance, "A barren vixen will kill for fun. Dog foxes will take the heads off and just leave the rest, sometimes chewing ears and tails. A vixen with cubs generally takes just what she needs to feed them." He believes that the vixen's lack of scent is nature's way of protecting her own, just as cubs have little scent until they mature.

Nose - Natural Ability and Learned Behaviour
I still marvel that hounds can own a line as much as four hours after a fox has left the lambing field. "They will hunt a faint line. Frost makes it more difficult for them and may well do away with the line altogether. A calm morning with a south westerly wind is ideal." It is fascinating to pondering the Fell hounds exceptional deep scenting abilities. Again, Stan has an interesting theory, "Mounted packs would not want hounds to drag on an old line. They want to get going, so if hounds hunt an old line they are lifted away from it. They aren't encouraged to do it, whereas ours are." It is an interesting

169

thought - how much is natural ability, and how much learned behaviour ? "Fell hounds can't be lifted like that, as you can't get to them. Deep scenting ability and fox sense, that is what the Fell hound must have. That is why the College Valley blood nicks so well here, and that of Duke of Beaufort's Palmer. He said Palmer was one of the best he ever hunted." Stan is very proud that Fell lines, especially that of Blencathra Glider '76 have proved so successful as an outcross in the south, "It's no good for Fell hounds to be stopping and looking back at you all the time, asking what to do next. Its much easier if they'll take it on." So what happens I ask, when hounds are well away from their Huntsman and check ? "They know their own mind. They won't keep driving on away from you, they'll pack up when a line has really run out and trace their steps back. You set off towards them and hopefully you bump into each other ! If they are nowhere to be seen then you can blow for them."

A Huntsman's Cares - and His Wife's

Stan believes strongly that a Huntsman's wife needs to be a keen hunting person to understand the commitment he must make, "It's not like a nine to five job. Especially with lamb worrying calls. You have to have an understanding wife." His own wife Margery is from the Melbreak originally and they met through hunting friends at a Hunt Social . She appears with steaming tea and hot crossed buns piled with strawberry jam, urging her husband to make me eat more. She smiles as he talks of what a Huntsman's wife has to put up with, "If you can't beat them join them I say." This has obviously worked well enough, "We've had so much pleasure from hunting. If I had my time over I wouldn't do anything else. We've made friends all over the country, just through hunting. It is a close knit community." It upsets Stan that hunting folk are abused by those opposed to the sport, and portrayed badly in the media, "There are no more genuine people. People from all walks of life all blended together, it's super, there are no class divisions. We are not killers. It is nonsense to think that without hunting

Margery Mattinson fulfilling just one part of the role played by a Huntsman's wife

170

foxes will not be killed, They will, and it will not be humanely either, not like hunting."

Stan thinks hard about the qualities a Huntsman needs, "A good countryman, preferably born in the area. Someone prepared to listen to his elders and learn. I was so lucky that way with Johnny, Harry Hardisty, Joe Weir, Antony Chapman. Then he will learn the right way. He must be keen on hounds and on the countryside. You must be very very interested in the job to be successful at it." His own method was to quietly let hounds get on with their job, "I never liked any interference, no hollering. Let them keep their heads down and they'll get on with it. Once you lift hounds' heads its difficult to get them back down again."

Full Circle - Master of Foxhounds, to the Blencathra

Mr Bill 'Bunty' Airey MFH died in the middle of the Season in 1996, as did joint master Major Phil Davidson MFH. Mr Joe Bennett MFH was left to cope alone, and needed help. He approached Stan, along with Dr Jim Cox a GP from Caldbeck. Both men accepted and became joint masters in 1997. It was a most unusual appointment for Stan, having begun at the Blencathra as a whipper-in, gone away to be Huntsman of the Coniston, to return as a master of the Blencathra, "It was very nice to be asked", he says modestly.

Barry Brings hounds to draw, April 2000
(Kay Gardner)

Yet Stan Mattinson is everything a good MFH should be in a country like this. He is a true countryman who loves hounds, takes great interest in their breeding, and understands fully the life of the hill farmer. We talk long about hounds and their breeding and rummage through photographs. After more tea I am on my way once more through the rain, wishing the Season were just beginning, rather than ending.

171

Tom Normington's skill as a horseman is well illustrated by this picture of him making light of a formidable obstacle on Harriet (Jim Meads)

172

Tom Normington

"I hope this is going to be fun, I don't want some dirge writing about me you know." These are practically the first words Tom Normington utters as I hand him a cup of tea which he piles sugar into. It would be difficult to write about Tom without it being fun. He is one of those irrepressible characters who would always make the best of a bad thing. A man with a disarmingly plain speaking manner, who knows his own mind, and believes that Life is for living.

I followed the Grafton from his last meet at Stene Park, a day of the clearest blue sky I have ever seen. Hardly ideal for hunting, but Tom made it a busy and enjoyable day for the many hunt staff and visitors who turned out. Lightly built, his skills as a horseman are second to none, a gift not all Huntsmen possess.

Of Miners and Nagsmen

Tom's Grandfather walked pups for the Rufford, and it was this that led to Tom's father, Jimmy being employed in the stables. Jimmy was one of four children, and the family's carriage hire business (including the local hearse) would not stand three sons. The old Stud Groom at the Rufford was not keen to employ the son of what he still saw as a mining family, but Mr Holliday MFH was not about to lose a good walk, and he was persuaded to give Jimmy a chance. Jimmy followed Mr Holliday to the York and Ainsty North. Tom was born at Barmby Moor near Retford, his father now whipping in. It was Jimmy Normington who first got Tom riding, being one of the old fashioned nagsmen. He would buy horses from a dealer at Kirkby Overblow, in Bramham Moor country. When they moved to the York and Ainsty South country, Tom was lent a pony to hunt. His partner in crime here was David Barker who went on to be an international showjumper, and Huntsman of the Meynell. There was a horsedealer there called Jimmy Gamble, who would bring 100 horses over from Ireland at a time to Stan Thistles Farm ready for the big sales, "All the racing and show jumping lads would come to see these horses ridden before the sales." The horses were ridden by Charlie Appleyard, later Huntsman to the Morpeth, and the ponies by young Tom. To ride so many different ponies and deal with all their quirks at such a young age is invaluable experience, so that later dealing with a difficult horse became second nature.

Whipper-in and Lead Driver

Tom left school aged 14 in the December of 1951 as in those days you left school according to when your Birthday fell. He started work in the Blankney Stables, where he stayed to the end of the Season. His father then went to the Fitzwilliam, and Tom went too. He was engaged to look after retired Huntsman, Tom Agutter's horses, which Lord Fitzwilliam provided, and accompanied him out hunting. When the second whipper-in's job came up at the Burton in 1953, Tom went there, to whip in to Charlie Mitchell. After three Seasons he left to do his National Service with the King's Troop Royal Horse Artillery. Already a very capable rider, he was made Lead Driver in just six months, which was unheard of, let alone for a National Serviceman. There were many Hunt Servants and jockeys in the Kings Troop, and it was a time Tom enjoyed very much. His Commanding Officer, Colonel Jack Spencer was a keen hunting man, whose other passion was Football. The Troop could almost have mustered a full international team. Tom was a good footballer, and went for trials with Charlton Athletic. He asked Welsh international Cliff Jones what the pay was like, as Charlton wanted to sign him up. There was a wage restriction in operation, and Tom discovered that a Hunt Servant's wages were far better than an international footballer's. How the World has changed ! Co-incidentally a hunting coat I bought at a sale a few years back belonged to Colonel Spencer, and bears the Royal Artillery Hunt Club button from when he hunted the Rezegh in Germany.

Tom's natural abilities as a horseman were fine tuned now, "When I went in to the King's Troop, I knew about good hands and leg aids. I knew just what to do, but I didn't know why you did it. It's a bit like someone learning to drive, you do it. But if you want to be a racing driver you need to know about the engine, its revs and so on. What they now call dressage was no different to what the old nags-men did before, it was just called 'nagging' a horse then."

From Army Discipline to Freeman's Way
Leaving the King's Troop he returned to the Fitzwilliam, this time to whip in to Jack Simister, "What you have to understand about Simister is that he had been taught by Tom Agutter. Now Agutter was

Time to hone skills. Lead Driver Tom Normington (left) with Wheel Driver Mick Smith and Centre Driver Tony Patterson of the King's Troop, Royal Horse Artillery at St John's Wood Barracks 1956

174

a Frank Freeman man. He was actually the only whipper-in Freeman had back. So in effect you were learning the Freeman way. Simister was smashing. Yes, he could be an old bugger ! But to him there was only one way of doing things, and that was that. It was the correct way. Once you accepted it, and did it you were all right. " Single men stood more chance of sticking to his strict regime, which left little time for family life. In those days hounds used to go on in to May and catch a May fox. Simister would then stop hunting hounds, and in his words 'let them down'. They would be sulphured and given Hankinson's worm balls, "The following week he would start hound exercise again ready for Peterborough Show. That was Summer, one week !"

Tom well remembers his first Summer, "If you want to turn any animal you don't turn and look at it, you turn the opposite way round so it can go behind your back. We were going through a village and there were milk bottles out." Tom turned correctly but did not change his whip hand to turn hounds over, and they knocked some milk bottles down, "Well, anything like that was a real crisis. He would go up in the air. He turned to me and said, 'Are you not ambidextrous ?' Well, I'd come straight out of the army and London. I had been in every kind of Club and bar you could imagine. I thought I knew a bit about Life but I'd not come across 'ambidextrous'. I didn't know what it was, so I said, 'I don't think so , Sir.' Of course that made it worse ! I looked it up in a dictionary when I got home !" Once Tom got in to Simister's way of doing things, life became easier, "My Sergeant Major could roust you up a bit, but he was a doddle in comparison." Simister would say, 'When you've been with me six months you'll see a gnat fly past half a mile away, never mind a fox!' Yet he could show great kindness, "There wasn't much money about then, but he would take you racing with him and give you a slap up meal, he would never let you pay. It was just his way, and he certainly made some good Huntsmen. You either made it, or fell by the wayside before a year was up." Hacking home one hot morning hounds caught 3 1/2 brace on the current Peterborough Showground at Alwalton.

Life in Milton Park was not without some light relief. In hard weather, Thomas, the butler would throw extra water on the lake to keep it frozen for competitions between house and estate staff. When Lord Fitzwilliam went away, Thomas would hold parties for the staff. Entertainments recalled by Tom included the young lads chasing the Irish housemaids down long corridors, sometimes with the aid of roller skates. Evidently his Lordship never did discover what was responsible for the strange marks on the floor !

Nearly A Huntsman

When Simister was injured, Tom took over hunting hounds for most of his last year, "It was a difficult time, all nature was dying because the corn had been dressed. There could be no stopping and it was really difficult. That Fitzwilliam country had a lot of plough even then and was the worst cold scenting country I ever hunted." With his father Jimmy as Stud Groom sometimes whipping in and brother Leonard second whipper-in, the Normingtons were quite a team. Tom was just 24, and Simister was to retire the following season. He knew he had made a good job of hunting hounds, and thought he would be given the horn. Lord Fitzwilliam asked to see him, and told him he could not employ him as Huntsman because he was too young. He swallowed his disappointment and stayed on another year to help Steve Roberts, who had come from the Cattistock, get to know the country, "You don't realise it at the time, but I know now how right he was. You may well be a good enough Huntsman when that young, but you lack the maturity to deal with the farmers and people. You just can't know enough about life. I still believe it is wrong to appoint very young men as Huntsmen."

To the Grass of the Grafton

Tom met his wife Ann at the Fitzwilliam, and they moved to the Grafton in 1962, "I followed Bryan Pheasey at the Fitzwilliam, and at the Grafton. We both agreed that whipping in to Joe Miller was like going to a holiday camp after Jack Simister ! That's not to say Joe Miller didn't do things properly, he certainly did, but it was very different."

The Grafton country was virtually all grass then, and not yet carved up by roads. It was a vast change from the open plough of the Fitzwilliam. Enjoying houndwork is one thing, but to enjoy the ride as well, good horses are essential. Tom says he has been very fortunate all his life in that respect, "I had horses from three marvellous dealers, Bert Cleminson in Yorkshire, later Archie Tomlinson in the Tynedale country, and when I came to the Grafton David Tatlow, so well known in

175

Mr George Fairbairn MFH, rated by Tom as the best Huntsman he has seen,
here with the Tynedale by Hadrian's Wall (Jim Meads)

the hunter world. It's the same with hounds, horses, and women ! You look for quality and class."

Joint master Colonel Foster, would never put his staff on a horse he would not ride himself, "There aren't many like that. He was a brilliant horseman, with brilliant horses. One of the real old fashioned hard-riding masters. I had three smashing years there, and I thought the world of Joe Miller."

Tynedale - Nothing To Touch It

Tom took his next step up the ladder when appointed Kennel Huntsman to the Tynedale in 1965, "There was no country to touch it, not even in Leicestershire. It was the best scenting country I've ever been in." Mr George Fairbairn MFH hunted hounds, impressing and influencing Tom greatly, "I've seen all the top amateurs and professionals of my generation, but George Fairbairn was quite simply the best Huntsman I've ever seen to hunt the fox with a pack of foxhounds. He was very under rated, because he was not in the right part of the country. He was a wonderful horseman, with the horses to do it, and the country to do it in. He was a very intelligent man, and really thought things through." This was very good scenting country, open with stone walls. Hounds would be out four to six days a week. "It would be that fast, we very rarely checked. When hounds got close to a fox he would sometimes lay down on top of a big boundary wall, and they'd be casting all around, because the scent was above them. When they got going you could cover them with a sheet, they had such quality. The heather was very high, and I've seen foxes squat down in it so that hounds run over the top of them, and he jumps up behind. Foxes were not always easy to find, and Mr Fairbairn never kept terriers in kennels. "He always said that half a good hunt was a fox well found, and did not be-lieve in bolting foxes. Hounds lose fox sense if foxes are always bolted for them." One day however at a place called Salmon's Well an old farmer said he knew where there was a fox. He led them to the place, "You would have a ditch dropping into a wooden trough and out the other side. At this place the outlet was blocked, so there was a pond." The old boy said he was going to put his terrier

176

in, "It was a long pipe, probably 40 feet long, so it must have been full of water at some point. I couldn't believe it. The terrier went in and the fox came up in the middle of the pond !" Apparently the old boy's terrier often went into this place with the same result. They really did not want to leave this country, but when the opportunity arose for Tom to go back to the Grafton as Huntsman, he knew it was his chance to fulfil his life's ambition, "We were very happy there as a family. All I'd ever thought of since I was a kid was hunting hounds. Being a Kennel Huntsman is all right, but you are not the Huntsman. Huntsmen were demi-gods to me, and when Colonel Foster asked George Fairbairn if I could go back in 1972, I knew I had to take the chance."

Huntsman at Last - Back to the Grafton

It was a chance he did not regret taking. The tradition of good horses continued under Colonel Foster, who was later succeeded by Sir Michael Connell and Mrs Ann Hawkins. Tom hunted hounds for all except the two seasons when Alastair Jackson joined the mastership, "They were wonderful times and we had such good masters. You cannot do the job without that organisation. We had some fun. I was only a second rate Huntsman with a second rate pack of hounds but we had a lot of fun, we did!" This does not do Tom's abilities as a Huntsman justice, as he showed excellent sport over 23 seasons at a time when the country was changing rapidly.

Amateur v Professional - Handling Hounds

Tom feels that those who say no amateur can be as good as a professional are wrong, "Of course they can be, as George Fairbairn was." He has also seen great changes in the way things are done, "Up to the War, hounds were handled differently. It was the way that had come down through generations. It was a very hard way. The old professionals had learned that one way, and it was really the amateurs who realised that it was possible to do things differently, by thinking it out rather than just doing it automatically."

This was mirrored at the same time by the changes in hound breeding, "Before my day, masters like Ikey Bell, then later Sir Peter Farquhar, and the late Duke of Beaufort along with Captain Wallace had realised that hounds' conformation was wrong." Frank Freeman had also realised this, devoted as he was to the old way of doing things. As hounds changed, so did the method of handling them, "Those amateurs had also realised that hounds had brains, and should be encouraged to use them ."

To Hunt a Pack of Hounds - Luck, and Quick Thinking

All Huntsmen need to be good hound men, and horsemen, with the personality to handle the job. To Tom's mind these qualities are not top of the list, "A professional Huntsman needs good masters, who will back him all the way. An amateur needs a good, loyal Kennel Huntsman." There is one thing that he puts above all this however, "Amateur or professional there is one thing they all need, and that is Luck. If Luck is on your side, fine. If it's not, you're buggered !"

He feels that many people just do not understand that the demands made on a Huntsman go far beyond the physical. From the moment hounds speak, their fox will be trying to outwit them. The Huntsman must try to be one step ahead, "A Huntsman has to have brains. People talk about brilliant casts, but all casts are no more than deduction. The brilliance of a cast depends on how fast your brain works ! A Huntsman has to have fox sense. If he's anything about him he will twig whether a fox is going straight, left or right-handed, which will help him cast. When hounds check he must work out why they have checked. From the beginning of the day you know which way the wind's blowing. You work out whether scent is good or bad on that day. Very seldom should you gallop at a check, or walk, it should be somewhere in between. You have to judge the pace of your cast according to the conditions on the day. A good Huntsman has all this ticking over." All this of course happens in the general haroosh of the chase, often with the pressure of a big Field. All decisions are made on the move and often in seconds. It is something very few people appreciate, "It's the mental pressure that gets you in the end, not the physical side. You are mentally exhausted at the end of the day." For this reason he believes it is very hard for one man to hunt hounds more than three days a week, "If you look at those packs which used to do six days a week, they always had two Huntsmen. Four days is more than enough."

Tom Normington and the Grafton hounds move off from his last meet at Stene Park (Jim Meads)

The Fox - A Funny Thing

All that said, he has enormous respect for the fox, and its intelligence, "They'll do funny things will foxes. Things you wouldn't believe." Once as hounds left a big wood, there was a line of car followers on the lane beside it. One couple were having their lunch with the doors open. Tom saw the fox go in through one side of the car, across the woman's lap and out the other side. I imagine they closed the doors pretty quickly !

Hound Breeding and Some Lines To Cherish

When it comes to hound breeding, Tom also has firm ideas, "It's very misunderstood is foxhound breeding." He believes that too many people just put a good dog to a good bitch and hope for the best without going in to the pedigrees, or line breeding to achieve what they really want, "With the number of top lines available you are very limited nowadays. You must look forward but breed back. It can take five or six years to get it right. We must never lose the really good lines, because they've all got their own characteristics. Eridge Ghurkha '65 (Old Berks Gulliver '62-Cherub '60), that was a good line. Duke of Beaufort's Garrison '58 (Duke of Beaufort's Garter '55-Arsenic '54) was another one I always kept. Heythrop Craftsman '62 (Brigand '54-Crystal '59) was a line you always wanted to see in a pedigree." The Old Berkshire Grammer '61 (Partner '57-Graceful '58) line, bred by Major W W B Scott from some of his best bloodlines is another he has found very good to hunt. He does feel that people have lost the idea of breeding hounds to suit a particular country, and dislikes the standardisation of hounds, "A pack of hounds is like a football team, you need different characteristics among them. Then they can do the job. Again it comes back to quality. If your hounds have got that they will hunt anywhere."

178

A Lucky Man

Now having retired to Gloucestershire, Tom still enjoys his hunting. Racing is another great interest, and in the Summer he likes to fish or play a round of golf with friends. His son Richard followed him into Hunt Service, but has now returned to his other love of racing, "Can we watch the 3.40 from Goodwood ?" Tom asks before leaving. A nice looking bay fills the screen, "I wanted something on that, but the bookie was shut." He adds a shade gloomily, "It'll win will that." When I offer to use my telephone account he cheers up no end. I take the 8-1, adding a little something for myself, and Tom's neighbour. Returning to the television, I note it has shortened to 7-1. Clearly must have been our money ! The horse wins doing handstands, and I fear Tom may do them too in the final furlong. I hope my account will not be closed as a result of our gamble. As the man said, it's all about Luck.

179

East Essex Huntsman John O'Shea with hounds at Panfield Hall.
(Jim Meads)

 180

John O'Shea

After travelling across to Essex in torrential rain and thunder, it was a welcome respite to arrive through a quiet leafy lane at the home of my old friend Annie Bazeley near Colchester, to find hot water, welcoming drinks and a roast supper awaiting. My terrier Minty celebrated our arrival by doing endless rounds of 'loopydog' on Annie's large and inviting lawn. After a whistlestop tour of the locality I set off the next morning with excellent local directions for the East Essex Hunt Kennels to meet John O'Shea.

An Irish Education - Horses and Hunting

As a boy growing up in County Tipperary horses and hunting were John O'Shea's life, "I was always skiving off school to go hunting. I went every Saturday and in the holidays." At just 14 he began work in the Tipperary Hunt Stables, "The set up there was spot on, run just like a racing stables, they had a Head Lad - not Stud Groom - a Second Head Lad, a Yard Man who was in charge of the grub and straw, about nine men in all. Captain Evan Williams, who had trained horses at Kingsclere also had the Knockaney Stud in Limerick, so if any horses were crocked they went there and swapped with another horse. They were all the very best horses. He was an ex-National Hunt Jockey and had won the Grand National on Royal Mail in 1937 and was very brave across country. There was nothing like the wire then, it was all grass and full of foxes." The job was seasonal, but finding work in Summer was no problem as National Hunt racing went on all year round in Eire, so John then worked with the racehorses.

A Long Way To Tipperary

It was not until he came to England that he realised how troubled his homeland was. As a youngster he was wrapped up in horses and hunting, but when he came to London to work on a building site he could see things with an outsider's eyes for the first time, "This was another world. I earned a lot of money on the building."

A Dorset Grounding - Hard Work and Discipline at the Cattistock

John's heart was still in hunting however, "I moved down to the Cattistock to work with horses at Creswells. I got friendly with the Kennel Staff, and the Kennel-Huntsman Joe Roberts asked if I fancied whipping in, and said if I started as Second Kennelman, I could get a whipper-in's job the following Season." It sounded just what John wanted, "I took the job on and I can honestly say I've never worked so hard before or since, not even on the building ! The flesh round was horrendous, and I only got one day's hunting as I never had time to go out !" As well as the sheer size of the knacker round, hounds were always fed cooked flesh, so the work seemed never ending, "Joe Roberts was a good hunting man, and if you could stick the work you had a good grounding. He took me on hound exercise and taught me the basics of whipping in then. Kennel discipline was an education really, and far stricter than racing stables." The one day John did hunt was a good one, but had a down side, "At seven o'clock Joe Roberts came over to my house and gave me a list of twelve knackering calls to be made. I went off in the Land Rover, and couldn't find half the places. There might be half a dozen farms with the same name. I was rolling around in the dark looking for dead sheep with collie dogs going at me. When I told him I didn't have time to go out hunting again he just smiled. It never did me any harm, but a lot of the lads now wouldn't believe it. Anyhow, he was as good as his word and got me a whipper-in's job with the Burghley, Lord Exeter's pack the following Season."

The Burghley

The Burghley hounds were a private pack, owned and run by Lord Exeter, and Kennelled next to the House. The country consisted of some Belvoir and some Cottesmore country, taking in some of the Fens. In contrast to what he had become used to at the Cattistock, John found life somewhat easier, and enjoyed being in the lovely setting of Burghley Park, "A lot of foxes were found in ivy on old buildings and roofs. There were three of us in Kennels. I'd got so used to tearing about I didn't know what to do with myself half the time !" Sadly the Burghley hounds were disbanded at the end of that Season, so John had to find another job, but he did not have to look far.

To the Essex and Suffolk with Eric Waldron

Eric Waldron was first whipper-in at the Fitzwilliam , and when he got the Huntsman's job at the Essex and Suffolk the following Season, he asked John to go with him in 1967. Staying for five Seasons, John met his wife Rosemary here, who did the Hunt horses. Now he too was ready to step in to a Huntsman's post.

Kennel Huntsman to the North Norfolk Harriers

John's first move as Kennel-Huntsman came when he went to the North Norfolk Harriers, "They are kennelled out at Guist now, Lady Coke's. When I was there they were kennelled just outside Cromer, and the master was Mr Shaw." Interestingly, for a man who spent so much time with horses, especially in Ireland, he says he rode the best horses ever here, "The best bar none. Oh, aye, wonderful horses. I hate big horses, but they had one there that was 18.2hh. He was some horse, too good for hunting really. He'd take on any bank or ditch. What a machine !" When not hunting hounds Mr Shaw enjoyed days with the Quorn and Belvoir where he bought these exemplary horses from Dr Tom Connors. John had great fun here with these West Country Harrier types. Harriers can be highly strung and I asked how he got on with them. "They were a bit quick, aye ! I made the mistake of getting them really fit, like you would with foxhounds. The first morning they were so sharp, whoosh, whoosh ! I thought this will be fun. I let them down a bit after that. You had to keep your wits about you with them all the time. They taught me a lot about handling hounds though. If you just kept strolling about quiet they were all right, but any sudden moves and they were looking about them and gone straight away."

Norfolk Generosity

This part of Norfolk is the most attractive and he enjoyed walking hounds out on the beautiful coastline, "We would go to the cliffs. The country all around Mundesley was really nice with fair bit of grass. The plough was light and fine, not sticky stuff." John liked the close knit Norfolk people too in this famous vegetable growing area. He arrived here not knowing the country at all, and messages left about picking up were sometimes fairly monosyllabic, "I soon got them out of that habit, the signposts were too few and far between ! When I went picking up the farmers really looked after me. I never had to buy vegetables all the time I was there. They are really, really nice people in Norfolk." The circular hare hunting however could never compare to foxhunting, "Mr Shaw was very good. He'd asked me to stay another Season, and I had agreed. When the East Essex job came up he said, 'Your heart's in foxhunting, isn't it ?', and urged me to go for it if I really wanted to. I thought that was very good of him, and have always been grateful for that."

Hunting the East Essex Foxhounds - 26 years on

Though the East Essex country is predominantly arable, it is very accessible, "There's nowhere we can't go, even when it's really wet. There are plenty of headlands, and set aside. We've no stock you see, so no wire or electric fences. Our senior master David Nott is a farmer and knows everybody. Oh aye, we are very lucky that way." Fields number between fifty and sixty, hounds sometimes out on Friday and Saturday, "I've been here since 1974, so you could say I like it ! Sure I know everybody, and the country but each day is still different. There's always something to learn with hounds." Essex is not a county that immediately springs to mind for good hunting, yet it still sustains four packs of foxhounds, with good support. Amazingly there has been just one new major bypass road since John arrived. There are some lovely pockets of country, "The north end is pretty much as it was, and is our best country. Bures and Findingfield are lovely, it's all completely rural out there with hills and valleys, beautiful. If anything it is better nowadays. Whereas there used to be more heavy

182

plough, the way it is farmed now means there is soon a covering of winter corn or rape. Once that's been sprayed in the autumn and had some good rain its just like grass as far as the hounds are concerned. When I first came there was no green at all, just plough. You couldn't pick hounds up and take them on to a grass field, as there were none, just field after field of plough. It is easier for the hounds now with that covering of greenery." John says that the fox population has increased in the last decade, but as elsewhere, the foxes do not seem to travel as far, or straight, "They always seem to be on the bend. You can't guarantee good runs in January and February any more. " Once hounds do get going though there is little to get in the way, "Oh ah, they can push on a bit. there are no roads or railways to stop them. Some of our adjacent packs aren't so lucky that way."

Hounds For a Plough Country - Surprise as the Welsh Cross Finds Favour

When I asked John about the type of hounds he favours in this predominantly plough country, there was a real surprise when he replied without hesitation, "Welsh cross. I think the Welsh hound is an acquired taste. Not many plough countries use them, but I don't find them too fast. They are a bit scatty in their first Season, but once you get them into your ways they are fine. They have tremendous cry, and certainly cover the ground. Last Season it was so wet here I was hardly ever in the same field as the hounds, so that independence works well. They have to do it themselves then. You have to trust them - they will come if you really want them. It doesn't do to upset them though. You have to get inside their heads, that's the thing, like I had to with the Harriers."

It Started at Badminton

I asked John how he came to have Welsh cross hounds, and yet again the hunting world proves a small place when it turns out that he has had many draft hounds from Badminton over the years, "They had always been good to me, and Brian started me off with some of the Welsh crosses." John received two little bitches Molly and Moppy '77, litter sisters of Peterborough Champion Monmouth '77 and his athletic brother Morgan '77 who so famously perpetuated the 'new' Welsh outcross, now so widespread, of their sire New Forest Medyg '69. "Moppy was quite outstanding, and that's what started me off with them really."

South and West Wilts Democrat '86

A later influence has been the broken-coated South and West Wilts Democrat '86 (Bacchus '83-Deluge '80) given to him by Captain Simon Clarke. "When I rang John Tulloch to ask about him he said, 'He'd hunt a fox through Woolworths on Christmas Eve ' ! *What* a good strong dog ." He certainly proved tenacious, and could be described as a 'non-change' hound who would stick to his fox come what may. "When he found a fox, that was the only one he'd hunt. We were out at Bures one day, and I was having one of those days when nothing goes right. Late in the day I put hounds in to a covert and they found straight away." It soon became obvious that a brace were in there, and when John heard a holloa at the far end, he quickly gathered hounds up to get away, and save the day. "It was quite big place and when we got away my whipper-in said Democrat wouldn't come. I told him not to worry, as I would go home that way and fetch him. We had quite a decent hunt and when we hacked back there was no sign of Democrat. I came on home and the telephone rang. It was a farmer and he said, 'Either you've got a hound tied up in wire, or he's shouting for you !' I went out there. It was four miles from where I had left him." Sure enough there was Democrat, marking his fox, furiously and in no hurry to leave ! John eventually got him away on a lead. He later showed me his son, who apparently has inherited the same traits.

Another Badminton Influence and a Low Scenting Outcross

A Peterborough Champion, Gravel '71 (Gaffer '68-Beryl '66) came to John as a brood bitch. Her paternal grandsire, appropriately enough, was Tipperary Growler '64, and her paternal grand dam Woeful '60 had also been an outstanding bitch who won the Peterborough Championship unentered in 1960, "When Brian brought them out I thought she'd slipped through by mistake ! We've had a lot of Badminton blood. The late Duke and Brian were very good to me. Whatever Brian said about a hound was always spot on. There was never any 'bull'. "

John has one Dumfriesshire cross bitch, Primrose, "She's by a Suffolk dog out of a Dumfriesshire bitch. I wouldn't want purebreds, but she has a very good nose and is really sharp."

"My Best Mate" - Paddy, of course

John came to pick up drafts from Badminton most years. Long-serving Whipper-in Denis Brown would help him load them up. Denis is a quiet man, who does not waste words, John quickly summed him up to be shrewd though, "He rarely said too much, but this one day, as we loaded the hounds, I was taking a doghound called Paddy '81 (Parker '77-Focus '78) Denis said, 'You realise you are taking the best working hound in the Kennel.' I took notice of that." John had asked Brian for a Stallionhound and now a three or four Season hound who had been successfully used by his own Kennel and others, Paddy fitted the bill. Aptly named he possessed lines to Carlow Grumpy '38, Kilkenny Teacher '45 and Tipperary Growler '64, one through the aforementioned Gravel '71. He also possessed the invaluable blood of Duke of Beaufort's Palmer '59 (Portman Pedlar '55-Precious '53) in some quantity. John was to find him indispensable, "He was so biddable and intelligent." He was still hunting well in his ninth Season, and was used by several neighbouring packs including the Thurlow and the Puckeridge. "Every day we hunted, he was out. He never missed and never had a toe down. He had depth and was muscular right up to the end with a good strong back." Paddy's only physical problem was his teeth, "We've a lot of concrete land drains here, and if a fox got in to one, Paddy would be there going at the concrete pipes. Gnawing those broke his teeth. He was a great dog to mark." One morning Paddy keeled over in the feed yard. A massive stroke killed him instantly, "That was a bad morning, I can tell you." The only consolation was that John was spared seeing the old dog decline, and having to make the decision all Huntsmen dread. For his old friend made the decision for him, as fit and strong as the day he had arrived. John shook his head, "He was the best foxhound I have ever known, aye. Like hunting with your best mate."

A Family Concern

At one time both John's sons worked with him, one son Paul doing the terriers, whilst his other son Patrick whipped in. Patrick is still here in his second season, having spent time at the Worcestershire, Grafton and in Kentucky, "It works very well between us, and he knows his job. He'll be looking to move on before too long."

There has occasionally been confusion between people concerning this John O'Shea with the John O'Shea who hunted the Cheshire. Apparently they are distantly related, but John told me a story to

John O'Shea brings hounds to an end of Season meet. Behind him are retiring joint master and joint Hon Secretary Mr Guy Lyster and his wife Gill, retiring joint Hon Secretary (Jim Meads)

illustrate this. One day four years ago he was out picking up, and returned to find the drawyard door open. In there were two greyhound pups, "Their papers were there, marked for John O'Shea from M Flanagan. He was the Kennel Huntsman at the Tipperary. I rang his wife. Turned out they should have gone to John O'Shea in Cheshire, who trains coursing greyhounds ! I had sent some hounds to Ireland by courier in the past, and the driver just saw the name, without looking at the address."

What it takes to be a Huntsman - Patience and Psychology

John has the relaxed approach to life so often apparent among his countrymen, and he believes this is an important quality for a Huntsman to have. "It's no good getting flustered. You have to keep your head even if all around you are losing theirs. If you get flustered, everything goes. You must keep calm and let the hounds do their work. Pressure is of your own making. Go out and do your job, and enjoy it." Again he puts emphasis on a Huntsman knowing his hounds' personalities, "You really do have to get inside their heads."

The Agility of a Fox . . .

Hounds once hunted a fox to the sea wall, "We'd had a nice hunt, and they crossed a big dyke on to a grass track beside the wall." John saw their fox go over the wall. The tide was lapping up the wall, and as he looked over he saw the fox running the vertical wall, "It was greasy as hell, and the hounds just went straight in to the Sea. there was this fox running like someone on the wall of death. It must have been speed that kept him there, he was flat out and at such an angle !" Hounds were struggling to get out as John blew for them. All were fine, but 'Charlie's' clever move saved him, "It's an amazing thing, the agility of a fox."

. . . and a Pony

Ponies too can be agile of course, "Years ago, I got away with hounds, there was just a child with me. I wish I could remember his name. Hounds were really going and we ended up in the Essex country. When we came to the River there were three strands of wire and a deep bank in. Hounds were over it and gone 'psst!' just like that. I jumped off and cut the wire. I said to the boy, ' Don't follow me, wait for the Field to come up.' He turned that pony's head and 'pssst!' shot straight past me. You've seen how a moorhen scuttles across water ? Well that's what that pony did, straight across. There was I, my horse up to his belly struggling to get out. The fieldmaster came next and broke his collarbone. One other horse got over, that's all. That pony was extraordinary, so agile. It really stuck in my mind. No way was that boy waiting, he was away with hounds !"

Influences

Tom Batterbee long serving Huntsman to the Suffolk influenced John, and he regarded him as a great plough Huntsman, "Looking back now, to when I was very young I realise Captain Williams at the Tipperary influenced me a lot. He never interfered with his hounds. They were the best pack of bitches I have ever seen without a doubt. I've never seen a pack go like them. I wouldn't want to be a fox with them about, you'd soon just be a cloud of steam ! They had 130 brace a Season. They were really sharp."

In Good Heart

Through pouring rain, I followed John's tall, lean frame across to the Kennels. It is an immaculate little set up, and from the road you simply would not know it was there. Even the building of a new housing estate next door has caused no problems. John also cares for the De Burgh and Essex Bassethounds. They came pottering in from the rain as he showed me some nice looking foxhounds, including Democrat's broken coated son. John tells me in his gentle brogue that he worries about the lads in Hunt Service today. He feels they lack the opportunity of a real apprenticeship in many cases, "I hate seeing them chucked in at the deep end." Another worry is the number of young amateurs he sees coming in, often with little experience, taking jobs and houses the young professionals need to progress. For all that though he believes the sport to be in good heart, despite the political climate. So long as there are professionals like John O'Shea providing continuity in countries such as this there will always be a future. I certainly found it a very heartening experience to find hounds thriving here in the county of Essex.

David Palmer Esq. MFH, seen here hunting the Ludlow
(Jim Meads)

David Palmer Esq MFH

It is not difficult to see how David Palmer earned the nickname Charmer Palmer. When we first met it was a filthy wet day, and I was evidently somewhat preoccupied. I later had occasion to ring him, and as we chatted about hounds he suddenly said, "You're not as frosty as I thought you were !" He subsequently asked me to join his lunch party at Builth and we became firm friends. He still calls me 'Frosty', and it is a name I now sometimes use when writing reports. I felt rather better about this when I discovered it had been the name of one of his favourite hounds. Once at Ardingly it was so cold and wet that those mad enough to be there at all huddled in the grandstand in a howling wind. I was reporting the Show, and my fingers were numb. The arrival of David bearing two whisky macs certainly made the world a better place. We watched the remaining classes, and he shivered so much my pen would hardly stay on the page ! At that time he had retired from hunting the Ludlow, and I was delighted when he rang one evening to tell me he was about to join the Worcestershire mastership, and breed the hounds. Our terriers played on the lawn of his Worcestershire Farm whilst he talked with great feeling about his hounds.

Early Days with the Albrighton Woodland
David told me, "Looking back I cannot remember a time even in infancy when I wasn't fascinated by hounds." Though not from a hunting family, hounds were always about and he would sometimes see them on exercise in his home village. He was at school with the son of Albrighton Woodland MFH Lionel Rowe. David started to ride aged about 12 and became a member of their Pony Club, his first day's hunting was from the Pony Club Meet. Throughout his early teens he spent many happy hours with this pack, and although, unlike many amateurs he came to hunting through his love of horses, the hound work soon became very important to him, "I was fascinated by the horses, hounds, countryside and foxes. I was completely bowled over by it, and that feeling has never gone away."

Mr David Palmer MFH with Mr Lionel Rowe MFH, who was such an influence

Wyre Forest Beagles
When David married Annette, he realised that keeping horses was no longer financially viable. Hunting by car held little appeal, so he decided to try beagling. He started going out with the Wyre Forest. "They made me so welcome. Of course I realise now that enthusiastic young blokes are like gold. Just half way through that first Season he was asked to whip in, "It was Paradise ! " When he saw the mastership advertised that same season in 1966, he applied, "I had no thought of doing it at all until then. I imagined the professional Huntsman would carry on and hunt hounds anyway. " No-one was more surprised when at interview the rhetorical question 'You will of course hunt hounds ?' was posed. The Huntsman of 24 years Reg Clarke could not have been more help, "I was so lucky. He had been with foxhounds until injuring his back. By co-incidence he had returned to his home village to work here. He was a very good teacher and really wanted things to work from the start." During the Summer David hunted with the Hawkstone and the Border Counties Otterhounds. He was one of an enthusiastic bunch of young men who watched Captain Wallace, Antony Hart and Ray Williams, "We watched and emulated everything they did. Tony Collins was there, Antony Adams, it was like a University course in hunting. We sometimes got roared at but it was great fun and very interesting." Another keen otterhunter was Derek Jones from the Penhow Beagles. The two became lifelong friends and Derek's knowledge about breeding beagles was to prove a revelation,

"What I had yet to learn about was the breeding side. Mixing more widely with all these people in the hunting world was an important part of the learning process." A major turning point came when he invited Derek to bring the Penhow for a day in Wyre Forest country, "We had a good first season in 1966 and hounds caught 14 brace. I was practising all my Wallace noises ! You can imagine, can't you ?" He laughs, looking almost embarrassed, "The following season we were attracting large crowds and there was a good social atmosphere. As a Huntsman you are a bit like hounds, success begets success and gives you confidence. When the Penhow came, I suddenly realised we were not even in the same league. They were incredible. My learning curve rose very sharply and I had new targets to aim for, new ambition." As a master hunting hounds it is not always possible to find time to see other packs at work, "It has to be a retrograde step really. The Pen How coming here proved such an eye opener." The Pen How Beagles had a very strong female line, "It was based on a wonderful bitch called Dummer Wedlock '57, and I became determined to breed our hounds up. I knew now that you could not improve a pack just by using good Stallionhounds. Both sides of the pedigree had to be good, and strong female lines are everything. We were never as good, but we got in to the same league. There is nothing like that feeling when you know you have good hounds around your heels."

Busman's Holiday in Devon and a Silver Horn

One annual event greatly looked forward to was a week long trip to Taw Vale country in Devon. The Wyre Forest country had an abundance of hares, and the Taw Vale had rather fewer. Sometimes the Wyre Forest would finish early to avoid catching too many Devon hares. One year the North Dartmoor visited the Wyre Forest and invited them for a day during their Devon sojourn, "Before the meet at Postbridge Mrs Nestling MH Taw Vale, who was a dear old lady, asked if I would like to hunt hounds using Kathleen's horn." Kathleen Varndell was Mrs Nestling's half sister, and was a very well known character. Kathleen's father Sidney was master and huntsman of the Crowhurst Otterhounds. For her 21st Birthday supporters had bought a silver horn, and she hunted the Crowhurst that day using it. When she came to Devon she hunted the Dartmoor Otterhounds. I had already heard much about her from friends who recalled hunting with her, "Kathleen was famous for blowing this horn without taking her fag out of her mouth, and I had seen her doing this when Mr Rowe took me out for a day." The horn, rather green was duly produced, "My hounds had been out every day and really weren't liking the gorse. I saw this field of swedes, about five acres, not what you expect to find on Dartmoor ! I put them in and Hugh Whitley who was acting as our host called out, 'You aren't in Warwickshire now you know. You won't find in there, they aren't Brussels sprouts !' He had hardly said it when, whoosh! up went a hare. We had a brilliant day. They ran and ran, and I never caught up to cast them. They did a huge circle and brought their hare back past the Field. The lead hound overtook the hare and they came back towards her to catch her. The only other time I saw a pack do that was the Exmoor who I once saw overtake their fox and run back to kill him." David handed back that lovely horn to Mrs Nestling, who insisted he should keep it, "Little did I imagine when Mr Rowe took me to see the Dartmoor Otterhounds that I would ever own that horn." He never hunted hounds with anything else from that day on. Though he loved his beagling and the tenacity of the little hounds he bred, who gave so much, he missed the haroosh of foxhunting. The Wyre Forest country was vast, stretching right across to the sea, and encompassed the countries of no fewer than 14 packs of foxhounds. This meant he kept very much in touch with the foxhunting world, as well as honing his organisational and diplomatic skills. One night he rang the master of the Clifton-on-Teme, John Shearer (who had also been master of the Albrighton Woodland) to clear a meet and was told that the mastership was splitting up, and that he should consider applying for the 1978-79 Season, "I couldn't really afford it, but the temptation was just too much !"

Clifton-on-Teme Foxhounds.

At last, after 12 Seasons' Beagling he was able to give up running and get back in the saddle in 1978, "I was lucky enough to drop on some good horses cheaply. It was bliss really." It was perhaps understandable that some members had voiced concern as to the new master's ability in the saddle, unaware of his early grounding. For the Opening Meet he rode a horse, Airboy, which could take on any fence from a trot. The keen new master was eager to impress, "I had a brand new coat, purple collar and twinkling buttons." Hounds found in a field of swedes - perhaps a Palmer speciality after that Dartmoor run, "I thought, 'Now I'll show them who can ride.' I'd already had a few on the floor cub hunting. I trotted at the gate and just before Airboy took off he trod on a swede, tripped and breasted

the gate." David was propelled vertically up his neck, a button catching the bridle on the way up taking it clean off. The rest of the twinkling buttons flew off one by one as the master went into orbit with his bridle, and Airboy disappeared into the wide blue yonder, "My whipper-in trotted up and said, 'Quick get on this and they'll never know.' He was on a little hog maned cob and my horse was a big chestnut !"

Strengthening the Female Lines - and Valid Shows the Way

Having learned his first hound breeding lesson with the Beagles David quickly set about upgrading the pack's bitches, "At the Wyre Forest I had naively tried to breed from good dogs and poor bitches. I now knew from that experience that exemplary bitches were everything, "Charles Stirling MFH Cattistock gave him some very good hounds. Derek Jones was by now master of the Silverton and gave him some very good ones, "One, Clifton-on-Teme Valid '82 was out of a bitch called New Forest Valour '75, a brilliant bitch given to Derek by Sir Newton Rycroft. Valid '82 was talented beyond belief and became the mainstay of my breeding." One day he saw Valid find a fox below an electricity pole, on a thick bank. "It was a place we only went to once a year. Twelve months later when we went there, she went straight to that pole. With Beagles and Foxhounds

Another big chestnut, but this time the partnership is very much intact !

there are always one or two that never really move from the last place they had the line at a check. We had a beagle called Warwickshire Worthy '68 at the Wyre Forest who was like that."

Learning the Hard Way - For Hounds and Huntsman 1978-82

The Clifton-on-Teme country has steep banks and thick woods, "I had a wonderful terrierman, Roger Powell who was very intelligent and taught me how to cope with those woods. It was a wonderful place to learn the hard way. It is well foxed but so thick that finding the fox is a terrific achievement in itself. I learnt then that finding a fox is such a lovely part of hunting. No human being on earth could get through those brambles but you have to teach your hounds to do it. They have to be keen enough to do it, however uncomfortable. You stand there and know they are going in. You listen for the crackling and every now and then a head or a stern appears yards away. Then, 'Yow ow ow!" It's *terrific* ! They won't do that unless they know where you are. It's no good putting them in and galloping to the other end to blow for them, they'll come round the outside. You have to wait and make enough noise so they know you are there, and that they are doing it for you. They'll go miles in then. I think that's why I've always been a bit noisy. Once they succeed like that, and keep succeeding they'll go in to the most vile places for you, find their fox and fight their way out to move him." To get a fox away from such a place is but short lived relief for in this country, just a few fields later the fox can go in to another place just as bad, "I think they were a very talented pack of hounds to do that and would have been quite something in more open country. It is so difficult for them, and stopping is so difficult too so most foxes get to ground. I was very lucky to have been given such good lines to use." Hounds once checked in a garden, where their fox was seen lying across the ridge of the roof. Foxes in trees were also a feature in Clifton country, and five once came out of a pollarded willow. One day Miss Mary Rouse Boughton of the Ludlow rang and asked, "If we offered you the mastership here, would you come ?" David had long dreamed of hunting this adjacent country, which was similar but more open, "There was more space between coverts, and it was even better then than now." That he would go was beyond question.

*Mr David Palmer MFH and the Ludlow hounds
crossing a stream. (Mrs Jean Griffiths)*

Fulfilling a Dream at the Ludlow 1982-96

The Ludlow had enjoyed much show ring success in earlier years and were a good pack. David is a great believer in breeding hounds for a country, and was very grateful for the total support of Miss Mary Rouse Boughton who backed whatever he wanted to do. He had already proved the success of a Welsh outcross in the Clifton country, "I left my cross breds behind at the Clifton, but brought the handful of bitches who had been their dams. Mary Rouse Boughton let me introduce cross breds here too." Both the Clifton and Ludlow countries need deep scenting hounds who can do things themselves as it is not always possible to be with them. Voice is paramount for the same reason. The streak of Welsh independence suited the country perfectly. David Davies Guardsman '79 and Teme Valley Lodger '88 were used as well as some of the Kennel's own Stallionhounds. The new out-crosses proved their worth. Another bitch was sent to Berkeley Pollard '77 (Portman Pilot '71- Coral '73), "That lovely blood nicked very well and did us a huge amount of good." As at the Clifton he also had some hounds from Michael Rowson at the South Shropshire. The mixture really operated, "They

190

Ludlow Hounds (Jim Meads)

were brilliant. I loved them. I had that feeling again as I did with the beagles, of knowing they were really good. To have those sharp, brainy little hounds by your side, knowing that when you let them on they would keep at it was wonderful. Hounds are such rewarding creatures."

Proving Themselves and Visiting the Beaufort

"I have always been fairly laid back really and loved big Fields because I knew my hounds would not let me down." This confidence was never more soundly proven than when the Ludlow visited the Beaufort Monday country. These smaller hounds just kept at it all day impressing all who saw them, and it is a day still talked about.

Frosty '86, a Great Kennel Huntsman and Dream's End

Valid '82 bred him Frosty '86 (Ludlow Freeman '83 -Valid ' 82), who was to prove a real star. She remained so fit that it was almost impossible to distinguish her from her daughters. On his retirement from the Ludlow in 1996 David was presented with a bronze of Frosty by Priscilla Hann. "That Brecon 'V' line is brilliant."

Another major factor in the pack's success was Kennel-Huntsman Austin James, "He loved them, and they loved him back. They were very happy. On hunting days they always looked to me, but once we finished they were his. He's a great chap and hounds really love him." David was here for 14 seasons, "The best of my time there was smashing. During the second half of my mastership farming changed, and the arable land increased. The younger farmers were still happy to see us, but the freedom we had earlier had gone." Eventually these changes, the familiarity with the country, and the 45 minute journey from his own farm to the Kennels took its toll, "It was unbelievable to me. I gave up because I wanted to after hunting hounds for exactly thirty seasons."

Capture Their Hearts, and the Rest Will Follow

Few can express the bond between Huntsman and hounds as eloquently as David. I asked him his fundamental theory as to what makes the hound/Huntsman partnership really tick, "My big theory is that what makes a pack good is only partly in the breeding. That makes a difference to nose talent and physique, but I truly believe that properly managed by a good Huntsman you could have very good sport with big, ugly, indifferent hounds. You must get their hearts in the right place. It all amounts to making your hounds believe in themselves. Once they have that confidence it snowballs and provided they believe in themselves most hounds are fast enough with good enough noses to do the job. Cry and nose are vital of course, and you always try to breed those in, and the better equipped they are, the better they will hunt. As I said earlier success begets success. You must set up the conditions for them to do it by taking them to coverts where they will find, giving them time,

191

and keeping the Field far enough back. You must encourage them properly without interfering at every turn. It makes all the difference. Too many Huntsmen try to hunt the fox themselves. I have seen some beautifully bred hounds produced by a second rate Huntsman who were hopeless. It is so important that hounds are managed by a man who understands them and can get to their hearts. That's what makes them *want* to do it."

A Unique Experience

For a Season, David hunted wherever he pleased and found this very refreshing. After Christmas he had what must be a unique experience, hunting three packs of hounds. Myles Salmon MFH Wheatland injured his back so he hunted them for two days. Then Austin James, now hunting the Albrighton Woodland injured his back and David hunted them for a week. Roy Tatlow MFH at the Clifton-on-Teme could not hunt hounds one day, so he returned to that difficult country. He is typically modest about this achievement, "The horn is a universal language." The Albrighton Woodland pack, which he feared might miss their Huntsman most of all followed him straight away, despite his strange horse, "Hounds want to hunt foxes, and once they stop looking for 'the boss' they fall in with whoever carries the horn." He makes it sound very easy ! David was enjoying many local days with the Worcestershire at that time, and it became a standing joke that he would ask their then Huntsman Julian Barnfield if he was feeling all right ! After this brief interlude, the novelty of responsibility-free hunting was beginning to wear off. Again with perfect timing the telephone rang, and he was asked if the Worcestershire mastership would appeal to him.

Golden Years at the Worcestershire

David was uncertain how mastership without hunting hounds would suit him, as he was entering hitherto uncharted territory. The Worcestershire are a good pack of hounds, with good country and plenty of support, not least from some very knowledgeable farmers. His first challenge came with the resignation of Huntsman Julian Barnfield, who was to return to his native Cotswold country. He searched carefully for the right man to succeed him, and found Ian Starsmore, who was at the Albrighton, "I knew he was right straight away, and this was borne out by the way he used the autumn for some very patient venery." Although he confesses that not carrying the horn was a strange at first, he quickly settled down to the idea, "I have such total confidence in Ian. I enjoy

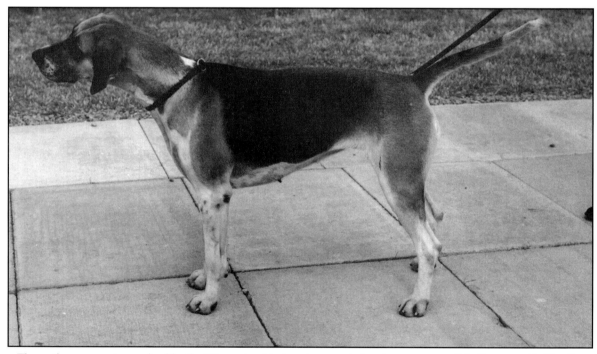

The author was not surprised by the Worcestershire's subsequent showing successes this Summer. At Honiton they won the Bitch Championship with Worcestershire Policy '99 (S Shropshire Ptarmigan '94—Caption '95) . It seems the Golden Years are only just beginning.
(Terry Crate)

192

Admired by many at the Ringside during Builth 2000, where they were runners up this beautifully matched Worcestershire quartet won at Honiton, where Policy who went on to take the Championship was joined by sisters Poppy, Posy and Polish.
(Terry Crate)

knowing enough about hunting to set it up for him. I involve him in the hound breeding, and we understand each other well. I am not remotely jealous, and he knows that I am not a threat to him. I enjoy the hunting without the pressure of having to provide sport. I have it made really, running the Kennels and staff, breeding the hounds and field mastering in the best of the country." He has also recently been appointed to the MFHA Committee. His son Giles accompanies him in the hunting Field, and sometimes gets sent over the bigger obstacles first.

Ian brought a bitch called Albrighton Glamour '96 with him. She is part Old English, and has now produced a litter. Cotswold Caistor '92 (Brocklesby Colonel '88-Bashful '88) has been used to introduce more Old English blood which it is hoped will improve nose and cry. A more experimental venture is a French crossbred called Bonaparte '94 (Dumfriesshire Bordeaux '92-Countess '89) , found for him by Captain Simon Clarke, "His bottom line is classic New Forest and the top line is a French dog on a Dumfriesshire bitch. He has that typical domed head and lugubrious expression, a wonderful voice and a very good nose. I was standing with three former masters of Foxhounds Ken Parsons, Frances Meier and Edward Davies when we saw a fox come out of covert, cut the corner off and go back in. Hounds roared up over the wire and could not pick up the line on the grass. He came up and locked on to it, 'Ow ow ow', taking the line back into the wood. They all went to him though they could not own it themselves until back inside. He could detect the line when even the Welsh crossbreds could not." He now has a litter of pups in the Kennel. We saw some useful young hounds from the Worcestershire at last year's shows. Now proving themselves in the field it would be no surprise to see the pack really make its mark in the next few years. David clearly relishes breeding them and watching them work, "I enjoy having Giles with me too. These are golden years for me." Golden years indeed even if the silver horn now stays in its case.

Bicester Huntsman, Bryan Pheasey
(Jim Meads)

194

Bryan Pheasey

Bryan Pheasey is one of those Huntsmen whose picture I had seen for years, but knew little about. He is a very unassuming man, who rarely talks about his career, with a deep love of hounds and a real sense of fun. I felt privileged indeed to visit him and wife Nora at their Oxfordshire home, where I enjoyed a delicious lunch, and a fascinating insight into the life of one of hunting's most popular men. Bryan Pheasey was born at Etwell. His mother a parlour maid and grandfather a saddler, "We'd always loved hunting as a family." When he was a boy his father was Stud Groom to Captain Sweeting, their cottage in the stableyard. Mr Pheasey would accompany Captain Sweeting, who had been wounded in the War, "They did two days with the High Peak and two with the Meynell. I used to clean all the tack. The Meynell days were worst as they'd be plastered in clay. Mother would play hell if I was still there after 9 0'clock at night. I was only a schoolboy then. My five bob a fortnight would be sent down in a proper wage packet from the Estate Office !" In Summer, ponies were taken for breaking and it was not long before young Bryan was given the smaller ones to ride. He then hunted them and once going freely they were sold on. It was all valuable experience for this already keen foot follower of the High Peak Harriers. One day in the 1935-1936 Season Bryan had been following on foot. Hounds finished at 4pm and he made his way back to the box. Boxes were rare in those days, this one having been constructed from a Rio Speedwagon which had been the first charabanc in Buxton. By the time he arrived, it had already left, and he was faced with a six mile walk home. He set off, and was approached by car followers - a novelty in those days - who asked him how to get to Bakewell. He said he would tell them if they dropped him off home first!

High Peak Foot Follower at a meet, Bryan Pheasey - bare knees and gloves !

A Brace of Buxtonians

Bryan first took Nora home from a Sunday school dance when he was 16. He volunteered for War service when he was just over 17, and was to become a wireless operator/air gunner. When Nora saw his crew cut she was less than impressed, "Haircuts were free, but if you didn't slip the barber sixpence he'd make a right mess of it", Bryan laughs. Undaunted, he wrote to her, failing to impress her again with his spelling, though with RAF education this improved. When he came home on leave he was asked to make up a foursome by some friends, walking in the Spring Gardens. His 'blind date' was Nora. They have now been married just over 50 years.

Bryan's first job after the War was as second horseman for Mrs Staveacre in 1947. Jobs were still scarce, "Work was with the arm not the head and I was lucky to get a job at all." George Steele, Huntsman to the High Peak then told Bryan the whipper-in was leaving and asked if he would be interested. He accepted, so he and Nora moved out of their lodgings with her parents who were Steward and Stewardess of the Union Club, to the Kennels in 1950.

High Peak High Jinx

Masters of the High Peak were the remarkable Misses Wilson. These twins were in their 70s by this time and still dressed identically. For hunting they wore beautiful green habits and specially made top hats. On one occasion they accompanied hounds to parade at the White City, "It made a marvellous spectacle." The whole thing was quite an adventure as the Hunt horses hacked everywhere and had never been in a box before, "George Steele was a good man to start with, his main asset being his enthusiasm for hunting. If you are keen on any sport you go along wondering what will happen. You

195

are excited by the prospect of it. That's how George got me feeling about hunting. Every day was something you looked forward to." The High Peak Harriers' country was entirely their own, so though hares were the primary quarry, foxes could be hunted as well. The Misses Wilson were not keen on hounds doing too much foxhunting, as they felt it made them too wild. George Steele however loved his foxhunting, and unbeknown to them would call round and take Bryan earthstopping the night before hunting ! "If we found one it was thrilling. Away they'd go to Maunsel Dale if we were in the North, or Dove Dale in the South." This was lovely stonewall country, unspoilt and wire free. Sometimes if hounds ran in to the Meynell end they would make a diversion to jump a hedge, for the sheer novelty. Such a novelty in fact that the horses would refuse as they had forgotten what hedges were ! Much of the central country was owned by the Duke of Devonshire, who hunted a little, as did his sisters.

When hard weather curtailed hunting, Miss Violet Wilson was unbowed, "Nothing will stop me enjoying some sport", she declared and went ice skating. Unfortunately she fell and broke a hip, and when hospitalisation became essential insisted that her sister be put in the next bed, so inseparable were the twins.

The Misses Wilson (Jim Meads)

Bryan enjoyed six seasons here, the Misses Wilson retiring in the fifth when Hunt Secretary John Morton took over. George Steele was a great influence, with infectious enthusiasm for the sport He had been at the Pytchley before the war and many believed him the best whipper-in in England, "He was some horseman. Whatever he got on just operated for him." He impressed upon Bryan the importance of loyalty and tact. They invariably rode home in the dark and sighting a car was a rare event. One night they heard a car coming and pulled hounds well over. An Austin Seven, lights like candles roared by, and never even saw them.

Counting Hounds - A Cautionary Tale

George Steele taught Bryan the importance of constantly counting hounds, and his reasoning was indelibly underlined by one incident which could have been disastrous. Hounds had met at Middleton Hall, home of Captain Waterhouse MP. After drawing one covert, Bryan made them a couple and a half light. He went back, but there was no sign of the missing hounds. At the end of the day, hounds

Bryan holds a High Peak Peterborough Champion under the admiring gaze of the Misses Wilson (Frank H Meads)

 196

were hacked back past the covert. It was now dark. The rest of the pack started to go in to the wood, they drew nearer, enticed by the sound of hounds singing. Those missing hounds had fallen through a rotten wooden cover into an old lead mine shaft. Quickly realising what had happened the others were pulled back, "I have never seen anything like it. Part way down there was a platform, also very rotten, which they had fallen on to. It was no more than about ten feet in diameter. It was a miracle that in their panic one had not been pushed off in all that time. Captain Waterhouse was a very brave man. Because it was his covert he felt responsible, insisting that he, rather than one of us, should be lowered on ropes to fix up a ladder and get them out." Had Bryan not counted those hounds both in to and out of the covert, no-one would have known where they had gone missing, and they would never have been found.

Out of Derbyshire

Bryan had set his heart on going to the Grafton, so when George Davis handed in his notice he applied in 1955. However Davis's job fell through, leaving Bryan without a position. Grafton Huntsman Joe Miller came to the rescue, ringing the Fitzwilliam. They still had a vacancy, and as time was getting on Bryan accepted. Though he stayed for only one season, it was a chance move which proved wholly successful and was to make a major contribution to his future career.

A Move in the Right Direction

The Fitzwilliam Huntsman at that time was Jack Simister, "That Season really set me on track. He took some standing, but he was dead right. Once we had to clear the course at Huntingdon racecourse, myself and the Cambridgeshire whipper-in. This happened every Bank Holiday, the horses were provided by a dealer, and if you hadn't been bucked off by 3 o'clock you were doing well !" At the end of the day Bryan walked back to the car with Simister who had been enjoying the day's racing, "I smoked then and lit a cigarette. He told me to put it out, as no-one should be seen smoking in a red coat. I hated to see that myself later on."

The Fitzwilliam hounds were big Old English types who did not suffer fools gladly. Their sheer size made them difficult to handle. Combined with a difficult temperament it did not make for an easy life. "The water was so hard there that hounds developed kidney problems, so we had to save soft rain water off the kennel roof. If you were 'on the wheel' one of your jobs was to go in to the lodges about 8pm and push all these hounds out, so that they would drink some of the soft rainwater. Well, you can imagine, on a hunting night those big old doghounds took some shifting. They were like lions !" Their intractable nature made many routine jobs quite hazardous. The whipper-in's belt had to have a slit in it, so that it could be looped to form a makeshift muzzle. Then if one of the hounds picked up a thorn on the way to the meet it could be safely handled.

"Mr Simister was a great man, hard but never showed you up in front of others. Nine times out of ten he'd say, 'Don't take any notice of me boy', on the way back in the box. He was just fired up, and had that sort of treatment himself. After that you put yourself in the right place. You had done things before anyone else had thought of them !"

Grafton whipper-in Second Time Lucky

The following Season George Davis did leave the Grafton, and Bryan was able to move. Yet he did not regret the year he'd spent with Simister ,"You got sharpened up."

Colonel Foster was senior master, "He was a man and a half. Once Joe had an accident and I hunted hounds, Colonel Foster then hunted four days. I had the privilege of whipping in to perhaps the best horseman I've ever seen, and not at all jealous if you could get in front of him in a good hunt. He employed me on May 1st and said 'Good Morning', then didn't say 'Good Morning' again until September 1st. His way, if he was unhappy with a whipper-in, was to talk to Huntsman Joe Miller. Joe was a really kind gentleman. I had five very happy seasons with him. They weren't the prettiest hounds, but it didn't stop them hunting and certainly didn't slow them down !"

Well Horsed - and Hounded

Horses were very good at the Grafton, and, Bryan often found he had a lot of horse under him, "One, well you just couldn't hold him. On the way to first draw some young hounds went on a hare.

197

I stopped them, and overtook the hare ! Then I was going round and round. I let him jump into the next field and went round that instead where the others wouldn't see me. A brace went away, and I jumped in right behind Joe Miller. Two miles on they divided." Bryan explains that if hounds divide, the whipper-in must watch the Huntsman to the last moment before stopping hounds, in case he changes his mind about which way he wants to go. Miller got further away, so he went after the other lot to stop them. They were now going so fast that even on this horse he could not keep up with them, "It was a matter of living with them, never mind stopping them." Accompanied only by John Shepherd, whose horse he had to cut out of some wire, they eventually got back at 4pm. By now the hard puller was dragging his hind toes, and Bryan's second horse had been taken home. Hounds would not be out much longer. They were all on, except Harvester. At 10pm Joe Miller rang to say he had been seen on the Canons Ashby road, and asked Bryan to fetch him. Harvester was a sharp hound, by Heythrop Harper '53 (Portman Lovelock '47-Cotswold Handcuff '49), "They were outstanding hounds. Like really wicked horses that have that bit of character." He reminded Bryan of those old Fitzwilliam hounds, and did not take kindly to being handled. He wondered how on earth he would catch the old dog, as he was nigh impossible to couple up. It was now midnight, and he couldn't help feeling this was his penance for the good hunt he'd had whilst everyone else had a moderate day. He spotted Harvester in the headlights, stopped the landrover, ran round to the passenger door, and opened it, "Box up", he shouted confidently, and to his surprise Harvester did. "He looked surprised as well, sitting there on the passenger seat !" It was a long and uneasy journey, the two eyeing each other sideways. The horse never pulled again, turning in to a brilliant hunter who evented, and was sold on, ending his days as the Fieldmaster's horse for some thirteen years in the Eglinton. Once Bryan was glad of a little mare's cleverness, although he got in to trouble. In his keenness to stop some young hounds off a hare he failed to see a single strand of wire between two hawthorn bushes. She jumped it and Major Drabble MFH reported him to Joe Miller for jumping wire!

The cleverest fox Bryan saw was with the Grafton. He saw him run in to a farm yard, through the sheep dip and out the other side. Hounds ran to the dip, and never did a thing for the rest of the day they were sneezing so much.

The Grafton country was very well run. Hounds were out three days a week up to April. Bryan still admires the pack's organisation, and adherence to a proper full Staff, "Kennelman Len Kingston was the best workmate you could wish for. He was a good pal, very strong and got through an enormous amount of work." These two devised a cunning scam to earn some extra cash. They managed to produce maggots of varying imaginative shades, and sell them to a fishing shop in Coventry, which proved a nice little sideline.

At the end of the fourth Season, with a growing family Bryan decided he needed more money. Fate intervened when a master of the Newmarket and Thurlow, Mr Neil Parker, brought some bitches over. He told Joe Miller that he was taking the Avon Vale the following season and Miller told him about Bryan. The following May 1st he went as Kennel Huntsman to the Avon Vale.

The Happiest Two Years
- Wiltshire Warmth

In 1962 The Avon Vale had a wonderful set up in the Spicer family's Spye Park, "They were the happiest two years of my life." Later Spye House was to burn down and the lovely grass country would be crossed by roads. Bryan found the people of Wiltshire warm and generous to a fault. "We'd come home from shopping and could hardly get to the door for vegetables, hams and so on. Always left anonymously. It was difficult to spend a night at home there were so many invitations." Though he never hunted hounds Bryan enjoyed his role as Kennel Huntsman to Neil Parker who was a good horseman and hunted hounds well, "In my first

Bryan Pheasey and Mr Neil Parker MFH
at Spye Park

198

Season there it snowed on Boxing Day, and it was mid-March before we hunted on a horse again. We'd caught 47 brace before Christmas though just hunting two days a week." The hounds impressed Bryan. They had been left alone, and at a check they would just get their heads down and get on with it. He had brought Harvester's brother Hamper with him, and he really helped them mark, "If hounds don't mark you don't know where you're up to, and I was pleased to think he made a contribution." After two Seasons the sought after Bicester job came up and Bryan applied. When he was offered it, Nora did not want to leave. Hardly surprising when they had found such an oasis. Bryan really wanted to hunt hounds however, and she could not deny him his chance. Many friends from those Avon Vale days like farmer John Giddings still visit 36 years on.

Hunting the Bicester

"The Bicester was a big job really. A vast country you couldn't cover properly even doing four days a week. So through cubhunting up to Christmas we did five days, then four after." Mr Smith Bingham was senior master and Mr Richard Cooper arrived at the start of the Season. He gave the Hunt a big financial boost, "He'd been amateur whipper-in at the Whaddon Chase and really made the place tick. We had wonderful horses all three Seasons he was there." Bryan now hunted the bitches, Mr Cooper the mixed pack. "He was a brilliant fieldmaster and really knew how to give the Field a ride, being an outstanding horseman. " He was succeeded by Mr Tony Younghusband from the South Oxfordshire. "Nothing deterred him, I saw him jump the parapet of a bridge to get to his hounds on a riverbank, places you'd never get to." Sadly Mr Smith Bingham then died and this was a difficult time for the Bicester. A Committee took over in 1972 with three Area Managers, Alec Bond in the North, "He was some man. It was a marvellous three man team Dr Preston in the South and General Darling in Tuesday country. General Darling was a kind fellow. One day he walked in to a yard and was told to 'Bugger off'. Not being used to this he was upset. At the fatstock dinner the farmer apologised and said he'd mistaken him for the man from the Water Board !"

Hunting was now down to three days, Bryan hunting hounds. It was a situation which could not continue as the country was just not being covered, and was adding to the unrest. Bryan was however enjoying hunting hounds all the time.

Captain Farquhar and the New Welsh Outcross

In 1973 Captain Ian Farquhar came in to be joint master, "He could not have been kinder. Mrs Farquhar was the most beautiful woman you'd ever see on a horse. The Captain and I would be standing looking at a place and she'd come flying straight by without hesitating." Captain Farquhar's joint master was Roy Strudwick, "He purchased a lot of land in the best part of the country. We got off to a good start, and he provided some very good horses." Bryan was happy with the hounds, and none looked better in their coats. He had some reservations when he was told by Captain Farquhar that he wished to introduce some more Welsh blood. Bryan was not a fan of broken coated hounds, though he freely admits he knew nothing about the Welsh hounds. The Welsh already at Bicester from Sir Peter's time was well diluted. He had enough experience of the hard Old English lines such as those at the Fitzwilliam however to give them the benefit of the doubt, "It was extraordinary. That new infusion of Welsh made the hounds nicer as people. You could take a thorn out of their feet or handle them in any way like that. Mind you, I had a job getting walks for them at first. It was like selling insurance ! When walkers got to know the hounds' characters they'd ask for more. They showed such kindness, those Welsh cross hounds." Vale of Clettwr Fairy '73 and her brother Falcon '73 founded this new dynasty, having been borrowed by Captain Farquhar. At the end of one day's hunting Fairy was missing. All attempts to find her failed. Captain Farquhar went out again late that night. One covert had a railway line running through it. He blew from the bridge and heard faint whimpering. He found Fairy lying beside the line, her skull fractured. He took her back near midnight. After a lot of patient nursing she miraculously recovered and produced three litters of pups, "We once crossed Fairy '73 with New Forest Medyg '69. Those pups were all little tikes."

Captain Farquhar never interfered with Bryan's daily routine. Bryan liked to take hounds on bicycle exercise all year. Only nearing Peterborough Show time would the Captain join in these excursions. He would let the puppies rake on and have more freedom than Bryan. Invariably there were odd scrapes, and Bryan was then left to resume his routine with a more hotted up pack, "It never did any harm but the last thing I wanted was excitable young hounds to take through villages." The young

199

'woollies' were particularly apt to be in at the sharp end of any trouble, to the Captain's amusement. Bryan's revenge would be to take a very hilly route if he thought Captain Farquhar was looking a bit delicate in the mornings. Bryan enjoyed working for him, "He never swore at me, not once. I used to tell him off sometimes though, chuntering at my hounds ! That's the sort of relationship it was. We were there to help each other." John Kennelly, now hunting the Atherstone, started in the stables. He was always happy no matter what befell him. Bryan once left him behind after parading hounds at Thame Show. On another occasion, he was sworn at by the master for galloping about on his horse. In fact the horse was a big strong one, and John a light lad who could not hold one side of him !

The Welsh Influence Makes Its Mark

The Medyg/ Fairy cross proved very successful. One doghound, Meredith '76 proved disappointing at first. One day they watched him from a railway bridge. A fox shot out of a bush, brushing past him. The penny dropped. Meredith suddenly realised what it was all about and just got better and better. He became a successful Stallionhound before he was killed on a road in the 1980-1981 season. Bryan continued hunting the mixed pack for the first three seasons, and admits he was not sorry when Captain Farquhar took them on as well in his fourth season, "I was getting older. Those Welsh hounds were really showing what they were made of. We had some of the best hunting this country has known. I remember three consecutive Tuesdays with a six mile point in the afternoon, one after a five mile point in the morning. Phenomenal." Another Welsh cross making his mark was Farmer '76 (Fresham '73-Vale of Clettwr Fairy '73), "You wouldn't believe what a hound he was. He had a gruff voice, so you always knew it was him, and that he was true." The social side of hunting was also in full swing with an exhausting number of parties and imaginative pranks, "It was a time of great fun. Everyone enjoyed their hunting and had smiles on their faces." The casting of Captain Farquhar as a Bishop in the Hunt Pantomime is particularly memorable to all who saw the performance. When a fall put Bryan on the sidelines he followed by car. Walking in to a big wood, he climbed a fire watchtower. As Captain Farquhar drew below, he lit a cigarette, oblivious to Bryan watching from above. He could not resist calling out, "You aren't supposed to smoke in a red coat !" The Captain almost jumped out of his skin. In 1985 Captain Farquhar left to take on the Duke of Beaufort's, taking some of the Welsh cross hounds and Charles Wheeler with him, "I was very, very sorry to see him go."

Another Amalgamation

Captain Farquhar was succeeded by Luke White, later Lord Annally, keen on his hunting and who had already shown his commitment as a boy by helping out in Kennels, and going on to hunt beagles. He hunted the mixed pack, Bryan taking up the horn again with the bitches. "He worked so hard. He orchestrated the amalgamation with the Whaddon. He visited every farm in their country we might possibly cross. He made it so smooth it might always have been that way, but it was an enormous undertaking." Bryan got on well with this conscientious man, and enjoyed the three Seasons he was there.

Going Out in Style

When Luke White left, Bryan was 63. Having scaled down the number of days he hunted hounds over the last decade, he now went back to hunting hounds four days a week, "I had a lovely time" he beams. " I don't quite know how I did it mind you ! I'd get up some days and it would be a rotten old morning. But you are so fit, that's the thing. You don't really realise it at the time."

Greatest Asset

Bryan firmly believes that a Huntsman's greatest asset is his wife, "Mrs Thame at Trafford House always calls Nora the Perfect Huntsman's Wife. That really makes me proud." Nora has become well used to long, erratic hours, and to feeding hungry young whippers-in, "She never let the lads go hungry" Bryan recalls referring to the likes of Frank Houghton-Brown, Charles Wheeler, John Day, Mark Sadler, John Kennelly, Ian Jones, and Martin Bluck. Bluck's father was Stud Groom at Astro Park and as a young boy Martin would often be carried home on the front of Bryan's saddle. When Captain Farquhar called for tea, he would become so engrossed in talking of the day and hounds that he would pile sugar in to his cup between smoking and talking, until the bowl was almost empty. Nora fixed this by putting a dessert fork in the bowl. It was some time before he noticed !

Family fun. Bryan (centre), his son David, granddaughter Laura Pheasey, grandson Charlie Barrett and Julie Barrett, Bryan's daughter.

Retirement

Bryan retired in 1989 after twenty five happy years at the Bicester. Then joint master Ian McKie said that he could choose a horse to keep. Bryan had six horses at the time. One did not belong to the Hunt, but was owned by Mr McKie's father-in-law, former master John Sumner. His favourite, The Snob, or "Snobby" had been quite cocky, so initially Bryan was given him to ride from time to time as it settled him down. Mr McKie swears he had nothing to do with Mr Sumner subsequently giving Bryan Snobby. They enjoyed a long and happy association, "He was the sort who would refuse a bad place rather than make a fool of you. A dream ride." When Snobby succumbed to colic aged 23 Bryan felt as if he had lost part of the family. He was found a little mare, "Now we understand each other we get along fine." He enjoys his hunting, often with daughter Julie. "I take her to open the gates. About two o'clock I usually decide that my horse has had enough, to the disgust of my grandson, Charlie !" Charlie is very keen, and all Bryan's grandchildren hunt. Nothing gives him more pleasure than when the family go out together. Both Julie and her sister Carol are very keen. Bryan's son David recently returned to the sport after a long absence, and his daughters Hannah and Laura also have the 'hunting bug.' When not hunting the couple take a great interest in their grandchildren's Pony club activities, keep an immaculate garden, and somehow find time for caravan holidays, "I would never swap what I've done. We've had great happiness throughout our lives."

A Story That Says It All

Though a great horseman, and a man who clearly enjoys his riding, Bryan derives pleasure from little things that happen along the way, particularly things hounds do, "Once, we were a couple and a half light. We had met thirty miles away, so by the time I'd had supper and driven back it was late. As I stood blowing for hounds by Hellidon Windmill, there was not a light in the village. It was a lovely clear night. I thought what a fool I must be ! Then, on this beautiful night, just as the Church clock struck midnight three hounds came trotting down the road in the moonlight. That made it all worth it."

W Edmund Porter MFH
(Jim Meads)

202

W Edmund Porter Esq MFH

The Porter family have a remarkable involvement of over one hundred continuous years with the Eskdale and Ennerdale hounds. I arrived on a sunny evening at the Porters' home in a lovely valley near Eskdale, and could hear Edmund hard at work in Kennels. He does all the kennel work single handed with help from wife Linda at busy times, and his enthusiastic sons David and Andrew aged five and nine, who look set to keep the family's involvement alive for many years to come. Edmund is an unassuming man, hard working, softly spoken, and quietly passionate about his hounds. He takes his role as Chairman of the Central Committee of Fell Packs very seriously, and is respected throughout the Lakes. The boys have disappeared playing 'hunting' - such a refreshing change from those who spend lives glued to the internet and virtual reality. Linda, a Coniston girl by birth, was baking for the Hound Trails the Hunt is running tomorrow evening. This draws in welcome funds from mainly non-hunting folk. the sport of Hound Trailing is quite separate from hunting and is still very popular in the area. As if by magic a delicious supper appeared, and conversation is lively. I was delighted to hear that hounds are to meet close to my lodgings at the Bridge Inn at 7am in the morning. I left with this happy thought and some fascinating bedtime reading - the Fell Packs' submission to the Burns Inquiry.

Tommy Dobson's Headstone (Kay Gardner)

A Family Concern

The Eskdale and Ennerdale pack was founded by local bobbin turner Tommy Dobson, known as 'La'al Tommy'. Dobson is one of Lakeland's legendary figures, an unlikely looking hero, small and bewhiskered. He evidently declined to shave his neck as the curious arrangement of whiskers kept him warm in winter ! Edmund directed me to Dobson's grave, and I walked my terrier through the valley to the isolated church on a cold and murky afternoon after hunting. The grave sports an impressive headstone, around six foot high adorned with a carving of Dobson, a hound's head, foxes mask, whip , brush and horn. It bears the legend 'subscribed to by over three hundred friends from all over the country'. Edmund's grandfather, Will Porter used to help out in Kennels as a boy, and became increasingly keen. Dobson eventually made him Huntsman, and on his death in 1910, having no family, he left the hounds to Will Porter. He hunted them until 1927 when his own son Jack (Edmund's father) took over as huntsman. Will remained master until his death in 1952. Jack Porter, then became master and hunted hounds until 1943. Art Irving was taken on to hunt hounds for Jack from 1944 to 1962. Edmund left school aged 15 in 1958 to whip in to Art Irving, taking over as Huntsman in 1963. His father made him joint master in 1979, remaining in office as senior joint master until his own death in 1991. Edmund has been sole master and huntsman since then, and his forty years' involvement with the pack was celebrated by folk from all the Fell Packs at the Bower House last year.

La'al Tommy Dobson with Edmund's Grandfather Will in 1900

203

Jack Porter, Edmund's father, Master of the Eskdale and Ennerdale from 1953-91 (Jim Meads)

A True Fell Pack

"I know I was born into it, but I had made my own mind up early on that hunting hounds was what I wanted to do. It was *all* I ever wanted to do." Caring for 56 hounds, doing all the knackering and skinning as well as general organisation is more than a full time job. Many puppies were in already and all will be back after Easter. June, July, and August are spent working on a local farm, with hound shows also taking up a lot of time in August. Edmund believes firmly in sticking to traditional Fell lines. "I breed amongst the other Fell packs. We used a Coniston dog this time. We used a Bewcastle dog the previous two years which was virtually Fell bred. You do have to use an outcross now and again. I have gone to the College Valley/North Northumberland, the Border and Liddesdale. "David Davies huntsman David Jones is a friend, and has brought bitches here to Stallionhounds in the past, sending a pup back to Edmund each time, so there are one or two Welsh lines. "We have some broken coats which go back to them. From time to time the broken coats come out. Three years ago we had a litter of three dogs, all rough, and three bitches, all smooth." Hounds must be light framed in this testing country, "They've some rough country to contend with right enough, including Scafell." He believes those who seek to use the 'Southern' hound here have got it wrong. Compared to their Southern counterparts these hounds appear to have straighter shoulders with their shorter necks, yet they are incredibly agile. "Feet are very important. They must have a hare foot to cope with walls and crag faces. I don't have favourites but some of our brood bitches are outstanding. I had one called Dally '68 (Trueman-Blencathra Darling) in the 70s who appears in a lot of pedigrees, as does Lyric '79 (Ullswater Miller-Silent). A lot of our bloodlines go straight back to my Grandfather's. He had two hounds called Kisskin and Jovial who won the couples class at Rydal in three consecutive years, 1925, 1926 and 1927. That's a true Fell line and you will find them in some of my hounds' pedigrees today."

Tradition - and a Few Changes

One would not imagine country like this changes greatly, but in the last twenty years there has been an increase in aforestation. Luckily there aren't the enormous forestry blocks here, but they have made a difference to the foxes habits, "The fox's environment has changed. We always draw these parcels of forestry, as foxes like the shelter they provide. In Grandfather's time, he would have gone straight to the higher Fells to find a fox, whereas we now go in to the lower lying forestry. They aren't really the same Fell foxes nowadays. You hear tell of foxes after bins and cat food in villages , which was unheard of here in the past. They don't travel the same distances now. They are far more used to people and so they do tend to feed near villages and picnic sites. They run in to the higher Fells when pushed, rather than living up there all the time. Also they run back and forth across valleys far more whereas they used to take off and go straight." I find it rather sad that this is just one more example of man's intrusion taking the edge off what is essentially wildness. There are more outsiders living in the area or 'off come' people as they are called here, often with holiday or retirement homes but few cause a problem. Much of the Hunt's country is National Trust with no fewer than 34 valley head farms belonging to them, "We keep our noses clean, and keep to the conditions of our licence. Practically all their tenant farmers are hunting people and those farms in the valley heads of Eskdale, Wasdale, Ennerdale and Duddon are sheep farms. That is why we exist really, to do a service for those people, especially now at lambing time." Lambing time in the Fells is late April, hopefully after

the worst of the weather. Unfortunately that is just when foxes are having cubs, and may seek extra meat. "Our busiest time is always late April and early May. The weather is a big factor. Some Springs we have a lot of call outs. Last year we only had eight lamb worrying call outs. Three years ago we had 26." Edmund explains that stormy, windy weather creates more problems. Not only does this make life harder for the foraging foxes, but the sheep dislike it: "So much depends on the ewe, and how she cares for the lamb. They generally do take care of their lambs, but on a bad 'clashy' morning the ewe doesn't want to bother with a lamb. That's when a fox will take them. Twins are also very vulnerable. A ewe can defend one lamb from a fox if she's a mind to, but she cannot protect two." The Forestry too is hunted under licence to the Forestry Commission. Forestry Fencing is a relatively new worry, "In the past if a hound was missing you would worry it was 'crag fast' (stuck in a narrow place in the rocks). Now if you've been in forestry you worry about the fences. Once a hound gets stuck in high tensile wire it cannot get out. You have to hope someone will hear them crying in time, so far we've been lucky." This last sentence is one to chill the blood of anyone who loves hounds.

Even here some road traffic has increased, particularly on the coast. To this end he concedes that the otherwise intrusive CB Radio can be useful to mobilise car followers and marshals with red flags to steady cars if hounds are near a road. CBs can also be helpful if hounds have got away and the lads who walk to the tops can tell him which way they have gone. Otherwise he is not fond of them at all. Edmund sticks to the traditional pattern of hunting the country, "In Grandfather's day they took hounds to stay on farms setting out the day before hunting. They would spend a week at a time away, hunting four days before moving on to the next valley." He follows the same systematic calendar, but brings hounds home each night. Warning cards are not necessary, as everyone knows hounds will be back at the same place and time each year. If bad weather means the higher Fells cannot be hunted then they hunt lower down, "We couldn't hunt Langdale, for example, for two days in February. We put in an extra day down the valley and caught four foxes." Farm visits are only necessary if meets need to be altered, or a farm has changed hands.

Secrets of the Fells

Enthralled, and caught up in the whole romance of Huntsman and hounds pitting their wits against the high brooding Fells, I ask what is the secret of being a good Fell Huntsman ? "Being light in the head, my wife says," giggles Edmund a shade bashfully, bringing me back down to earth as Linda joins us again, "You've to be a real dog man, to do this. You've to understand your hounds above all else." He is a firm believer too in the old adage that foxes are caught in Kennels - by the way hounds are fed and looked after, "They have to be properly fed and cared for to produce the work in the field." Nowhere too is knowledge of a country more essential. Forget knowing the best places to jump, or which gates open. Here knowledge of the safest sheep trods, footpaths and vantage points can save many a hard mile, "Fell Huntsmen are all locals, with a good knowledge of the country. Over the years you get to know the ways of foxes too, and where their earths are. It can save you a lot of climbing." He likes hounds to get on and do the job themselves, and dislikes any outside interference, "If hounds are hunting they want leaving alone." He does not like hollering either, "It only unsettles hounds. Mind you, my hounds are pretty independent and don't take a lot of notice." I quickly made a mental note not to forget myself and holloa if I viewed a fox in the morning.

Edmund Porter MFH with his hounds on a rugged cliff face (Jim Meads)

On Duty

I crept out of the Bridge Inn at 6.30am, to head for the meet at Wasdale no more than 3 miles away through winding stone walls, and pastures of restive sheep. The morning was cool and dry with weak spring sunshine. Crossing a cattle grid I rounded a bend to a breathtaking surprise. A huge glistening expanse of water, reflecting sleep scree covered slopes beside it. This is Wast Water itself, which appears to stretch on forever. At the valley head far beyond can be seen the intimidating heights of Great Gable and Scafell, both mountains still liberally covered with snow on the tops. I bore left as directed past more verdant sheep pastures, beyond which lay a thick sloping band of rusty bracken, dotted with boulders and lurid yellow gorse. Above lies a band of high crags and rock. Edmund arrives with hounds, unboxes and takes them straight to the green pasture below, where a fox has been taking the vulnerable twin lambs. They are keen to get on with the job, noses down, and soon feathering along a blue grey wall, across the lane, and through the bracken, already beginning to speak. Edmund followed below, with only the odd melodious call of encouragement. When they reached the rocks, hounds split, and it was riveting to watch their single mindedness as they danced lightly over the huge granite rocks. The sheer scale of the crags dwarfed them , Edmund a small red dot moving among the audibly loose scree below. They hunted with great cry along the crags, and over the top, out of earshot by 8.30am. There are no roads that side, so it was now a matter of patience, no hardship in such awe inspiring surroundings. I walked across the bracken, my terrier investigating many peaty places. There were few followers. Occasionally further along the lane I met one or two who had CBs, and news of hounds. A few hounds were left and I watched two hunting the crag quite happily alone. One stayed for a long time hunting an old line over the granite. He hunted on away in solitude. We heard some hounds right handed, and they had evidently made for the valley head. I made my way there in stages, stopping now and then when I saw sheep movement, or found a good vantage point. Those hounds ran on to Great Gable and over. They were seen by some sharp eyed regulars running through the snowline on Scafell top, where they eerily vanished. The valley head beneath these great heights boasts some habitation, a pub and a small rustic church. I passed one hound coming along the road, on his way back to the meet. The morning became increasingly cold, and I too made my way back to walk towards the crags, hoping for some sight or sound of the main pack. Another hound joined me here, near the box. I sat with my back to a rock, sheltering from the wind. Suddenly a movement caught my eye high in the intricate pattern of rock, something shifts, kaleidoscope like. Hounds, followed by that elusive red dot ! They pick their way down through the rock and cheerful gorse in bright sunshine, a sight that will live with me forever.

A sight that will live with me forever (Kay Gardner)

Edmund Porter and his hounds in the breathtaking Wasdale (Kay Gardner)

Edmund's stride says it all. Hounds hunted well to mark their fox and account for him. A successful morning's work. The other remaining hounds must be gathered. Edmund returned to the box, and blew. A couple appeared from different directions. Now he must go to the valley head and try to find those that crossed Scafell. The Blencathra met on the other side. "Typical if my hounds tire a fox for Barry to catch!", Edmund jokes. By the time we drive there the morning has changed. It is now dull and cold, raining slushy ice. He goes beyond the church, and climbs., pausing now and then to blow, or call. Slowly but surely hounds began to arrive, cautiously making their way down the scree, their huntsman unsighted. In this vast landscape they are tiny specks even through binoculars, yet the regulars can still name them. This is a fascinating conclusion to an unforgettable morning. When all those hounds had appeared he was still two light. One was back at the meet, another had been gathered up by a farmer. Hounds have many friends up here and it is easy to see why. Back in my room I read the Burns Inquiry submissions, written straight from the heart by folk who seldom go in for letter writing. Quite simply hounds are their lives, their recreation, and their social life revolves around their pack. Hounds provide a much needed service as exemplified this morning. To these people hounds are part of the family, they are born on the farm, walked there, spend their summer holidays there each year, and if possible retired to their walk. When the dreadful day comes, each hound is afforded the honour of a proper burial on the Fells he has hunted all his life. I found hunting in this beautiful part of the world both humbling and spiritually uplifting. That evening at the Hound Trail Edmund simply asked, "Will you be back then? I think you might be smitten." Judge, dear reader, for yourself.

Edmund blows for hounds at the end of a successful morning's Lamb Call at Wasdale, April 2000. (Kay Gardner)

207

Michael Rowson
(Jim Meads)

Michael Rowson

When I arrived at the South Shropshire Kennels on a warm June afternoon, Michael Rowson appeared, surrounded by a pack of cheerful woolly terriers. He tells me they are descended from a bitch he bought in 1961 called Penny. Though not far from Shrewsbury the Kennels nestle in a calm oasis of green. Views are clear and far reaching. He pointed to a distant clump of trees in the Summer haze, "The Stiperstones are that way. I was born just beyond them." He showed me the Kennels and hounds, who are dozing quietly beside a field of goats and hens. His wife Norma has just arrived home and after a quick cup of tea we set off for a whistle stop tour of some of the best country. It soon becomes clear that these deep grassy valleys and open mountains are sheer heaven for a true foxhunter. We see only sheep as we climb the beautiful Long Mynd. Michael points out the lead and barytes mines were his grandfathers worked, and the farm once occupied by his late sister. Landmarks of good hunts, tricky fences, deep earths and hospitable meets are plentiful, as one would expect from a man who has lived and hunted here all his life.

Beyond the Stiperstones

As a child Michael Rowson longed for a pony. There were stables at nearby Winsley Hall and his mother happened to meet Mrs Brown, wife of the Stud Groom. She told her about their pony mad son, and Mrs Brown suggested he go round and see her husband Ted, "I was out like a shot on my bike when mother told me." In 1954, aged 12, he attended his first cubhunting meet at Harnage Grange home of senior joint master Mr Towler. "I was taken by Mr Bonner-Maurice, a lovely kind gentleman, father of Major Ted Bonner-Maurice MFH of Tanatside fame. Cecil Gooch hunted hounds, with George Peverley whipping in. I was completely overwhelmed by the magic of it all, and decided there and then that I wanted to be a Huntsman." Soon he was hacking horses to meets as far as 18 miles away, and home in the dark, "I must have hacked thousands of miles, and just lived for the weekends. I think it would be *dreadful* to hack 18 miles home now !" At night he relied on the horses to show him the way home, and they never let him down, "We would take six or eight home together. I wasn't that familiar with the country then. Kids didn't travel about like they do now. Any child whose father had a car was rich." These happy weekend excursions continued all through Michael's school days. He was desperate to go in to hunting, but his mother wanted him to make something of his life, "I had passed my 11+ and got to grammar school and I don't blame her. My family were all local, Dad was a bus and lorry driver, and both my grandfathers worked themselves to death in the mines, which ruined their lungs. When you are young and all the adults around you tell you that you are being stupid you start to believe them after a while." He compromised, agreeing to go in to farming. Again his mother insisted he go about it the right way and study at the Farm Institute. He dreaded this, thinking it would be like school, but to his surprise thoroughly enjoyed it. The knowledge he acquired there would later prove very useful when he was asked to carry out post mortems on fallen stock. On leaving he started work for a local corn merchant, where his knowledge of the area proved invaluable.

The Snailbeach Harriers

He was now about twenty and enjoyed rabbiting with friends, using his terriers and a spaniel cross sheepdog, "The terriers would give tongue, but I felt we needed more music, and went to buy a beagle." He returned with two beagles, and soon found himself the repository for all manner of unwanted pet beagles. The addition of three harriers from Mr Bay de Courcy Parry MFH ('Dalesman') really made things go with a swing. Then Bob Buswell came to the United as Huntsman. His son Richard also kept beagles. Then Richard left to live with his mother, leaving twelve couple of beagles behind. Michael smiles wryly, "Well, I didn't need much persuading to take them on. I always had a pony or

two by then. I think the rest of the village thought I was completely mad !" Except for some other keen lads including George Adams, now Fitzwilliam Huntsman and David Boulter, now in Ireland. All these boys lived in the village of Snailbeach, and were to become very familiar with Michael's Harriers. "David worked on a farm, where the other lad liked Sundays off, so he worked the Sundays and came hunting with me on Saturdays." Another regular was Tom Wilson, a former miner, "He was a real sporting man. His ashes were scattered on the grass yard as he said he would still be able to go hunting on the hounds' feet. His grandson Nick has just gone to the Tynedale as Kennelman." Michael arranged all the meets, a feat which would be impossible now with so much land owned by the National Trust and Forestry Commission. The quarry was mainly hares, though sometimes a fox jumped up. One night they marked one to ground near the Bridges pub below the Mynd. Michael had to pull them out of the hole ! Richard Buswell later returned to whip in to his father, and went to hunt hounds in America. Mr David Palmer, then hunting the Wyre Forest Beagles was introduced to Michael by that first rate hound man Ray Williams, founder of the Wyre Forest Beagles and Master and Huntsman of the Border Counties Otterhounds. They have remained great friends, despite Michael 'poaching' some of what was technicallly Wyre Forest country. After hunting, followers gathered back at the farm where they had met where hounds were fed and popped in to a box. The ensuing parties went on into the small hours, once to 5am.

Helping out at Annscroft

Michael spent the rest of his free time helping Jack Warburton out at the South Shropshire Kennels, sometimes going with him to shows or hound parades as well as the odd day's whipping in during the Season. Then Jack had a very bad car accident, ending up under the wheels of a lorry coming home from Peterborough. Mrs Lindsey Wallace (now Mrs Sykes) MFH rang Michael to see if he could help out, "I did all the hound exercise for her that Summer, and she hunted hounds that Season. I would do an hour and a half's exercise with the kennelman, then sometimes a knacker round. I would rip back and do my lot quickly, perhaps taking them some of the cooked flesh. Then it was off to the office to do my bit of corn selling. I didn't get much sleep, but it was *great* !", he adds with relish. Being in the local Young Farmers Club where he knew so many people, and his hunting contacts were a great asset to his work. Somehow amongst all this he found time to indulge his passion for reading. "Books aren't the answer to everything, I know. But I liked to read. I still have limited time for it, so feel I must not read fiction, but prefer biographies and books written by great hunting men. You can always learn something. Wherever we go I have to look in the secondhand book shops."

The Opening Meet at Winsley Hall 1965. Joint master and Huntsman Mrs L A Wallace MFH (now Mrs Sykes), Secretary Lt-Col J Munro, Michael Rowson, acting whipper-in, Mr John Whalley MFH, Jean Raper and Sara Stevens.

The Ultimate Temptation

When Jack handed in his notice, Mrs Wallace MFH approached Michael, "She said, 'What about giving up those beagles to be our Kennel Huntsman?' I was 26 by now. I never would have applied but when it was offered to me it was too much of a temptation !" His mother was none too pleased, but his father, who died only a week before my visit, was, "He always had ferrets, terriers and the odd greyhound. He was a very doggy man. So you see the Hunting gene was there, and doing those horses at Winsley Hall sparked it off." So in 1968 Michael achieved his long-held ambition, becoming Kennel-Huntsman/whipper-in to the South Shropshire Hunt.

Fulfilling a Lifelong Ambition

Michael had seven Seasons in this role to a succession of young amateurs. When Captain Barrow came to the South Shropshire, horses for the Hunt Staff were in short supply, "He brought two lovely hunters with him. We begged borrowed and practically stole others !" These were named after the people who had lent them , Jack Griffiths, Arthur Wainwright, Gerry Murphy and Tom Jones. For the Opening Meet, Michael was to ride an unclipped, hairy pony, "He was a cracker." It was customary then for a photographer from the local newspaper to attend, so during the meet, Michael was put on one of the more splendid looking hunters, swapping on to the pony as they moved off ! Two coverts were drawn blank, and hounds were put in to a big wood which was always an assured find. As Michael stood on point he heard hounds running away from him. Behind him, he heard a bang, but thought no more of it. He listened hard for a 'Gone away' the far end. To his surprise, he heard hounds racing back towards him, to the right, and out of covert behind. When he got out, hounds had checked. "Captain Barrow was doing his best Tom Smith cast. There was a farmer standing nearby with a gun over his arm. He said, 'There's a dead fox here Mike.' He had thought hounds were hunting another, and shot this fox, which accounted for the bang! It was *the* fox. I had read a lot of books about hunting, but none of them told you what to do in these circumstances !" Michael tucked the fox under the long flowing mane of the chestnut pony, and trotted up to Captain Barrow, who was still casting diligently. "There he was, trying to get these hounds on 'Y'ert try old lads.' I just pulled this fox out and said, 'Is this what you're looking for, Sir ?' He *did* splutter !"

A True Foxhunter

1973 saw the arrival of Mr Marek Kwiatkowski as Master and Huntsman, "What fun we had. For two Seasons we laughed from morning to night." He then went on to the Meynell.

When Mr David Herring took on the mastership, he and Michael shared hunting hounds up until 1978. Michael then became Huntsman, a role he enjoyed for 16 seasons. His enthusiasm for hunting hounds never waned, though he has stayed all his working life in the area he was born in, and he only ever missed eight days, "Had I been ambitious to go somewhere more fashionable I would never have had the true venery I've enjoyed here. The more fashionable the country the more pleasing of the ladies and gentlemen you have to do. If you don't, then you don't last. That means you have to be less true to your hounds and keep pushing the job along." A situation which clearly would not suit Michael Rowson, who is a true foxhunter through and through.

Teamwork Behind the Scenes . . .

Kennelman George Jones came to work with Michael in 1975 and stayed for 13 Seasons, "He was a workaholic, as long as he could go hunting he would work day and night. He did our terrier work and made an excellent job of it. Our children grew up together and we never needed a babysitter as his wife Joyce would always do it." Present Kennelman Philip Edwards started helping in the Kennels when just nine years old, "He loves the hounds and is very good with them. When he was just a schoolboy I would get home from hunting to find the rest hounds out in the grass yard, and all the yards done, so that I came home to a clean Kennel." When he left school he came to the Kennels on a Youth training Scheme and has never left. He too did the terrier work for several seasons.

. . .and in the Field

When Michael first arrived, Roland Young, a local farmer whipped in, and did a good job for several seasons. Steven Perkins helped him, "He was one of a famous hunting family from near Church Stretton. When Roland gave up, Steven's father John took over. No professional could have done the

job better, and he always turned himself and his horse out to perfection. His eyesight was amazing, and many times he turned a moderate hunt in to a good one." Since 1991 professional whippers-in have been employed. The first of these was Michael's daughter Diana. Declan Feeney now Kennel Huntsman to the Meynell spent two Seasons here, and Will Bryer who could have forged an alternative career as an artist, followed, now whipping in at the Cottesmore, "It is not easy to get honest, hard working staff, and I have been very lucky."

Some Memorable Hunts

Just because a country is not 'fashionable' does not mean good hunting is not enjoyed. There have been many good days. Once hounds hunted a fox the length of the Long Mynd. A seven mile point, "Unfortunately, near the end I thought they were marking in forestry and sent the horses home. They went further and further away into the dark. That was on Monday, and it was 1 o'clock on Tuesday morning before I had them all back and fed !" Another hunt which sticks in the mind provided a 9¾ mile point in to the United country. "My horse was done by the time we got to the six mile point, so I had to take to a vehicle which did take the shine off it somewhat. We were in unrideable, uncharted country in the end, and it was dark before we got to hounds. We never knew whether they had that fox or not, but as they were only two fields behind him halfway through and continued the pressure, I would like to think they did, for their sakes."

The Carlow and Beaufort Influences

So far as the hounds are concerned there were two major influences. In the early 1960s, when the Carlow disbanded Mr and Mrs Wallace obtained two bitches, Waspish, and Crystal '62 (Kilkenny Cricketer '58-Saucy '58). Crystal was bred from, "That line has continued, and flourished. I would think more than half the Kennel now go back to Crystal."

During Mr David Herring's mastership in 1975 the Duke of Beaufort gave him bitch called Sonnet '71 (Sailor '63-Bella '66). "Sinbad '95 (Exmoor Pewter '89—Songbird '90) goes back to Sonnet. We had some very, very good foxhounds in that 'S' line with looks as well. Sinbad's sister, Singsong '95 was best brood bitch at Ardingly in 1999."

The Girl With Everything

There have been some lovely hounds emerge from the South Shropshire Kennels in recent years. None more so than Charlock '91(Exmoor Daresbury '87-Craven '88), who was perfection itself. Michael recalls that her dam Craven '88 (Berkeley Freshman '84-Cornet '84) was nothing exceptional. "She had a superb litter brother called Craghill though." His praise for Charlock is unstinting, "She had everything, and had such a lovely personality. She was never any trouble at all. I regard her as the most beautiful bitch I have ever seen. No judge ever found a fault in her. You always need a bit of luck in hound shows, but every prize she won, she more than deserved." The prizes were many, for she took the unentered Championships at Builth, Harrogate and Peterborough in 1991. She then claimed all those three Championships the following year, "I don't suppose we shall ever

South Shropshire Charlock '91. Invincible on the flags and in the field (Jim Meads).

212

have another like her." That her feet remained perfect into her eighth season bears testament to the merits of sound conformation. Her abilities were not limited to the show ring, "She would draw, hunt and *how* she would mark ! It was always difficult to get her away from an earth. Some girls have everything, looks, beautiful hair, lovely personality, *and* they can sing. That's how I look on Charlock."

Showing Success

Showing hounds successfully has undoubtedly been a big part of Michael's career, but still it was hunting hounds which he found most fulfilling, "I have enjoyed the showing, and it is probably why I am more widely known, but I would love to have been known as a Huntsman rather than a show-man." Yet it has obviously given him pleasure to see his 'home' pack's success on the flags, "You do need luck in showing, and everyone sometimes wins when they should not, or loses when they should have won. I believe it should not be taken too seriously, and always try to leave the ring with a smile on my face." This mild mannered and laid back man has a very energetic showing style, "I want to make sure they give every ounce. If you have to do something you want to put everything you can in to it. You have to put the preparation time in as well, if you want to stand a chance of winning."

Four Peterborough Champions in a Decade

Winning the Doghound Championship at Peterborough with Crockett '87 (Exmoor Bandsman '81-Charcoal '81) in 1989 was wholly unexpected, and this first Championship win did please him greatly,

"If you aren't expecting to win, it feels even better." He recalls one year at Builth. "It was some years ago. I had a dog called Breadbin '80 (Wheatland Diplomat '76-Gracious '77) who had come second, and I took him in to the Championship as I thought he might get Reserve. We had another dog called Gardener '80 (Heythrop Pixton '75-Graphic '77), and I said to Roland, 'He might as well come in too.' Breadbin never got a look in and Gardener was Champion. Captain Barclay was judging and really liked him." Breadbin '80 and Gardener '80 were out of litter sisters Gracious and Graphic '77 (Meynell Growler '74-Bribery '71) respectively. The South Shropshire's continued show ring successes put them in the spotlight, and this changed matters somewhat. It is one thing to experience sweet success unexpectedly and revel in the achievement of a small pack, but staying at the top brings with it the burden of pressure, "I cannot imagine how a jockey must feel, riding a hot favourite for the Derby, but when we took Charlock '91 to Peterborough, in 1992 following her Harrogate and Builth

Michael Rowson at Builth
(Terry Crate)

Championships, we were odds on to win. Everyone was expecting it - the champagne was chilled and waiting. It would have been *dreadful* if we hadn't won. Mrs Sykes said to me after we won, 'You must be thrilled.' I replied, 'Madam, I am just so *relieved*.' I really was." Two more Championships followed with Doghound Champion Sinbad '95 in 1997 (Exmoor Pewter '89-Songbird'90) and Clever '97 (VWH Guinness '92 - Claret '92) taking another Bitch Championship in 1998. Both Sinbad '95 and Clever '97 are maternal grandchildren of their first Champion Crockett '87.

Let Hounds Speak for Themselves, and be True to Them

In Michael's best Season in 1983-84 hounds caught 76 brace, "Tally isn't everything but in sheep country it goes down far better with the farmers if you can say that hounds have had 40 brace by Christmas. It makes them feel you are worth having." When it comes to the skills required of a

213

Huntsman, he has firm ideas, "It is not so much about inspired casts and all the showy bits. It has more to do with the ability to know which hounds are putting you right, and which are putting you wrong. The greatest compliment a Huntsman can receive is if someone says, 'He may as well have stayed in bed, the hounds did the lot' ! A Huntsman must know what to draft, what to keep, and what to breed from. If his meets are well arranged, and he can take hounds to a covert where they will find a fox, that is worth far more than beautiful horn blowing and bull !"

Family Support

Michael's two daughters Clare and Diana are both mad keen on hunting, but with different approaches to it. Clare wanted to go to University and get a good enough job to pay for her horses to hunt on. Diana takes a more practical approach, and set her heart on following in father's footsteps, "'I am so proud of them both, Clare has worked with great determination to achieve success in the world of finance and business." Diana's chosen career in Hunt Service came as no surprise, "She always wanted to do it, and would get up in time to come on hound exercise before school. She would be out in front on her bike or pony to flag traffic on corners. She had a wonderful grounding. I would have loved it at her age." He is very conscious that his daughters had a great advantage over him, "Because of my job they have always been able to have good ponies, as all my bosses kindly allowed me to keep them here. It is such an advantage if you can learn to ride across country at that age. Something I never had." Michael has enjoyed great support not only from his daughters, but from his wife Norma, who was from Brayston Hill, and despite not being from a country orientated background loved it from the word go, "Norma took to hunting like a duck to water." He soon got her riding one of the ponies he could not resist buying at local sales. The two were introduced by his only sister, who sadly died of leukaemia aged just 44, "I was living here as a single man, and being a good sister she would come and have a tidy up for me. She worked as a receptionist in a hairdressing salon, where Norma worked, and brought her here one weekend." Norma has readily filled the breach to help Michael on exercise or in the hunting field whenever he found himself short staffed. In addition to all this, and looking after their visitors she does all the gardening, "She has been a tower of strength. Being a Huntsman's wife is not an easy life - there is a great deal to put up with !"

A Father's Pride Stretches Across the Atlantic

After his own frustrated start Michael never discouraged Diana's ambition. The fact that she had the disadvantage of being a girl in a male world did not worry him either. He had already seen two lady amateurs hunt the South Shropshire, "I was absolutely thrilled to bits. " They got on very well when she whipped in to her father, "Di is full of fun. We had a great time." The two obviously share a similar sense of fun, for Michael's is evident throughout the evening. She hunted hounds for two days when her father had a rare absence, catching two brace on her first autumn morning. After this initiation, Di took a two year Equine Course at Hartpury College, before going to Australia for a Season, where she whipped in to the Adelaide Foxhounds. She returned to whip in to her father for another Season.

Michael Rowson with wife Norma, daughters Clare and Diana (Jim Meads.)

Moving to the Meynell and South Staffs she whipped in to David Barker for one Season. She then went to America in 1998 where she still whips in to the Midland Foxhounds in Georgia. Michael has visited her there, and she recently returned home for a few days to see in the year 2000, "They have some good sport there after the coyote, though its quite different to foxhunting. They can be three times the size of a fox. A lot of the hunting is in forestry, and they can go at any time as there is no stock or arable land to worry about. There are always parties after hunting. Di is even more of a party goer than I used to be !"

No Other Hobby Will Do

Michael freely owns that he misses hunting hounds terribly. He puts this feeling down in part to having turned his hobby into his Life. "I don't have other hobbies. I can't get worked up about cricket or fishing or anything like that. I *wish* I could." He now fills the role of Kennel Huntsman, but no longer goes out on hunting days. He is at pains to explain that he gets on well with the young amateur Mr Andrew Cook MFH, who now hunts hounds, and that his decision not to whip in was made because he simply does not enjoy it. Richard Evans, whose father Leonard hunted the Ludlow now whips in, "We are very lucky. He is Stud Groom too. They are doing a good job. I had a great innings, and I am in my 33rd Season here now."

Influences and Dalesman's Help

Though they never worked together Michael had great admiration for Bill Lander, "I used to take bitches to the Heythrop. He was wonderful with hounds and people." The two frequently met at Hound Shows, and were neighbours for many years when he came to Sir Watkin Williams-Wynn's.

The greatest influence on him personally however was closer to home. "I have always been terribly proud that old 'Dalesman' helped me so much. Living just 30 miles away at the top of the United country he became something of a mentor, "I was just a youngster with my few hounds. He seemed to take to my enthusiasm for the job. Even when I was a corn merchant's 'rep' I was still just a frustrated Huntsman !"

Follow Your Dreams

Michael believes that whilst the material things in life can help it run along more smoothly, happiness is more important, "I have never regretted going in to Hunt Service. It is a wonderful life. If I had not, I am sure I would always have regretted it, and wondered whether I should have. Someone once said, 'Follow Your Dreams.' I did. That's me."

The Moon Rises Over the Long Mynd

Before I left, very well fed and looked after by Michael and Norma, who even offered a bed for myself and a lodge for my terrier if required, Michael showed me some of his hunting diaries. These would make fascinating reading, becoming more detailed as time went on, and with daily notes about which hounds cut out the work. He has added pictures and letters. After recent publication of a piece about the Snailbeach Harriers he received a letter from John Walcot, who whipped in for a while. He recalled one evening as darkness fell, discussing how they should gather up hounds. Michael had replied, 'Don't worry, the moon will soon be up.' It was, and the hunt continued. For me that summed up Michael Rowson's tireless enthusiasm for hunting. By the time I left the air was cool and shadows lengthening. I did not feel inclined towards bypasses and traffic, so took the scenic route, cutting back over the irresistible Long Mynd. As we climbed steeply, a huge full moon rose high in a pale blue sky. My terrier watched the rabbits darting about in the moonlight. It was not hard to imagine Michael up here with his Harriers, and what fun they must have had.

Michael Rowson (Jim Meads)

Martin Scott Esq., MFH and the VWH Hounds, November 1977
(Jim Meads)

216

C M F Scott Esq

My first day with my adjacent pack, the VWH, in 1985 was Martin Scott's last day hunting them. Shortly af terwards he became County Chairman to the then British Field Sports' Society, for whom I was a Local Secretary. He set about this challenge with character- istic enthusiasm, setting up a supplementary PR Com- mittee for North Wessex, and has now moved up to be Chairman for the Region of Wessex. I soon learned that Martin is a man of very firm beliefs, who gets things done and is not content to be a mere figurehead. Direct and fair, his fierce loyalty to his band of volunteers is reflected in their dedicated hard work, many having served for over a decade. Things have not always gone smoothly at the top in the last few years, but in times of crisis, in this as all else, there is no more loyal friend or sympathetic ear. Hunting regularly now with the Duke of Beaufort's his is a familiar figure, always in the right place, quietly doing his own thing. That he ranks hounds, puppy walkers and farmers among his favourite people comes as no surprise. In fact to any- one with a dedication to hounds he is a source of endless snippets of information about a day's sport, or the work of individual hounds. He always has time for a passing word, unlike some who gal- lop on leaving only mud splashes for posterity. His is the rare knack of imparting knowledge without being imperious. He has a wickedly dry sense of humour, often accompanied by a look of mock dis- dain, or even hurt, belied only by a glint in the coolest of blue eyes. There frequently follows an un- mistakable laugh. I have long become accustomed to the accusation that I head every fox on Wednesdays and Saturdays. Bitten by a celebrated hound called North Cotswold Landlord '44 for pulling his stern you might think he had learned his lesson some fifty years on ! Scenting revenge, not to mention a rarely inspired piece of investigative reporting, I enquire about the scar so famously left by Landlord. Not a hope. It was on his face, and has recently disappeared. . .

Beginnings

Martin's grandmother died in childbirth, and his grandfather, a former international rugby player also died, so his father Major W W B Scott had been brought up by his Uncle Charlie, a joint master of the North Cotswold from 1908-21. The illustrious career of Martin's father, joint master of the United, Portman (twice), North Cotswold, West Water- ford and Old Berkshire foxhounds is one of the most legendary of its period. Given his first Birthday meet at the tender age of two, his pony with a basket saddle, young 'Scotty's' foxhunting future already looked assured. His constant companions, terriers and hound puppies (West Waterford Lottery '48 often sharing his pram) played their part in what was to become a lifetime's passion for hounds. Add to this his early friendship with Captain Ian Farquhar, partners in crime at kindergarten and much else, and his fate was sealed. Small wonder the chauffeur allowed hound puppy Portman Lollipop '49 to occupy the front seat, leaving the two little boys to their own devices in the back !

Martin Scott with his father Major W W B Scott MFH

Early Memories

Martin recalls an early wet day on a good pony with the Portman, and the thoughtful help of Percy Durno at the Heythrop, "He told me what to do out hunting in that wonderfully polite way." Much early sport was had with the Heythrop where he can never remember a bad day. In at the end of one particularly good hunt, along with John Barrow, he was offered the brush by Captain Wallace, "I was only eight or nine, and said politely 'No thank you. Sir Peter Farquhar has already given me one', as I thought you were only supposed to have one !" A moderate grey pony which went flat out stopping only at

217

fences, put him off somewhat. Major Scott was now at the Old Berkshire, and fractured his skull extremely badly. However, the silver lining to this particular cloud came in his purchase of several cobs on which to hunt. The bond he struck up with one of these, an old grey called 'Omo' probably saved the teenager's early nerve, "He lolloped along, happily popping little fences and I could stop whenever I wanted to." His time was now divided between the Old Berkshire and the Heythrop, a pattern which continued into his army career, when he got as much hunting as he could during leave. His hunting career began in earnest in 1968 when he went as 'Third whipper-in and bloody boy' to the Heythrop. Captain Wallace, now at his zenith was a tremendous help and influence at this time. Tom Bailey was revered as Kennelman here, a post he had already occupied for 36 years, and Martin had already known his son Sidney since Pony Club days. Bill Lander was Kennel Huntsman and first whipper-in, Tony Edwards second whipper-in. Martin helped in Kennels during the summer, went fencing with Geoff Tomlin, and even did the terriers for a while. This was a period of hard work, and learning a huge amount more or less by a process of absorption. The absorption became on one occasion literal. As anyone who has tried it will tell you there is a knack to washing down yards with buckets of water effectively. The yards took about seventy bucketfuls at the Heythrop. Martin's enthusiasm in this quarter was not matched by his efficiency at first, and he splashed Tom Bailey once too often. Without hesitation, Tom launched a full bucketful at him, to 'sharpen him up' on what was thankfully a very hot day. Watching Captain Wallace hunt hounds was in itself an education. One piece of advice which proved invaluable was to "Settle a mixed pack early on, and they will hunt on their own." His method of always ensuring a really honest hound was on each side of him during a cast, say on a road, has also held good. This was a period of unforgettable sport with plentiful foxes in a country whose organisation lacked nothing. When the popular joint master Mr Colin Nash was laid up at the Old Berkshire, Martin's whipping in duties were divided for a time between the two countries. It was a busy time swapping his green coat for a red one and back again, and he fears he may have got it wrong once or twice ! With so much experience under his belt and an enthusiasm nothing less than insatiable he began to look for a pack of his own. The Eridge became available at the same time as the Tiverton, but he never regretted his decision to go for the less urban West Country.

The Tiverton

Thus in 1969 began eight gloriously happy years. Though the Tiverton country could be frustrating from the point of view of getting about, it was a terrific wild place for hound work, "On a holding scent it was at its best, as you could keep with them, but with the hills on a good scent you really couldn't keep up." Lady Amory MFH impressed upon him the importance of getting hounds away together in such country, and never were Captain Wallace's words of wisdom about settling a mixed pack more

With lifelong friend Captain Ian Farquhar LVO, MFH

apposite. His first Kennel Huntsman was Rodney Ellis (now MFH Tedworth). On his first day the young master arrived at the Kennels, doubtless eager to impress, knife honed for action. Skinning his first calf, he was so keen that he sliced the skin to ribands. Rodney tactfully suggested, "Never again, Sir." Bob Street later succeeded Rodney and was also a great addition to the team.

One senses that Martin would have been in his element here devoting himself to his hounds and kennels, while wife Jilly helped with the horses. He is full of praise for his wife, who became his joint master. Though this has its advantages (to quote Nigel Peel, "One can quite legitimately hold masters' meetings in the bath,") there can undoubtedly be some tense moments. Jilly recalls one day when the artist John King was out. She was whipping-in, and her husband turned round with the immortal words, "If you can't help bloody well go home!" This moment was captured in a sketch for her by John King. Another incident, anything but funny at the time, caused a good deal of amusement in retrospect. Martin was going for a day with the staghounds, and Jilly was loading up. His horse kicked her full in the face and as she lay in a heap Rodney ran, shouting for Martin to come quickly. Martin, hounds ever uppermost in his mind imagined that the pack had escaped, and ran down the lane from their cottage blowing his horn. History does not relate what his stricken wife said to him in the ambulance, but when she returned from intensive care she did manage to see the funny side. Another long-suffering female was Belinda. Regularly abandoned in the hills to be rescued by some thoughtful member of the Field as Martin disappeared after his hounds she too was most forgiving. This rather rotund mare developed a laid back approach to the insults and indignities regularly thrown at her. Two days a week could no longer satisfy Martin's hunger for sport, and he began to yearn for a four day a week country. Opportunities were limited, with just 15 packs still operating this frequently, and so when the VWH vacancy arose it was seized with relish.

The Vale of the White Horse Hunt

Here Martin renewed his long association with Kennel Huntsman Sidney Bailey who had whipped in to Major Scott, who hunted the Heythrop when Captain Wallace and Percy Durno were both laid up. With both men possessed by a deep love of hunting it was set to be a winning combination, "Sidney was more than helpful. Here I was coming in and taking away half his hunting, and he really couldn't have done more. He would show me the most likely places to find, and I have always had complete faith in his assessment of hounds. He has the most wonderful quiet control of his hounds. We are still great friends." This is a more difficult scenting country than the Tiverton, and not all the hounds Martin brought with him could make the grade in Gloucestershire. He left a good pack in Devon, and with typical self-deprecation adds, "They caught a lot more foxes after I left !" That most knowledgeable and well loved foxhunter Major Jock Mann MFH was sorely missed when he died as a result of a hunting accident in Martin's second Season. The price for having four days' hunting a week was losing the precious close contact with hounds which he had so enjoyed previously. He did as much hound exercise as he could to get to know them, but still missed regular contact badly. Hunting in Gloucestershire was a very different affair from hunting in Devon, where all the followers had known the hounds' names, and houndwork was by far the most important factor of any day.

In 1985, Martin relinquished the VWH, and the period of transition from Master to member of the Field proved unsurprisingly hard for a man still in the prime of his life, and who had until now breathed, lived and dreamed hounds. He confesses that his first Season not hunting hounds was a pretty miserable one. Happily, Fate stepped in. With the arrival at Badminton of his great friend Captain Ian Farquhar, Scotty's love of hunting was restored. He hunted regularly with the Beaufort, still doing two days a week from start to finish. Watching his friend rise to the challenge of this demanding post, and the introduction of new bloodlines proved fascinating, "The Beaufort people were very friendly and welcoming, and I am lucky to have a certain amount of levity there." He still breeds the VWH hounds where his encyclopaedic knowledge of pedigrees is highly sought after, and they have become established at the forefront of the modern foxhound for looks as well as outstanding working qualities. He can rattle off most hounds' credentials at the drop of a hat, and is always happy to share information with anyone who shows an interest. There have been occasions when I have been bumbling along with a hound show report, and cannot find something on a particular hound. A call to Scotty, even if he is in his bath, never fails to produce the information required. Daughter Milly hunts with him on Saturdays and that she shares his interest in houndwork whilst bravely taking on the country, gives him great pleasure.

Martin Scott flanked by Mark Hill MFH, VWH and Huntsman Sidney Bailey
(Terry Crate)

Hound Breeding

A leading authority on hound pedigrees and breeding Martin undoubtedly inherited this flair from his father. Major WWB Scott was instrumental in the metamorphosis which took place in the foxhound, with the introduction of Welsh blood. By skillful use of Sir Edward Curre's, Mr Ikey Bell's and Captain Jack Evans' bloodlines at a time when Welsh hounds were far from popular, he made a contribution which should not be underestimated. His foundation bitch Portman Maxim '31 still appears in pedigrees at the Old Berkshire and Heythrop, "Whenever I asked my father's advice about hounds he would simply say 'look 'em up'. He was a very honest hound breeder. I started looking in the Stud Books in 1968, and made my own split pedigree book. I would plan matings, and then ask him if they looked all right. He did advise me not to breed closer than the fourth or fifth generation." Line breeding in this way has become Martin's policy. He explains, "When I came to the VWH it was relatively soon after the amalgamation of the two packs - Bathurst and Cricklade. Hounds were of varying types. I wanted to breed a more level pack, and line breeding is a good way of doing this. It was circumstantial rather than a conscious decision." He still maintains the separate female lines in the Kennel, cherishing the Cricklade and Bathurst female lines. Bugle '76 was a particularly good example of an old Bathurst female line, and had her whelps in a tree down by the stream. When he was at the Tiverton Mr Colin Nash gave him a hound called Old Berkshire Grammer '61, bred by Major Scott. A great character, with a wonderful voice and very good nose, Grammer '61 was still getting whelps in his tenth season, and greatly enhanced the Tiverton pack. His grandson Ginger '76 died sadly young, but not before he begat some good VWH progeny. One of these Gingham '80 was dam to what Martin believes the best litter he has bred there - Barber, Barton Barker, Baker, Barmaid and Bashful '84 (Berkeley Borwick '79 -Gingham '80).

220

Star Qualities

Two bitches hunted at the Tiverton which he terms 'stars' were sisters Reckless and Redwing '69 (College Valley Ranter '66 - Heythrop Perky '67). These were bred by his predecessor Mr Alan Sturges, well-known as a long serving steward at Honiton. There are too many favourites to name but Tiverton Gaudy '74 (Forager '69-Gravity'71) and Pittance '72 (Forager '69 - Heythrop Perky '67) got a special mention. The VWH bred Topper '75 (Preacher '70 -Total '72) was ranked very good, as were Safeguard and Sandwich '73 (Duke of Beaufort's Crowner '69 -Savoury '69), VWH Trouble '74 (Presto '67-Tonic '72), and VWH Wary '74 (Duke of Beaufort's Warden '68-Pretext '71) who remained outstanding in her work despite suffering a broken leg. Tiverton Panda '73 (Graveney '70-Old Berks Pretext '66) was a notable non-riot hound who goes back tail female to the aforementioned Portman Maxim '31. To achieve his level pack Martin merged the blood of sires such as Heythrop Peacock '73, and his son Brimstone '76, or Heythrop Draycott '77 with that of Tiverton Ginger '76 and Cotswold Gentry '76. That these sires were full of Portman blood was not a particularly conscious decision, but worked out that way. The more recent kind loan of Portman Bedford '89 from Edward Lycett-Green, MFH, enabled him to get back to Old Berkshire Grammer '61 and to add more College Valley/North Northumberland blood to that of Tiverton Ginger '76. Using the neighbouring Cotswold Glencoyne '84, by Blencathra Glider '76, underlined the value of the Fell cross. The success of this Fell blood following on from the proven College Valley nick prompted the decision to go straight to the College Valley using their Dalesman '92 and Governor '95. Sidney Bailey is brilliant at assessing a hound's individual attributes and Martin puts implicit trust in him, knowing he would never advocate breeding from a hound that was not honest in its work. "When Sidney tells me which bitches are in season, I have a look at the board in the Kennels to see who he *hasn't* told me about !" Martin's favourite Stallionhound was General '80, and he likes breeding back to him, and his brother Genius '80 (Cotswold Gentry '76-Charcoal '77). He believes VWH General '80 to be the best Stallionhound he ever hunted, possessing great fox sense, which he passed on to his grandson VWH Guinness '92, who has been widely and successfully used.

I have long held the belief that too few masters breed hounds to suit a particular country, and this is borne out by Martin who says, "Better transport has enabled too many people to breed for fashion. Too much use of dogs bred on similar lines means we are in a muddle, as they all go back to the same stuff. That is why I felt it was necessary to do something different, and go to the College Valley. Having got the level pack I wanted, I was able to do it, but *not* until I had what I really wanted." He warns, " You must *not* experiment until you are *absolutely certain* what you have got." He also agrees that the modern trend for shorter masterships does nothing to help the continuity of hound breeding. When time permits he hunts elsewhere, and enjoys watching the VWH hunt in Cirencester Park, "A wonderful place to watch houndwork if one can get away from everybody !" Recently he has also had days with the Cottesmore, North Cotswold and College Valley/ North Northumberland. The work of College Valley Daniel '95 and Worthy '94 particularly catching his practised eye.

Martin Scott explaining the finer points at the VWH Open Day (Terry Crate)

Judging

In the Show Ring, Martin's practised eye also comes into its own. Anyone who has seen him stalking decisively about the ring is left in no doubt whatsoever that this man knows just what he wants. He judged his first Puppy Show, the Dulverton East in 1969 with Mrs Pat Smyth, MFH Dulverton West. Her husband Fred succeeded her in the mastership. Speaking of them with a genuine respect, he says, "They were tremendously popular. She really was a very special person." In 1970 Martin was asked to judge at his first major Hound Show, the South of England, with the late Duke of Beaufort. This was the last time that particular Show was held indoors.

"The Duke of Beaufort was great fun to judge with. He made you do all the work, and stopped you when you got it wrong !" A far more preferable teaching method to that of some senior judges whose underlings are reduced to quivering 'yes men'. Judging one's first major show with such an eminent judge is never without a degree of nerves. Anxious to get things right Martin purchased a new bowler for the occasion, and stayed nearby with his cousin Sir Walter Scott. It was a hot Summer, so he left the windows of his car open overnight. His cousin was habitually up and about early. Around 5am he noticed his terrier, the ominously named Trouble, playing with something on the lawn. Closer inspection revealed it to be Martin's new bowler. Not until the Show was over did the young judge learn that his cousin had rushed indoors with the hat, patching it up hastily with glue, boot polish and Indian ink ! Now himself a senior and highly respected judge Martin travels the length and breadth of the country every Summer, and has judged at all the major hound shows, taking in five Royal Foxhound Shows at Peterborough. His integrity in the ring is a particularly valuable quality. For all his authority in this sphere Martin remains one of the most approachable of judges, always keen to help the young or inexperienced learn more. His services have also been called upon four times in the USA where he enjoys staying with that great hound man Mr Benjamin H Hardaway III MFH. Reading Hardaway's book It is not difficult to see why the two men have so much in common, sharing such enthusiasm for hounds. Martin adds with a wry smile, "I am also a good listener !" Tiverton Caper '75 appears in all the Midland Pedigrees today. Major WWB Scott sent 17½ couple of hounds to the USA in 1939, evacuees from the threat posed by Adolf Hitler. Most of these went to his great friend Mason Houghland, whose grandson Mason Lampton now hunts the Midland Hounds and is married to Hardaway's daughter Mary Lou.

Martin Scott (centre) judging the Beaufort Puppies with Capt. Brian Fanshawe (Terry Crate)

The Future

At the outbreak of War, Major WWB Scott put on his uniform and took his hounds hunting on a Sunday, in case he did not come back. Such action would now be typical of his son.

Looking ahead, Martin says, "I am very positive about the future. I am a great believer that it lies in our own hands." He hopes that his work for the Countryside Alliance helps put something back in to hunting, "My volunteer helpers in the Region are second to none. I could not do anything without them." Martin is always the first in the front line when we are called upon to demonstrate. Nothing rattles him more than people who take our sport for granted. Except perhaps Huntsmen who blow for their hounds rather than going to fetch them. Members of the Field who don't give hounds room, who follow him and chatter, and think of nothing but jumping fences are given short shrift, "People not paying attention to hounds ", he growls, "And untidiness. Girls

Familiar figure with the Duke of Beaufort's (Jim Meads)

without hairnets. Boots without garters and spurs !" Lest you think you have stumbled into an interview with Victor Meldrew, I will close with one lasting memory. Picture this tranquil scene. It is late March, and we have enjoyed a long day in the steep wooded valleys around Hawksbury Upton. My companion and I have been walking all day and it is now 5.30 pm. Hounds have run uphill yet again, and out of earshot, we sit on a bank, to enjoy the last of the Spring sunshine, hoping perhaps they will run back to us, or pass on the way home. The song of blackbirds fills the woods, and the warmth combined with the after effects of a long day makes us sleepy. Even our terriers are dozing. A stream babbles gently in the background. Suddenly, galloping hooves thunder above. Dogs alerted, we scramble to our feet, to see Scotty hurtling downhill towards us, hat aloft, "Didn't you see that fox? Lovely big fox, he went all along there. I thought you might have given them a holloa." Our startled faces prove too much. A grin spreads from ear to ear, "They've gone home. What are you waiting for ? Good Night girls." With a cheery flourish of his hat he is gone far down the hill, the birds silenced by the echo of that infectious stentorian laughter.

223

Tim Unwin Esq. MFH at a meet of the Cotswold.
(Kay Gardner)

 224

Tim Unwin Esq

Over the years I have found Tim Unwin to be a meticulous man who can always be relied upon when detail is required. Beneath the calm exterior lies a methodical thinker who cares deeply about hounds and farming. Future generations will undoubtedly look on his long mastership of the Cotswold as a very important one, not only for that pack but for the legion of others which have successfully used its bloodlines to the greater benefit of the foxhound. Cotswold hounds are noted not only for their looks, but for their work and tremendous cry. No hound has been bred from by Tim that did not have great cry, and this has paid dividends. Few have the flair for breeding hounds possessed by Tim Unwin, who has skilfully blended a variety of types to produce an enviably level pack. Looking at hounds after the Puppy Show in 1999, it was only by nit picking one could find a fault. Even the oldest had good feet, an important quality so often neglected. He still takes a prominent role on the local Countryside Alliance Committee. He will always be found supporting farmers when any crisis looms, and was instrumental in helping Martin Scott and his Committee fight the County Council's ban on hunting. Having enjoyed some interesting days with the Cotswold myself, and long being an admirer of their hounds, this was to prove a fascinating morning.

A Cotswold Upbringing

Born at Arle Court near Cheltenham, hounds have always been part of Tim Unwin's life. His Uncle Collie had a pack of Beagles, later taking over the Boddington Harriers. He hunted both packs mounted, beagles in the Vale and Harriers in the Hills. Tim remembers Lt-Col Cyril Heber Percy MFH from Cowley Manor hunting hounds before the War, "In the early years of the War I remember him coming home and taking a prominent part in hunting hounds, wearing ratcatcher." During the War Mr Kemble acted as master and Miss Rosita Seldon Truss whipped in, practically running the Kennels. When the War was over the twin Misses Wilson, took the mastership, "They rode 'twin' horses too and you were in an awful muddle taking your hat off all day because you never knew which you had said, 'Good Morning' to !" Tim's father was Vice Chairman and after two seasons a special meeting was held at Witcombe Park, home of Major Hicks Beach to interview two applicants for the mastership. "To some people's surprise, a fairly young man called Captain Ronnie Wallace, from the Ludlow got the job. His enthusiasm and knowledge of the Cotswold country, where his father lived resulting in a unanimous decision. As word got about that this young Huntsman was a bit different, we were getting very large Fields at places like the Puesdown Inn on Saturdays, bordering the Heythrop country." Tim remembers long hacks to these meets, and home again, and the prominent role terrierman Charles Parker took in proceedings, "George Knight who had been Kennel Huntsman at the Ludlow came with him. He was wonderful and sadly died in office. In modern terms Captain Wallace was 'head hunted' by the Heythrop, taking with him Raymond Barrow from Farmington who had been Fieldmaster, and later became a joint master of the Heythrop. Charles Parker also left with him. The Cotswold mastership was taken on by Sir Hugh Arbuthnot, who had whipped in to Wallace at Eton, and followed him to the Ludlow, "It was a very successful mastership and he was joined by Mrs Jackie Brutton of Springhill." Tim recalls meeting at the Air Balloon roundabout, on the A417, "Perhaps two cars would pass during the meet. You wouldn't even think of crossing the road there now !"

Getting Serious

When Tim did National Service with the 17th/21st Lancers, his hunting became confined to leave. When he left to farm he took up hunting 'seriously.' He was Fieldmaster for Sir Hugh and Assistant Secretary to Major John Talbot. When Sir Hugh went to the Duke of Buccleuch's, Mr Bob Phillips came to the Cotswold from the Garth and South Berks. After three seasons Tim joined the master-

ship, continuing in his role as Fieldmaster. When Captain Brian Bell came Tim continued until 1967 when the mastership of the neighbouring Cotswold Vale Farmers' Hunt became vacant. He applied successfully, allowing him to carry the horn for the first time.

Fun in the Forest

So began a very happy time for a man who confesses farming and hunting to be his Life, "They were wonderful people. It was exceptional if farmers hadn't been there for several generations. There was a great atmosphere of solidarity which always comes with stock farmers." It was the perfect place to begin hunting hounds without the pressures of big and sometimes unsympathetic Fields, "Their whole attitude to hunting was so refreshing. It got them away from the farm, and if they had a good day it was a bonus. I felt no pressure at all, because I probably wanted to have good sport more than they did." He opened up the Forest of Dean, "Consequently I was able to start in the first week of August and conclude on May 1st. It was a great bonus , as I had to go to the Kennels at Boddington every day to walk hounds out, and of course hunting them was much more fun, so the longer the Season went on, the better! " His dedication included fetching hounds from Boddington for those early meets the night before hunting, and keeping them overnight at his home. At 3.30am they would load up the horses, "Hounds slept contentedly in their box. We would go off to the Forest at that ghastly hour and come back at what seemed like teatime." Bert Smith took care of the Kennels and he relied on amateur whippers-in. When Captain Bell resigned from the Cotswold, Major Milne came to see Tim and asked him to apply for the mastership. It would appear the Heythrop were not the only 'headhunters.' "It was literally about May 1st 1971 when I left the Cotswold Vale, that the tapes were cut to open the M5. I never actually saw traffic flowing on it during my time there. It ruined the best of the Cotswold Vale though they luckily had some country West of the Severn as far as Ross-on-Wye and the Forest of Dean."

Back to the Cotswold

So began Tim Unwin's extraordinarily long mastership in the country where he started hunting as a boy, had served as Fieldmaster and Assistant Secretary, and had never left during his sojourn into the Forest of Dean. He returned as a fully fledged amateur Huntsman, already showing the feel for hound breeding which was to become such a prominent feature of his long mastership.

Strong Female Lines . . .

Captain Bell had used his experience of the Berkeley bloodlines to good effect, and Mr Bob Phillips had used Heythrop and Badminton Stallionhounds, "He bred an outstanding bitch called Pastime '66 (Duke of Beaufort's Palmer '59-Cactus '61). I used copious helpings of Heythrop blood, one of the earliest stallionhounds I used being Heythrop Lonsdale '70 (Clinker '66-Lottie '63)." Also instrumental at this early stage were three draft Beaufort bitches Major Gerald Gundry MFH had sent him at the Cotswold Vale, "They bred me some useful future Stallionhounds." Two of these bitches were Mischief '68 (Tipperary Growler '64-Mona 65) and Gaslight '68 (Tipperary Growler '64-Wakeful '65). What Tim liked about these two was the strength of their female lines going back through the Beaufort Kennel of the previous century, "Strong female lines are the important thing in breeding." Duke of Beaufort's Mischief '68 was put to Heythrop Lonsdale '70 to produce Moleskin ' 74, "He had a voice like a bull and was a vital link, producing a very good litter, which included Stallionhound Porter '79. He in turn produced a super litter of bitches including Bonnet '83 who was as red as a fox, and Bonfire '83 who was in the winning two couples at Peterborough."

. . . Produce Good Stallionhounds

Perhaps the most notable sire produced from the Cotswold Kennel at this time was Gentry '76 (Heythrop Grossmith '71-Teapot '71), "He appears now in top lines in many Kennels." Martin Scott regards Gentry '76 as one of the best outside sires he has used, explaining, "He is one I like to breed back to." Gentry appears in the pedigrees of the VWH Stallionhounds Guinness '92 and Gardner '95. Teapot '71 (Berkeley Telstar '64 -Policy '68) was bred by Captain Bell. A little homework reveals that Telstar's sire was Old Berks Tewkesbury '61, a half brother to Old Berks Grammer '61, bred by Martin's father, Major W W B Scott MFH. Tim reveals that Gentry did not really approve of hound shows. "He tolerated them, but hated them really and never looked happy."

Groomsman '75 (Heythrop Grossmith '71-Policy '68) sired Crofter '81 (-Compass '76). It was Crofter '81 who sired Grocer '86, who was to become the pack's second Peterborough Doghound Champion.

The role played by those earlier mentioned bitches, is fascinating, for Teapot '71 and Groomsman were both out of Policy '68, a daughter of Pastime '66, and Compass '76 was a granddaughter of Duke of Beaufort's Mischief '68.

The Top
The Cotswold took their first Peterborough doghound Championship with Grappler '05 (Wheatland Grappler '78-Clematis '81) in 1987, possessing size as well as quality. Clematis was by Gentry '76. With Grappler's son Carter '89 (- Corrie '84) another fine hound the Cotswold Stallionhounds were really making their presence felt. Amory '90, a son of Berkeley Albion '86 has also become a useful sire. His dam Clover '85 died just after whelping and he was hand reared by Mrs 'Pinkie' Dickins. Both Corrie '84 and Clover '85 were by Crofter '81.

Pilgrim '88 (Berkeley Pontiff '85-Corrie '84) showed great promise and was best young doghound at Peterborough. Sadly a thistle went wrong deep in the ball of his foot.

When Grocer '86 (Crofter '81-Gossip '81) became their second Champion Doghound at Peterborough in 1988 the consistency of the Cotswold hounds had reached its zenith, "The third cross of Heythrop blood had worked through, and things were boiling nicely." It is one thing to reach the top, but staying there is another matter. It might have been thought the Cotswold could not top this. Yet there was more to come.

When Clematis '81 was put to Blencathra Glider '76 she produced two outstanding Stallionhounds, Glenrock and Glencoyne '84. The latter became the most famous, and in 1991 these two sired both Champion and Reserve at Peterborough for the Wheatland. Glencoyne '84 also went on to sire Heythrop Glazier '90, who took the Peterborough Doghound Championship in 1993.

Mr Tim Unwin MFH (centre) admires his second Peterborough Doghound Champion Grocer '86. On his left are judges Mr David Herring MFH and Captain Charles Barclay MFH. Cotswold Kennel Huntsman Roland Sheppard is showing Grocer (Jim Meads)

The Masterstroke - Blencathra Glider '76
I have always been fascinated by the successful use of Blencathra Glider '76 at the Cotswold which was to prove such an outstanding outcross. Those Fell hounds with their porcelain quality are something very special. The steep valleys of the Cotswolds seem in retrospect a logical place to use them. I asked Tim how he came to use Blencathra Glider in particular, "I was hunting in the Fells one Spring with the Blencathra, hunted by Johnny Richardson. Hounds were waiting for a fox to bolt from a clitter of rocks. It's a lovely time to watch hounds, when they are on their toes. They were at the height of expectation and there was a dog in the middle, very serene, very in control, with lovely quality shoulders. I asked, 'What's that very nice looking dog ?' Johnny replied, 'You'll not find better that that, that's Glider.' He was not a young dog then. I saw one hound hunting that day in his eleventh season! They are bred for great stamina." He admits that the Fell hound can look a little upright in the shoulder but puts this down to the optical illusion created by their shorter necks. Having recently returned from the Fells we swapped thoughts on this extraordinary country, "Possibly because of that rather romantic setting up there one gets carried away by the whole thing." If the successful use of

227

Glider is anything to go by, there is no harm in getting carried away now and then. His son Glencoyne '84 is simply one of the most influential Stallionhounds of recent years, "I've never heard of a Glencoyne that didn't hunt." Through his son Heythrop Glazier '90 the line has been perpetuated, "It is not a particularly good line for getting doghounds, but there are some very good bitches. Glencoyne has certainly made his mark."

Old English also Proves Successful

Not only did Tim use the Fell outcross, he also used an Old English line most successfully. Cotswold Kennel Huntsman Roland Sheppard had come from the Brocklesby, "I sent him up there to find me a decent one, and he came back with Colonel '88. He only hunted a few days with us, and did nothing startling." His progeny have proved successful, and Roland obviously did a good job, for Colonel produced Caistor '92 (-Bashful '88), who in his eighth season is still hunting and getting good whelps.

A Transatlantic Flavour

A trip to judge in America, where Tim hunted with Mr Benjamin H Hardaway III MFH sparked an interest in American lines, "We were hunting in May, in very hot and dry conditions. They were pretty impressive, hunting in fine voice. Due to Ben Hardaway's generosity, Captain Brian Fanshawe had a Stallionhound called Midland (USA) Hardaway '89 at the Cottesmore." Though by the time Tim saw him Hardaway had been stifled, assured of his good hunting abilities he decided to use him, "You would never know what effect six months quarantine has on a puppy, not yet developed. He had been used at the Cottesmore and Cattistock who are now into the third generation, and think a lot of them." Hardaway got Tim a striking tan Stallionhound called Harker '96 (-Dorcas '90). For such a big dog he is incredibly light on his feet, "Yes he floats, doesn't he ? He has a great voice too and is a terrific jumper which can be very useful these days with so much wire netting. I took him to Peterborough just for people to see, never expecting to be in the shake up. He was third in the Stallionhound class, I was highly delighted and he liked it too !" Harker is now with the Hursley Hambledon, and has already got some nice progeny about, "He is based on an old Cotswold female line which goes back to Percy Candour '39, one of the foundation bitches of the pack really. It also has a touch of the Blencathra Glider '76 blood."

This extraordinary ability to blend different bloodlines has been a major factor in Tim's success as a breeder. To pick the right lines, which will nick in together is an art which should not be underestimated, "Hardaway had Stud Book blood. Quite a few American hounds are what they call cross-bred, as there are a lot of Studbook hounds out there. Ben Hardaway has some lovely quality hounds. He has used College Valley, Old Berks, Heythrop, all the best. It's easier for them to get blood out there than it is for us to get this way because of the time and cost of quarantine."

Changes - For Better and Worse

In the last 30 years hounds have changed enormously, "Thirty years ago you might have difficulty finding one or two nice ones at a Puppy Show, now you struggle to find faults. After the War there were fewer good hounds about. You can't breed good points if there aren't the good hounds to do it with. Then draft hounds got about and Stallionhounds emerged, particularly from the Portman and Beaufort."

"One of the great things is that you see results very quickly in hound breeding. You can put things right very quickly. Conversely you can muddle it up very quickly too. Using young hounds is not really the right thing to do, but you can cheat occasionally to get out of trouble. It needs thinking about though." With fewer long masterships and many less experienced masters taking packs on Tim feels that the experienced breeders have more responsibility to keep things on the right track, "Those who have not been in it very long cannot have a natural assimilation of the art of venery, because it is new to them." The trend towards standardising hounds also worries him. He feels that few people breed for a country, "It may look good, but it is not. With more traffic and urbanisation the last thing you want in some places is a hard driving, fast pack that you cannot get to. In some countries it may well be desirable to slow things down. It would be quite a feat, because if you are looking for a Stallionhound, few Huntsmen will put their hands up and admit, 'I've got a slow one' ! You would have to go further back, to slow bitches. I believe it may be desirable in some circumstances." He cites a master at the Carolina Hound Show, where he was judging, "He came up to me afterwards and said, 'Seems

228

you don't like ma hounds ?' I said I thought they lacked the quality to be on terms with a fox in dry conditions. He said, 'Ah've always gorn to the slowest dawg Ah can find.' I replied not to take any notice of me, as he was obviously doing a very good job ! He *wanted* plain, slow hounds."

Don't Just Ogle - ask !

Tim emphasises the need for caution in the use of show winners, "The young may ogle prizewinners and think they are going to transform their hounds. Far less borrowing of Stallionhounds goes on now than previously, so it is harder to judge if a hound will suit your country. It alarmed me when we had show winners that people would rush up and ask to use them. Only the minority would ask, 'Is he a good one ?' I would tell people openly that Grocer was all right, but not ten out of ten. He lacked a bit of drive at fences and so on, though in his defence he got a hole in his foot and never fully recovered. He was good but not top notch. He proved a good Stallionhound and passed on sound working quali- ties to his progeny." He admits it can be daunting for a young master to ask the more experienced 'old guard' if their precious prizewinners are any good, "You have to be subtle. Ask if he has a good voice, or good nose. Beware if they say, 'Quite good', or hesitate before answering. You can draw a lot out like that !"

Tim feels that the present rule where a draft hound may not be shown is short sighted, though he owns that a breeder could be somewhat miffed if his hound was beaten by the draft, "On the other hand, it is reflected glory. Look at a pack like the North Cotswold, for example. They draft all their doghounds. It seems a pity that if one of those turns out to be Stallionhound quality, no-one can see him. Hound shows are a 'shop window' and even if not the place to decide on using a dog, seeing hounds gets people talking about them."

Handling A Pack - Trust and Patience

"As we have just said, the breeder who wants to breed for a country has a difficult job these days. Fashion is a dangerous thing. The more quality a hound has, the faster he will be. The faster he is, the better brakes he must have, like a fast car. There is nothing worse than a hound with such speed he takes the pack two fields on. Then they all look at each other and say, 'Hang on, I thought some- one had the scent ?' Really good hounds will stop, and show you." He believes that a great deal of a pack's response in these situations is down to handling, "A pack excited by an excitable Huntsman will flash on, hoping they are right. The good ones gallop back to where they last had the line and then you find the Field all over it, so you are doubly mucked up."

Tim believes a Huntsman's greatest asset is to have the confidence in his hounds to let them get on with the job. He concedes that more lifting and casting is inevitable now with the hazards posed by roads, "The less mucking about with them the better. How often one sees hounds run into country that is difficult to cross because of wire and so on. Hounds check, cast, go on, check again and do it all themselves. Too often a Huntsman tries to cast hounds before giving them credit for getting there and allowing them to make their own cast. It is fatal, because then they start to think, 'We've lost it, where's the Huntsman?' The biggest quality a Huntsman can have is to sit still and do nothing, and let them sort it out for themselves when they check." This confidence, and quietness are the key to successful handling, "If hounds are in full cry two fields away it's no good blowing your horn to stop them, or shouting and yelling. You can do it until you are blue in the face. They don't hear you. Get to the lead hound and do it quietly. You won't achieve the impossible. The possible is quite difficult enough !"

Don't Fuss , Just Look Them in the Eye

 Doing things with the minimum of fuss is paramount as is a positive attitude, "If they put up a brace you must decide quickly what to do, a good whipper in will help get things right." The early autumn mornings are invaluable for building understanding between hounds and Huntsman, "Young hounds will make mistakes. If a hound comes back to you after doing something wrong, so long as it looks guilty, that is enough. You only have to look at it - just as you would look at your dog - it knows straight away that you aren't pleased. Do that as often as you can to strengthen the thread. Don't ever carry on to find another fox until you've settled things down. The other hounds will let the sinners know how they feel too, growling and saying, 'Where the hell have you been ? We've been waiting for you !' It plays a vital part in getting them steady."

229

The Cotswold Country and Shooting

The steep wooded valleys and high brashy fields of the Cotswolds certainly provide plenty to think about, "It's not an easy country, never has been. It is cold scenting, but clean, with little stock about so you can get some very fast hunts. It is subject to atmospheric change too, with fog and mist on the escarpment." As in so many places the greatest change Tim has seen has been the increase in traffic. Shooting has increased, but he believes it is now at saturation point, "Virtually everywhere has a shoot, but you just have to get on with it." Luckily commercial shooting is not a great feature, so few areas are blanked out for months on end. Most shoots are still small and home based. The biggest shoot operates four or five times a week, "The foxes are still there but it's very hard to get in. There are some heavily syndicated shoots where guns come in and contribute nothing but money." Tim fears that the crisis in agriculture has at times led to a reversal of accepted practice, so that the shooting keeps the farm afloat, rather than being purely a sporting interest. Many of the keepers in Cotswold country are keen on their hunting though, so coupled with Tim's meticulous organisation problems were few, "I remember once in the 1980s I knew we were close to a Shoot. I'd just got hounds stopped and someone told me there was a whistle in the valley." Fearing dire consequences he moved on. He spoke to the Keeper that night, who said, "Why didn't you come to my whistle? The fox came straight through the beaters." The following season in the same place the Keeper and his son were hollering either end of the valley, "The worst thing is that you become very conscious of it. It makes you cast where you *hope* the fox has gone, away from the Shoot. You have to cheat your hounds. You sort of stop them and swing them away, and cast where they know the fox has not gone. You can see them thinking, 'What's wrong with the silly old so-and-so ?' They must think you are pretty stupid. If you can do it quietly they soon forget particularly if you can push them on to another fox. "

Learning From the Greats

I ask Tim who he has been most influenced by, "Dermot Kelly once said to me that if you hunted with Captain Wallace for even a day you were so inspired when you returned it made you a better Huntsman for a day or two, until you slipped back into your old habits. He did everything quietly, without a whipper-in swishing after the hounds all the time. As a young man I was not wholly aware then of just what I was seeing. It was only later you realised you had seen something special. Sir Hugh Arbuthnot was so laid back that he would not help the hounds and they had to do everything themselves. Captain Wallace liked to influence things and assist the hounds when they needed it. I was so lucky then. I had days with the late Duke of Beaufort, 'Master', which were always a magical performance too. I hunted with Sir Peter Farquhar and Bill Scott . Those men gave their lives to hunting." He feels today's amateurs, and professionals have to contend with a very different world, "The countryside is

Tim Unwin and the Cotswold Hounds on a misty morning (Terry Crate)

changing. Less of it is owned by country people. Farms of 100 acres or less become pretty paddocks. It is far more complex to organise a country now." Increased traffic and indiscriminate fox control make the really long hunts impossible, "I don't believe there are so many old, and I mean old, foxes about. Either they are picked off when on their travels, or run over. Consequently foxes that are found are less likely to travel far, as their knowledge of the country is not as good as it might be."

Memorable Snapshots . . .

It is the little things hounds do along the way that can make or break a good hunt, and it is these which stick in Tim's mind, "I remember a bitch I bred at the Cotswold Vale, Ladle '69, hunting full cry down a tarmac drive at Edgeworth, despite the smoke from a bonfire. I heard that a hound I drafted took the whole pack down a road last Season. One of the bitches I had from the Beaufort could take a line down a road. It's nice to think these qualities can be passed on. It happens countless times over the years." The thrill however is still as great. He recalls vividly a day near Pimbury Park. Hounds had checked on plough and Tim cast them. A puppy of the first American cross dwelt back, "Soon she was going ' bow wow wow'. I was hesitant to go with a puppy, so just cast the rest

Tim Unwin MFH at his last meet as Master of the Cotswold (Kay Gardner)

past her. As soon as they reached the headland they hit it off, and away we went. That was a very exciting moment, for an outcross to spark like that when hardly entered." It is not just the individuals who make a day special, "There are days when the whole pack does something rather pleasing say in a strong wind which drifts them off the line and suddenly they gallop back to where the original line was." Perhaps the biggest thrill of all though is that of anticipation when hounds first open, "For a fisherman the first strike, the first tug on the line is the most exciting. The analogy in hunting is when you find your fox. The first challenge is always the most exciting one, knowing that the whole thing is about to start."

Tim regarded Carter '89 (Grappler '85 - Corrie '84) as one of the best he bred, "We were drawing along the Chalford valley near Oakridge one very warm autumn day. It was Carter's first season and when most of the pack had drawn on he dwelt by some brambles. He had a very fine voice and opened. It sounded right, so I took the others back. Sure enough he had found a fox."

. . . and Still the Thrill of the Unexpected

Tim continues with 'snapshots' - moments which stick vividly in the mind, always with great enthusiasm in his voice as he speaks warmly of his hounds, "Once at Seven Springs hounds ran to a sports field, surrounded by chainlink fencing. I had a cobby little puppy, lacking in quality who I hardly thought worth keeping. Do you know she was the only one who got over that fence. I sat there thinking, 'How the *devil* did you get over that bloomin' thing ? You shouldn't be *able* to do that. You've got it all *wrong*!" I can well imagine an exasperated Tim saying this aloud to the puppy, who must have looked very pleased with herself, "It was such a lesson that handsome really is as handsome does, and that sometimes the sheer determination to do something far supersedes beauty, however desirable it may seem."

A Continuing Legacy

Few these days stay in mastership for any length of time. Tim's record of thirty three continuous season's as a Master of Foxhounds, who hunted hounds in the same County for thirty one of those from 1968-1999 is a remarkable one. His wife Primrose, also a native of Gloucestershire has always been supportive, particularly to the younger members of the Field. The couple's six grandchildren all hunt. Retirement must have come as a dreadful wrench, but Tim is enjoying 'hunting around.'

The continuing legacy of those superlative hounds lives on in so many pedigrees, and will continue to influence the looks and ability of the Foxhound forever. The words of Shakespeare seem apt, ". . . as for a map does Nature store, To show false art what beauty was of yore."

Clarence Webster, Warwickshire Huntsman
(Jim Meads)

232

Clarence Webster

Schooldays - or Not

Clarrie's great grandfather hunted the Linlithgow and Stirlingshire, and his grandfather hunted the Lanark and Renfrewshire, "You'll have to ask brother Jim, he's the expert on family history. We're connected to the Johnsons as well. I'm named after Charlie's father, Clarence." Clarrie was born at the Taunton Vale Kennels where his father was hunting hounds. In 1935 he moved to the Essex Union, and this is where Clarrie's childhood hunting memories begin.

When War broke out in 1939, staffing was reduced, Clarrie's father being left with just the Stud Groom and Kennelman who had served in World War I. Thus Clarrie took one day off school a week to whip in to his father aged just 14. His weekly letters explaining 'a chill on the tummy' were leniently accepted by schoolmaster Mr Gardner, a regular bicycle follower, who would invariably enquire how the day had gone! Co-incidentally my own Grandfather Gardner was a schoolmaster who followed hounds by bicycle, but sadly I cannot claim them to be one and the same. Sometimes both Clarrie and his brother Jim would whip in. He told me "Clarrie liked to hang about the second horsemen because they always fed him sandwiches !" Clarrie remembers Jim coming home sometimes and complaining to their mother that his father had been getting at him all day, "It was all right really though. We might have got a rollicking, but once we were home it was all forgotten."

Real Education

Clarrie was called up himself at the age of 18 and served with the Royal Horse Artillery in Northern Italy, then spending two years serving in India. Demobbed he returned to whip in to his father. In 1951 he succeeded Tim Langley as whipper-in to Jack Simister at the Wynnstay. Not everyone enjoyed working under this strict disciplinarian, but Clarrie enjoyed the experience, "He was a brilliant Huntsman and a very good chap. We just seemed to click somehow." Clarrie enjoyed riding the superlative horses provided by Mr Matson in this well fenced, good scenting grass country. He whipped in to Simister for three seasons, and on his departure stayed one more Season with Charlie Wilkin. It was here he met his wife Ennis whose father worked on the estate. She explains that her mother was a keen racing woman and named her after a racehorse. The Wynnstay Kennels were beyond belief, the hounds enjoying red tiled floors and fireplaces in each lodge. One can well imagine them reclining in this luxurious setting at the end of a hard day.

The Final Move

When Clarrie went as first whipper-in to another legend, George Gillson at the Warwickshire, he could not have forseen it would be his last move. Gillson left to hunt the Meynell and Major Profumo, Meynell MFH came to the Warwickshire in 1956. Clarrie was asked to stay as first whipper-in and Kennel Huntsman. When Major Profumo left in 1958 he became Huntsman, a post he occupied in this most enjoyable of hunting countries until 1982, "When I came to the Warwickshire it was still very open. There were no hunt jumps." As so often was the custom then hounds hacked everywhere. When a box did arrive, George Gillson went in that leaving Clarrie and the second whipper-in to hack on, "I remember one night coming past Lower Lemington and through Cherington, there was a dance on. This was before I was married", he adds hastily as Ennis arrives with the tea tray, "I said to the second whipper-in, 'Let's go back,' so we did our valeting, had a bite to eat and came back on a motorbike to the dance." As Huntsman there were numerous good days, but one still stands out most clearly in his mind. It was February 1964, and hounds had met at Barton on the Heath. After a fast twenty minutes to Wolford Wood, they found again in Barton Spinnies. Going away at the end of the covert they crossed the old green lane, running through Gravel Coppice. Here they swung left handed, then straight for Wolford Wood. This left many of the Field behind. Crossing in to Heythrop

country to Evenlode they turned left handed over Chastleton Hill, circling through the gardens of Chastleton House, and beyond, still running left to the Little Compton Road. Then they swung right now as if for Rollright. They recrossed the road to the valley where they marked in Salford Osiers. This had taken just 55 minutes. Snow still lay four or five inches deep on top of the hills, and this made no difference whatsoever to the way they hunted.

Mr Denny Green whipped in to Clarrie for a number of years, his wife Charmian becoming joint master of the Warwickshire when still Miss Jackson. Denny recalled, "One day, Clarrie jumped a fence, and the horse's girth broke. There he was in mid-air on the saddle as his horse went on. It must have been a split second but he seemed to be in the air for ages. He hit the ground, still on his saddle. Miss Boultbee Brooks saw this and kept saying, 'Poor Clarence, poor Clarence.' I can still see him now flying through the air on that saddle, it looked so funny !"

The Country and People

It is hard to choose a favourite bit of the country, but Clarrie confesses, "I liked the Pytchley end of the country, around Shuckborough and that side on a Wednesday. Those lovely hills around Todenham were always good, and that would be the best bit now." Once a month Clarrie and Ennis would meet up with the Maidens, at the neighbouring Pytchley for a meal. Denny Green recalls one meet at Flecknor, when the Warwickshire hounds met fifteen minutes earlier than the Pytchley at Staverton. The Pytchley fox ran in to the Warwickshire country, and spotted by Clarrie near the railway, hounds were laid on. This provided a very nice 45 minute hunt, when apparently the Pytchley had a fairly mediocre day !

The late Mr 'Gaffer' Forsyth, so well known throughout the hunting world did the terriers for Clarrie, "There was no greater friend. If we needed anything in Kennels, it was done." One morning whilst walking out, Gaffer drew up in his car, "Clarrie, I saw a wonderful sight on my way home last night. A fox came across the Kennel field with a chicken in his mouth. It's marvellous to think he was right where hounds are now." The two men laughed at 'Charlie's' cheek, and Clarrie returned home. To find all his chickens dead !"

Like all hunting countries the Warwickshire has changed, but is happily still not blighted by the roads so many packs have to deal with, "You wouldn't believe your eyes now. The country when I arrived would have been at least 70% grass. Gradually it became ploughed up and would be 70% arable now."

Hounds in the Field and a Historic Championship

Regarding hounds Clarrie has firm views, "We only ever went to the Beaufort or Heythrop for Stallionhounds when I was there, and it nicked in extremely well." In the field his preference was for a

bitch pack, "I found them so much easier to handle than a mixed or doghound pack." Yet he concedes that the doghounds have their day, "On moderate days they will persevere for you when bitches will fly on, but on balance I still preferred bitches to hunt." Comparing packs he notes, "The Wynnstay were a good old sort. Slower than these, but good all the same." He has seen the Warwickshire hounds change over the years, "When I came there was just one lemon hound. All the rest were tri-colour and very like the Belvoir type. It was only when we changed to Heythrop and Beaufort sires they became so much lighter."

Clarrie Webster with the Warwickshire Hounds on exercise outside Tysoe Church (This picture was taken by Mrs A C Lambert, used as a picture postcard and sold by the WI.)

Clarrie Webster and the Warwickshire Hounds in kale (Jim Meads)

Warwickshire hounds have long been renowned for their working abilities, and to this day in my opinion no pack has better cry. There have also been some very good looking hounds, the Warwickshire taking no fewer than 16 Peterborough Championships at the turn of the century. In a happy echo of these halcyon days Clarrie showed two Doghound Champions at Peterborough, the first of these being Partner '68 (Duke of Beaufort's Palmer '59-Accurate '63) in 1970 at the old showground. This was only the third time in 20 years that this prize had not gone to Chipping Norton or Badminton, breaking an eleven year monopoly of the Doghound Championship by hounds from the Beaufort and Heythrop packs. Partner was very highly regarded in his work and also won the Stallionhound class. This strong red and white hound's victory had come 61 years after the Warwickshire's last Peterborough triumph, but a second Peterborough Doghound Championship for Clarrie followed quickly in the form of Grafton '73 (Heythrop Wiseman '68-Gravity '68) at the new Showground in 1974. Miss Boultbee Brooks was required in the ring to accept the prize, and rather than go round she put a chair against the fence and climbed over, Sir Marcus Kimball waiting the other side with another chair. "She was a lovely Lady, marvellous. The Duke of Beaufort was judging and said he'd never seen anyone jump a fence at Peterborough to collect their prize !"

Inevitability

There was never any question in Clarrie's mind that he wanted to go in to Hunt Service, though being light he had the chance to go in to racing with Lord Mildmay and Peter Cazalet. There was no doubt either that Clarrie and Ennis would retire in the Warwickshire country, "Yes, we love it", he says with real feeling ,"What a lovely bit of the world". Clarrie hunts regularly and hacks a splendid looking former show horse, Manuscript, formerly owned by the late Ian Thomas, dressmaker to HM the Queen. The horse lives next door and the two have formed a close bond. Clarrie enjoys nothing more than pottering about the country he knows and loves so well, "We stand on top of the hill and watch proceedings", he adds with a twinkle in his eye, "Have a criticise !" Clarrie gives the impression of being a very unflappable man, for whom nothing is too much trouble. It is easy to see why he believes patience to be a Huntsman's greatest asset. Unassuming with a laid back voice which still bears traces of his Essex upbringing he pulls his cap firmly on to go and check up on Manuscript. When not hunting, or hacking on Manuscript he tends his garden and enjoys growing his own vegetables. If hounds finish nearby Mrs Green MFH invariably calls with them at the Websters' cottage, which this most hospitable of couples really enjoy as much as their visitors.

235

Jim Webster when he was whipping in to George Tongue
(Jim Meads)

236

Jim Webster

Brothers Jim and Clarrie Webster have deep rooted family connections with the world of Hunt Service. Their grandfather, Will Webster married the daughter of Harry Judd, Huntsman of firstly the Ludlow and latterly the Lanark and Renfrewshire. Will Webster then succeeded him in that role. "Harry Judd's other daughter married Bert Thatcher who hunted the Zetland. Our Uncle Harry hunted bassets. He was in the Veterinary Corps and was killed on the last day of World War I."

Jim's father was Huntsman to the Taunton Vale, where both he and his younger brother Clarrie were born. His father bought Jim a pony when he was about six. Unfortunately it bucked him off and he was dragged across a field, hung up in the irons, "I was frit to death ! It put me off riding all together." After his father left his next post at the Wynnstay, he came to the Essex Union. Frank Buckingham, a great polo player lived opposite the Kennels, "I used to see him when I walked home from school." He was a formidable man, "Everyone was frightened of him." He told Jim's father to send him over after school to fetch a bag of apples. Dutifully doing what he was told, Jim, then about 12, went to Buckingham's yard. To his horror he had a saddle put into his hands, "The last thing I wanted to do was get on a pony, but I was too scared to say a word." The pony was saddled up, Jim told to get on, and he never looked back. He regularly rode ponies to the polo ground, eventually becoming confident enough to ride one and lead one, "I never played polo, but was the water boy, helping keep the ponies cool." When his parents went on holiday to Somerset they returned with a roan pony called Biddy, "That was me set up, in my little bowler hat ." It seems that the weekly 'chill on the stomach' was hereditary too, for like his brother Clarrie he also suffered from this complaint regularly in winter ! "I loved my hunting. We used to put the pony on a train and everything."

Early Days
He tried to get a job at the Brocklesby first of all, "I was only about six stone and they had big heavy iron beds for the hounds which had to be lifted. They said I wouldn't be strong enough. Bert Peaker was Huntsman in those days. His sister looked after him, and we had pigeon pie after hunting." Little did he think then that in years to come he would return to the Brocklesby to use their Stallionhounds.

Consequently, when Jim left school he stayed on at the Essex Union for two years, working in Kennels and looking after two horses and some ponies for Mr Heatley MFH. He hunted regularly, sometimes carrying a terrier. He found working for his father something of a strain and decided it was time to leave home.

George Tongue needed another boy as third whipper-in, "I'd had enough experience in kennels by that stage to keep my head down and get on with things, so it worked out all right." When Jim arrived in 1939 there were ten men in kennels. When war broke out, second whipper-in Dick Perkins went straight into the army, first whipper-in Harry Evans also went to war leaving young Jim to whip in to George Tongue. This he did four days a week for a Season, until further staff reductions became necessary in 1940 George Tongue found him a job as whipper-in to Billy Pope at the Grafton where Joe Miller had also joined up, "Hours were long . We'd leave kennels at 8am, hack say to Weedon, hunt and come back across country. There was never any need to worry about the hounds, just run your eye over 'em in gateways." Whilst at the Grafton, Jim himself joined up.

War Service, and an Unexpected Bonus

After initial training he had a choice of regiment, and decided he would like to go to his native Essex Yeomanry, "So off I toddled to be stationed at Malton in Yorkshire." Many of the officers stationed here hunted with the Sinnington. Returning from a tank course at Barnard Castle, Jim found a note telling him to report to Captain Gee, the Adjutant. As he left, wondering what he had done wrong, he noticed that his bed was covered in parcels. Captain Gee was himself an Essex man, and being keen on his hunting knew all about the Websters. Far from receiving a rocket, Jim was told that he was to whip in to the Sinnington from the following morning. The mysterious parcels contained his hunting kit which Captain Gee had asked his father to send on. Now Jim really started to worry. How was he to get dressed up for hunting in the Barrack Room, and report to Captain Gee's car, when all the other lads would be square bashing ? "Do you know, I passed them all on parade in my red coat, spurs the lot, and not one of them said a word. They didn't even blink. I couldn't get over how brilliant they were, and I was never teased about it once." During this time the Sinnington's Huntsman George Gulliver had a bad fall, smashing his jaw on the road. There was no question as to who should take care of hounds, and in order to do the daily kennel work Jim was given a motorbike ! On hunting days, Lady Feversham provided horses for him, and he enjoyed his days in this lovely grass vale. It was certainly an unexpected bonus for a lad about to go to war. He even hunted hounds one day, but it proved a bad scenting day late in the Season, and nothing went his way, "I wasn't asked again !" For the whole of that Season he whipped in and looked after the Sinnington hounds. Then he was sent away on exercise for the serious business, preparing for the D Day landings. He was sent to Normandy, and went through that campaign, "We joined with the 8th Armoured Brigade, Leicestershire Brigade, Sherwood Rangers, and Hertfordshire Yeomanry, to form a floating Brigade, sent wherever we were needed." He carried Will Webster's hunting horn in his tank, once recovering it from his tank when it had been wrecked.

Post War - Cheshire Interlude

Returning from the War in 1947, Jim advertised in Horse and Hound for a position in Hunt Service. He received a handful of letters and with the help of his father and Mr Heatley whittled them down. Mr Heatley advised him to go to the Wynnstay. His reasoning was that the pack had not hunted during the War so would need building back up , which would teach Jim a lot. The pack also had Jack Simister at its helm. It is extraordinary how many Hunt Servants were made by Simister, though others doubtless fell by the wayside under his strict regime. Jim had endured Normandy, and leaving his father to work for George Tongue was well used to hard taskmasters. One of the first jobs he was given by Simister was to scrub the green kennel walls with a bucket of water and a brick ! He fell in well with Simister and stayed for two seasons. Meat was still rationed at this time, and Jim lived in a small flat without electricity. George Seale, the kennelman was in charge of getting meat - from the butcher, I hasten to add - and invariably got chops, "They weren't up to much, nearly all waste. Anyhow, we scrambled through. Luckily the farmer down the road killed a pig from time to time. They looked after me very well always, so I was lucky." Lucky indeed, for it was whilst walking hounds down to this farm to fetch milk he met his future wife, Sheila, who cycled that way to work. He moved to the Cheshire in 1949, hoping to get a big enough house to enable them to marry. The house however was given to the second whipper-in, and after another two seasons Jim was no further forward. Then he received a letter asking him to return to the Belvoir, the fact that he knew George Tongue's ways, and that Tongue knew him was a major factor. Jim's younger brother Clarrie followed him at the Wynnstay in 1951.

Back to the Belvoir

Everything went well at the Belvoir, Jim hunting hounds regularly towards the end of Tongue's time there. After five seasons he was given the huntsman's job, and enjoyed a long and happy time here. "We had brilliant horses, all through my time. You could see by the end of it though that the country had changed a lot. All that lovely vale was grass when I started. You would jump 25 fences in no time at all, and it was open, not queuing up at jumping places like now." George Tongue and George Barker were great friends. Jim often got the job of driving George Tongue to parties and so on.

Prince Charles and the Late Lord Daresbury MFH, judging the Belvoir Puppies shown by Jim Webster
(Jim Meads)

239

Jim Webster and hounds in the Vale (Jim Meads)

Old English . . .

Huntsmen with the long established Old English packs have a limited choice when it comes to breeding hounds. "I used to go to the Buccleuch, who had some good hounds. We used a lot of Brocklesby too, and they used a lot of ours." Jim became something of an authority on Old English hounds, becoming particularly familiar with the Brocklesby Stallionhounds, as well as his own, "In Leicestershire you would have 300 out on Saturdays, with a lot of visitors. You needed hounds to keep driving on, especially when they hit plough."

. . . and Irish

Jim was asked to judge the Limerick Puppy Show along with Warwickshire Huntsman, George Gillson. They waited apprehensively at the airport, Gillson chain smoking. The flight seemed to take an age to be called, "I said ,'Don't worry George. There's two nuns over there, we'll keep an eye on them as they must be going to Ireland.' It turned out our flight had gone, along with the Stallionhound I was taking, and the nuns were going to France !" The two Huntsmen walked outside to ponder their predicament, "Who should be out there but Evan Williams, master of the Tipperary." The story about the two Huntsmen and the two nuns therefore spread rapidly across the Emerald Isle. The next flight was late in the afternoon and by the time they had taken a train to Limerick, the day seemed a very long one. The following day Evan Williams invited them for lunch and to look round the Kennels, "We saw Growler '64. George said he was a big dog with a long neck and a bell on the end of it ! That's what George thought of the great Growler ! We had some fun in Ireland." Jim was often asked to judge in Limerick. He even looked after the hounds for a fortnight when Hugh Robards got married. He was always well looked after and entertained. His regular Irish trips were a great help when new blood was needed. Cooper Atkinson and Ron Harvey also accompanied him on occasion.

240

Wonderful Country, and the Importance of a Good Second Whipper-in

Back in England the Belvoir country was wonderful to hunt in, "The farmers were brilliant and there was never any trouble. Mind you we liked to get a run into the Quorn country when the wind was in the East." Jim retired in 1986 after hunting the Belvoir for thirty seasons.

When it comes to what makes a good Huntsman his reply is instant, "A good second whipper-in always makes a Huntsman good, that's what I was always taught. When you are hunting hounds you are thinking about them. Your whipper-in should have a good eye for a fox, and think about where he is going. He should know the country well too. I believe that is true anyway. Some people try really hard, but just don't have an eye for a fox, for birds moving and so on. My son Richard has it, but he's not in Hunt Service. He is very good when we follow by car."

Jim's own whippers-in at the Belvoir went on to have illustrious careers of their own. First there was Bill Lander, who went on to the Heythrop. Then Charlie Appleyard, a good horseman who went to hunt the Morpeth. Dennis Boyles who hunted the Devon and Somerset Staghounds also whipped in to Jim at the Belvoir, "He was always keen on Staghounds, right from the start." Then there was Stewart Coley, latterly Huntsman of the Avon Vale, and highly thought of by Jim.

Of Superstition and Gardening

Jim confesses he is a superstitious man who hates going under a bridge if a train is crossing. The number thirteen he also avoids. Recently he underwent heart surgery, having become very immobile. He can now enjoy his garden again, and potter down the lane, which was unthinkable two years ago. His garden is clearly his pride and joy. Brother Clarrie telephones whilst I am here, and we have a word. Jim has seed potatoes ready to deliver to him, "I hope he's not telling stories about me", he chuckles. The two remain close, and clearly the similarity does not end with hunting. I leave, walking my terrier near Belvoir Castle which glows in the bright Spring sunshine. A church nestles in a sea of green in the village below. The only sound is that of lambs, and with its well planned coverts it is not difficult to imagine what it would be like to hunt this beautiful Vale.

Charlie White on 'Chestnut' with the Essex & Suffolk

242

Charlie White

Charlie White's is a face familiar in many parts of the country. Following a childhood in Dorset, to his last job with the North Cotswold at Broadway, Worcestershire, with many stops in between from south to the home counties, East to West and twice to Wales. Latterly he earned fame in the show ring with the lovely bitches of the North Cotswold. I visited him now in retirement, on a glorious June day for driving across the rolling Downs of South Wiltshire and Hampshire, into the very heart of West Sussex.

From Bicycle Pillion to Pony at the Portman

From his home at Ferndown in the Portman country, Charlie White remembers following the Portman, aged about four on the back of his father's bicycle. By the time he was twelve he had graduated to a pony and hunted every Saturday that meets were within hacking distance, the furthest of these being at Kingston Lacy. His pony did all this as well as the usual gymkhana activities on a diet of gorse chaff. This is something I had never come across before. Charlie explained that this entailed two hours' work every night, "Father fed it through the chaff cutter wearing hedging gloves. It put as much life in to them as corn, but went through them like grass. I've even raced them on it." Charlie's early ambition was to become a vet. He had failed his 11+ as he had only come out of hospital the day before. Passing the 13+, he had to make up two years of science, and was not allowed to take Latin. As this scuppered any chance of him becoming a vet he lost all interest in his education, "I left at 15½ instead of staying on until 18 as I should have done."

From Milkman to Second Horseman

His first job after leaving school was a milk round, which he did with a pony and float. Then he saw that the New Forest Buckhounds were advertising for a second horseman. Applying successfully for that job he stayed at the New Forest Buckhounds for one season, where he rode second horse to the Huntsman, Jack Slightham.

In Hunt Service with the Chiddingfold and Leconfield - and Out Again

On the retirement of Mr Corbett MH, well known in the carriage world, Charlie left the Buckhounds, securing the post of second whipper-in to the Chiddingfold and Leconfield, "The man I learned most from was the Kennelman here, George Seale. He had been at the Wynnstay for 15 seasons, and had also been with Bob Champion at the Ledbury. Prior to that he had whipped in to the Portman. He went on to the Quorn as Kennelman for twelve seasons. George was a real Kennelman, not a Knackerman. He was one of the best, rather like Tom Bailey, who I only knew from taking bitches up there." During this time Charlie met his future wife Patricia, from the old Cowdray country, at Petworth Youth Club. They married, and soon realised that his weekly wage of £3.15 Shillings would not be sufficient to put together a home. He came out of Hunt Service and worked on the land to do overtime and save some much needed cash.

Second Time Lucky at the Southdown

A year later Charlie had the chance to go to the Southdown, whose Huntsman had been first whipper-in at the Chiddingfold and Leconfield during his time there. It was tempting, but the young couple had just settled in to a new council bungalow, and did not want to move again. A year later, in 1954, the Southdown job came up again, "I went to have a look, and stayed three seasons as first whipper-in until 1957." Here he had his first opportunity to hunt hounds when Huntsman Fred Cockerill was off with pleurisy for six weeks.

243

Charlie on Timber at the Essex and Suffolk

Under Jim Bennett's Influence at the Old Berkeley

Like many young men at this time Charlie moved about the country, his next job taking him to the Old Berkeley, in 1957 also as first whipper-in for another three seasons. Huntsman Jim Bennett was also a Dorset man, whose home had been no more than five miles from Charlie's, though the two had never met previously, "The day I went on trial there, I made a mistake. We came to a gate, and I rushed to open it. I got told off, as he wanted to jump it. He did jump it, and I followed." It proved such a good day that even with second horses hounds went home at 2.30pm. Jim Bennett was to prove Charlie's greatest influence as a Huntsman, "Hounds always went well for him, as did the majority of horses. He was a very good chap across country." His Kennel routine was faultless, no detail over-looked. Each Friday he would go to the bank whilst his wife did the shopping. He would return armed with polishes, 'Tide' soap powder, 'Brasso' and everything imaginable for keeping the place immaculate, "It was always spick and span. While he was out each Friday my job was to take the deck scrubber and wash all the lodge walls with 'Tide' water." He recalls riding the showjumping 'rejects' they had from Alan Oliver's father here. One day he saw Jim Bennett on one of these, 'Socks', jump the corner of a hedge, and back again, "I found a lower place and that was nearly five foot. Phil Oliver said, 'I didn't know he could do that!' as Socks was supposedly not good enough to show jump." Another day he saw Jim ride across a footbridge, with a seven foot drop into the water below, and jump the stile at the end, "I followed him, and found my mare wasn't as clever and stepped straight off the side !" When Jim Bennett broke his ankle, Charlie hunted hounds. He clearly enjoyed his time there, "I never went to another place like it for kit either. I had four coats in three seasons, a new pair of boots and breeches every year. We had macintoshes to wear to the meet, whipcord, gloves stocks, even a pocket knife !" When he left he was presented with a silver horn as well as a cheque.

Climbing the Ladder at the Essex and Suffolk

After this excellent grounding, Charlie's next move in 1960 was to prove a longer one. Going to the plough country of the Essex and Suffolk as first whipper in, the following season he became Kennel Huntsman/First whipper-in. After another two seasons he shared hunting hounds with Joint Master John Jiggens until 1967. Whilst here he had two particularly good horses. 'Timber' he had on loan from his amateur whip, and once he got going well several people were interested in buying him.

Charlie did not want to lose him, so bought him for himself. He was very adaptable, jumping wire and wide ditches with ease, "He was clever but frightened me to death going so fast into things. You couldn't stop him, or turn him round even in deep plough. Turning him in to something high didn't stop him either, he'd just jump it." Charlie tried everything, not even a gag could hold him. Then one of the whippers-in Jock McLelland who had been in racing stables suggested trying a breaking bit with bars, "He still pulled but you could guide him with it. If he was wrong at a fence he would stop. He was very clever." Charlie's other great favourite was the more angular 'Chestnut'. He had been through dealer Dick Porter's yard a couple of times because he bucked so badly, and was a real character, with several tricks. "You might have been out all day, or just on hound exercise. It didn't matter, because half a mile from home he would decide the person on his back should walk !" We had a kennel boy, kennel girl and whipper- in, and we would all go on hound exercise together. The Suffolk side horse did four days a week then, so we liked to get them all fit together. One day, I looked round, and there was Chestnut trotting by, Linda trudging along behind." Charlie could not resist asking her why she had got off, knowing full well what had happened ! "He was a lovely horse, my daughter thought the world of him. When he was fit his old ears were on the go all the time." The Kennels and Stables were separated by an engine room which housed the generator, "We used the 45 gallon diesel tank as a mounting block. When you put your foot in the pedal, that horse would buck all the way round to the Kennels, so you couldn't get on him, but hopped around whilst he bucked and bucked." For all this he only put Charlie off once, "He was about to go in to an electric fence. I shouted and turned him away from hounds, giving him a smack down the ribs. He bucked me straight off !"

Never a Dull Moment

There was never a dull moment when Mr Jiggens hunted the bitches. He made certain of that. If things were a little slow he would send Charlie on to give a holloa, "It wasn't easy trying to get out of sight in that flat country. Do you know whenever he made me do that, they would run on and mark to ground. I used to tell him he was the jammiest Huntsman ever !" He would often be sent on to find a refill for Mr Jiggens' flask. There were two opening meets, one in Essex and one in Suffolk, and innumerable parties and pre-hunting breakfasts.

A Memorable Hunt - Thirty Five Years On

Charlie showed me an Essex and Suffolk Newsletter, 'Covertside' which recalled a very good hunt in its 'Twenty Years On' feature. Now thirty five years ago, he added his own memories of this exceptionally good run. From a meet at Chelsworth on the 15th December 1965, hounds found at Wagger at 2pm. Passing Preston Church and Kettlebaston Rectory for Home Wood, they ran past Hitcham House Farm over the meadows at Chelsworth, where they crossed the River. Here Chestnut's nearside rein broke, and Charlie continued the rest of the hunt riding one-sided ! Running on to Semer Wood they crossed the road to Ravens Hall. Some people gardening here had seen their fox some 15 minutes earlier. Scent must have been very good as they ran on through Howe Wood in tremendous cry. The light was fading fast as they went into Groton Wood. As the moon came up they ran harder than ever, and had to be stopped on the road at 4.45pm. This was a point of nearly ten miles, and twenty as hounds ran. A good hunt like this is always memorable, particularly when hounds run on as the moon rises. At Christmas time it is somehow even more special, "You are always pleased, as a Huntsman, when someone else remembers it too", says Charlie, referring to the newsletter piece. As they hacked home in the moonlight many people ran to their garden gates to wish them 'Happy Christmas.'

A Model Master of Foxhounds

Colonel Hitchcock was a model Master of Foxhounds, "He was the sort of chap I admire. He talked to everyone. If we were trotting along on a frosty morning and he saw a tramp at the side of the road he'd stop and talk to him, 'Bit bloody cold last night?' You'd see him at the County Show with Royalty, and he was just the same. If more masters and huntsmen were like him there wouldn't be half the trouble. People looked forward to seeing him. He had been at Dunkirk, and every couple of years his batman would come to see him because he liked him so much. He was full of fun and could put on a Suffolk brogue. When my daughter started hunting aged about nine he would ring up and say, 'Vinny going out tomorrow ?' If I said no because it was too long a hack he would say, 'Well tell her to get down to my place in the morning and she can come with me. He would look after her, and bring

her back. That's the sort of chap he was." The Essex and Suffolk Supporters gave Charlie a horn at the end of his last Season, and at the point-to-point one of Dick Porter's horses put him off twice in five minutes by dropping its shoulder!

Monmouthshire and Clamber '63 Proves his Worth

Charlie's next move was to another contrasting country. He moved West to hunt the Monmouthshire in 1967, and stayed in this wilder, hilly country for five seasons. He took Timber and Chestnut, who sadly only lasted through cubhunting. Whilst here he had one of his most memorable hunts, "We met at Wyndham James' Trevedda Farm, the Loogey. Years before the Pandy Foxhounds had been kennelled there, hunted by Wyndham's father. Hounds found in the gorse above the farm. They ran up to the top of the Loogey and down. Wyndham said, 'We can't go up and down this mountain. If we split up one of us will stay in touch.' His brother Morgan rode the top with me as my whipper-in, Jack was off with a fractured skull. I was riding one of Jack's horses we'd bought from Dick Porter in Essex to keep it fit. Hounds kept going up and down on the sheep tracks. A lot of the time they were amongst the sheep, which was making it very difficult for them. Every time they checked one hound put them right. He was called Essex & Suffolk Clamber '63 (Clarion '58-Lavish '59). His dam was by Duke of Beaufort's Lister '55 and I bred him for the Essex and Suffolk plough. He was no oil painting, rather straight in the shoulder, but he coped with all that sheep foil. Every time he spoke the others went to him, even though they couldn't own the line themselves." Finally hounds ran on, out of the Monmouthshire country, to just above Hay-on-Wye in the Golden Valley, "We were now in snow which lay higher up the mountain. Thick fog came down just as if someone had flicked a switch. Hounds lost their fox, and I cast all around but they could not pick it up again. The fog lifted as quickly as it came down. This was a 16 mile point, only Wyndham, Morgan and myself there. We owed it all to Clamber, for we should never have got that hunt without him. Wyndham still talks about it, and when I went back for a day by car recently it was still being talked about, nearly thirty years later."

Charlie was not a great one for Hound shows, but did win the English Championship at Machen with a bitch he had bred at the Essex and Suffolk. He was sometimes called upon to judge, "I upset one or two at the Brecon Show. People came up saying this would win, or that would win. My daughter was in the crowd and told me that after the first class there were mutterings because I'd put down something which had won elsewhere. She said ,'Oh, I expected that.' When she told them who she was, they asked her what I would do next !" He has judged a number of Puppy Shows, and this year is returning to judge the Monmouthshire with Captain Foster.

'Timber' - Clever as a Cat

Timber was still going strong, and was game to take anything on, "One day we came to a place I'd never jumped before. I must have been feeling brave or stupid with hounds running well. There was a pair of five bar gates, a ditch, angled five yards away from the gate at one end, a yard away at the other. There were two strands of wire on this boundary fence. I steadied him for the ditch and he popped over the rest. Four fields on we lost our fox, so I went back in to our draw. Everyone else was waiting there, no-one had followed me !" Now with more time, he got off and tied the wire back to the gate. "He jumped it and changed legs so quickly for the next bit. That's the worst fence I ever jumped." A field further on there was a deep ditch, with a cut and laid either side on a hump. Timber slid and couldn't take off. He ended up in the ditch, standing up. Charlie had to stand on his saddle to get out. There was no room to turn him round as the ditch was deep but narrow. He told his whipper-in to take the reins with his whip and say nothing until he was clear of the horse, "Once I'd climbed out I said, 'Come on old boy, you got in, we'll get you out.' He scrabbled round to sit up, like a dog begging. I gave him a minute or two and said 'Come on' again. He jumped straight out, without any scrabbling." After this remarkable vertical take off, Timber landed on his feet, not on his knees as might be expected.

To the Banks of the Tetcott

Next, Charlie went even further West to the banks of the Tetcott where he hunted hounds for four seasons. His much loved and very adaptable horse Timber carried him here, dropping dead on Easter Monday at the end of the Season. Charlie had hunted hounds from him for eleven seasons, and he coped equally well with the plough and dykes of Suffolk, the hills and drop fences of Monmouthshire and the Cornish banks.

Charlie White at work in the feed room

Back to the Principality

After four Seasons in Cornwall Charlie returned to Wales, this time to hunt the Curre in 1976. This was very similar to the Monmouthshire, with nice country but a fair amount of wire and drop fences. After six Seasons here as Huntsman, Charlie returned to Sussex to be Kennelman to the Chiddingfold, Leconfield and Cowdray.

Kennelman of the Old School from Sussex to Berkshire

I asked Charlie how he felt about no longer carrying the horn, as it is not a transition all Huntsman can make, "I missed it, of course, but I'm the sort of chap who is happy as long as I'm with hounds." During six seasons he worked under Peter Collins and his brother Bob here. He also helped Bob parade the Hampshire hounds when he was without a whipper-in recently. When Mr Nigel Peel moved to the North Cotswold in 1988, Charlie went to the Old Berkshire as Kennelman to the late John Smith. That Season Mr Peel contacted him, and asked if he would go to the North Cotswold the following one.

247

Charlie White and the Monmouthshire Hounds

Final Curtain at Broadway

Charlie's role when he arrived at the North Cotswold Kennels in 1989 may loosely be described as Kennelman, "I worked in the Stables but mainly in the Kennels to help Guy Allman who had been taken on as Kennel Huntsman, and who I already knew. I filled in any gaps really. I carried on helping out with hound exercise and walking out when Clive Shillam came." Little did he think that in the twilight of his career he would be called upon to be Kennel Huntsman and first whipper-in again in 1991.

During his time as Kennel Huntsman at the North Cotswold, Charlie became well known in the show ring. As he had already told me, he had never been too keen on this before, and had done very little. The success of the North Cotswold's bitches was on an upward curve however, and they began to take many prizes. Charlie's last Season 1996-97 was to prove a troubled one. He had a nasty shock when a horse he was riding broke its elbow. Later on when hounds hunted in to the Heythrop country his horse side stepped in a gateway, pushing his ankle against the post. Charlie hunted the rest of the day, and it was only on the following morning he realised something was badly wrong. X rays revealed broken bones, and he missed six weeks. On his first day back he hunted hounds as Mr Peel went to a funeral. The one redeeming feature remained the pack's showing successes during his last summer of 1996.

Grapefruit's Sweetest Victory, as Predicted by Martin Scott

From her early appearances in 1995 North Cotswold Grapefruit '95 (Duke of Beaufort's Mostyn '92- Greeting '91) was the talk of the showing circuit. Possessing quality, depth and presence, she really filled the eye. She had won the prize for the best unentered bitch at Peterborough and looked as if she would take all the beating. Though beaten in the Championships at a sweltering Ardingly and Builth Wells, her subsequent win at Peterborough, following in the pawprints of her maternal Grandsire Cotswold Grocer '86, more than made up for any disappointment. She was the pack's first Peterborough Champion, "It was really nice, and I felt I had achieved something. That morning Martin Scott who always judged our Puppy Show said to me, 'You'll be all right today Charlie. I've seen a lot

248

of hounds this year and you've got a really good chance.' He was right. He always says what he thinks doesn't he ? So many judges go to Puppy Shows and come out with how well the hounds look and how good they are. I've heard him say that they aren't up to the usual standard. That's how it should be, too many are frightened to tell the truth. More judges should be like Mr Scott."

Retirement in Sussex - and Carrying the Horn Again

Charlie's retirement has not been uneventful. He was called upon to hunt the Chiddingfold Leconfield and Cowdray, "From the Opening Meet, Mr Robin Cursham had a fall. I was out, round the other side of the covert. I was asked to carry the horn for the rest of that day, and we got drenched." He hunted them for a fortnight, "I was happy to fill in for the odd day after that." He did so again last Season when Huntsman Peter Collins was laid up, "We caught a brace, without much of a hunt on either, but

Charlie White at Ardingly
(Terry Crate)

we did what we had gone out to do." I asked how he managed, hunting a pack of hounds strange to him, "They are looking for their 'boss' until you move off. Everything that happens is basically the same, though the horn and voice varies of course. Once you find, it is no problem at all."

Counting the days when he has acted as substitute, Charlie has hunted eight packs of hounds in varied countries - the Southdown, Old Berkeley, Essex and Suffolk, Monmouthshire, Tetcott, Curre, Chiddingfold, Leconfield and Cowdray and the North Cotswold. I asked him what makes a good Huntsman, "You should not make a fool of your hounds, as some amateurs are apt to do. You cannot play tricks on them. You need to rely on them, and if you trust them, they will trust you. Try not to take too much notice of people who say, 'I *think* he went this way'. Doghounds won't stand messing about, if you once mess them about, next time they look up and say 'Bugger you!', that's why Mr Jiggens liked the bitches. I always think bitches are more like giggly girls ! "

Charlie still enjoys his hunting, whether on a borrowed horse, or by car. He catches up with friends at the Hound Shows, particularly Builth Wells where he meets so many he knew from his years in Wales. His cottage is tucked among the trees away from hum drum roads. He assists his wife in the garden, where fourteen duck recently attacked one of the borders. It is a great place for birdsong, and before I left we watched a woodpecker on their bird table. Small wonder he has returned to this part of Sussex three times.

249

Subscribers to 'A Short Cast Back'

Jo Aldridge, and Nipper
Mrs Sarah Ash
Mrs S A Ashmead
Mrs Iona Baber MH, Chilmark Beagles
Mrs H D Bailey
Mr & Mrs M C Barkwith
Julie Barrett (née Pheasey)
Simon Bateman Esq, Grafham, Huntingdon
Mrs Annie Bazeley, Boxted, Colchester
Mr & Mrs Maurice Bell, Wensleydale Foxhounds
Lord Patrick Beresford
R J Berkeley
Clarice & Ernie Blackwell, Farthingstone
Carol Boswell (née Pheasey)
Dara Brady
Alf E Burnett Esq, Lincolnshire
H B J Busby Esq MFH
Reverend Celia Carter, Avening, Gloucestershire
Lady Arabella Casey
Myra Chappell
Les Cheesley Esq, MH
Capt. Simon Clarke
Martin Claxton , Huntsman Percy Foxhounds
Tony Collins
Mr & Mrs J Cooke, Taynton
Terry Crate Esq, Ilminster
Robert Denny Esq MRCVS
Alex Denny
Janet Denny
Robert Dent, Leyburn
Mrs Mary Dickerson, Badsworth Hunt Supporter
Paul Duckett and Amanda Hutchings
C Dunstan, Devon
R H G Faber
Dr Sara Farmer, South Yorkshire
Camilla Ferranti
Charles Fielding Esq
John B Gardner
Countess Goess-Saurau
Leslie Goddard, Sherston
Mrs R D Green MFH, Warwickshire
Paul Greenwood Esq
Mr & Mrs J O Greves, Oxfordshire
Brian Gupwell, Badminton
Bob Hall, Didmarton
John Harries
Mrs Sheila Hasler
John and Margaret Hatherell
C Hemmins Esq, Longstowe, Cambridgeshire
Mrs Diana Hewitt
Albert Hickson, Kennel Huntsman Radley College Beagles
Judy Hobhouse, Somerset
Howard Holloway Esq
Michael Holt,Coleshill
Mr & Mrs M J Hoskins
Flt-Lt Peter C Hunt
Vic Hurst, ('Video Vic'), Kenilworth
Fred Ind
Mr & Mrs Alastair Jackson
Mr & Mrs C Jerram, Dauntsey, Chippenham
Charlie and Sheila Johnson

Sally Jones
M J Keel Esq
Ian and Sue Langrish
Tim Langley
Mrs J J M Latham
Mrs Joan Leonard
Miss Gwyn Lloyd, Alderton
Mrs Bruce McKenzie
James D Mallett, Huntsman North Lonsdale
D J Mallett, North Lonsdale
Mrs Lesley Mead,
Jim Meads
Mr & Mrs I N Mitchell
Mrs J Mitchell, Grittenham, Wilts
Mrs Winnie Morton, Fadmoor
Mrs Joan North, Charlton-on-Otmoor
Iain Osborn Esq
Derek Owen Esq, Denbigh
David Palmer Esq, MFH, Droitwich,Worcestershire
Miss Avice L Pearson
John Perkins, Hatton, Shropshire
Brian and Nora Pheasey
David, Candy, Hannah and Laura Pheasey, Bicester
Lt-Col J H Pitman
Clive Preston Esq
Mrs Greta V Radford-Smith
R J Righton Esq
Mrs A L Rook
Miss C J Rowson
C M F Scott Esq
Brian Sedgley Esq
J T Seymour-Williams Esq
Dr M E Sheard, RAC Beagles
Mr & Mrs Richard Sherwood, Dorset
P C C Sidebottom Esq
David Smith, Thornbury
B W T Smith
Mrs Patsy Spanoghe
Jim Squires Esq MH, Chilmark Beagles
Mr & Mrs Robin Squires
Mr & Mrs J Stebbing, Fairford, Glos
E Stevenson Esq, Wick and District Beagles
Mr and Mrs A Stirling, Timsbury
Mrs R W Stratton
Tony Street Esq
Mr & Mrs F A Underwood
Tim Unwin Esq
The Hon Mrs Mark Vestey
Mick and Chris Vincent
The Waldron Family, Haydon Wick
Diana Warner (née Colbeck)
Clarence and Ennis Webster
Mr & Mrs D G White
Charlie White
David Wilmington, Ilminster
Michael Windell , Allengrove Farm, Luckington
The Rev F J L Winfield
Mrs J Winfield
Dale Woodall, Mendip Farmers' Hunt
Mrs S M Woodhouse, Wotton-under-Edge
C R W Wysock-Wright

Index of Hounds Mentioned in the Text

Index of Hounds Mentioned in the Text

Index of Hounds Mentioned in the Text

Index of Hounds Mentioned in the Text

254

Index of Hounds Mentioned in the Text

256